streamlined

A Metaphor for Progress

The Esthetics of Minimized Drag

streamlined

A Metaphor for Progress

Lars Müller Publishers

CONTENTS

Paul Jaray: ideal streamlined shape
for a body close to the ground,
c. 1920. ETH library, history of science
collection.

Franz Engler, Claude Lichtenstein

1   American highways, c. 1940.

2   Gotthard Schuh: tram-stop, Zurich c. 1935.

"... denn die Gestalt der Wirklichkeit
ist immer reicher als die Linienführung der Grundsätze."
("... for the shape of reality is always richer
than the lines of principle.")
Robert Musil, Der Mann ohne Eigenschaften, I,
(chap. 121)

This book deals with a concept that is both popular and imprecise: 'streamlining'. As so often happens, popularity and imprecision are dialectically related in this case. The notion of 'streamlining' sends out signals in many directions, and thus the images and interpretations conjured up by streamlining are appropriately diverse. Some people associate it with scientific research, others with individual artistry, others again see in it the obvious excesses of a consumer society. One person will go so far as to see streamlining as the dictatorial power of physical laws, while for another it will be as good as synonymous with 'superficial styling', with forced expressiveness and the arbitrariness of everyday culture. This book is intended to show that the boundaries between science and everyday culture are permeable (in both directions), that science too is concerned with 'creating form' and that in most cases 'streamlining' has an identifiable and plausible content.

The notion of the 'streamline' originated in science. The definition is as follows: "Streamlines are lines whose local direction corresponds with local flow speed." However, it is no small step from this scientific definition to the language of design and its field of associations with streamlining; streamlining refers to the body itself, the streamline runs along the body – or at best through it, if it is internally hollow – but in any case outside its material form. An object is fundamentally 'streamlined' if the medium that is flowing past (or through) it – i.e. air or water – remains as free from turbulence as possible. It is obvious that fulfilment of this requirement depends upon the shape of the body. But the nature of 'streamlining' as such can hardly be deduced scientifically; the concept is not an unambiguous definition, it is more like an identification of character. It derives from the sphere of application, and thus its many associations are rather like a response to the pluralistic social use of the word. If the truth is told there is not one kind of streamlining, there are many 'streamlinings'. This is why it was able to develop into a popular catchword between the wars. (For this reason we shall treat the idea as singular in this introduction, not for reasons of didactic pedantry, but to allow the aroma to develop as richly as possible.)

The archetype of speed and shape lay in sharpening to a point. When the Phoenicians' superior ships are mentioned we think of them as slender and pointed, to offer minimal resistance. In the early years of this century racing cars attempted record speeds by drilling through the air with their pointed noses; this was an idea borrowed from ballistics. Jules Verne also had a projectile-shaped train steaming towards the moon; here only the pointed shape of the locomotive indicated that something special was going on. Today we are amused by the mixture of imagined high speed (supersonic range) with the pictorial repertoire of the cosy little trains of the day. Today, 120 years later, it is years since we first went to the moon, and all that has practically been forgotten. Are we really so forgetful, or did manned space flight need a powerful pictorial idiom like streamlining? Even the 'Atlas' rocket was not streamlined at all by the standards of science-fiction fantasies, from Flash Gordon to Tintin.

The period between the fantastic visions of a writer like Jules Verne and today's discarded memories has been influenced by movement more than any before it. And where there is movement the cry is also heard for faster and more comfortable movement and – concealed from the public for a long time, but a persuasive argument today – for greater effectiveness. In the first half of the century efforts towards achieving these goals can be summed up in the powerful notion of 'streamlining'. Faster – more efficient – more comfortable and elegant – more ecological: this somewhat simplified historical sequence links various qualities to the idea of 'streamlining'.

When the top speed of a means of transport was still seen as an indication of how quickly one could get from one place to another, the hunt for records was a virus affecting large parts of the population. Record speeds were a matter of general knowledge – for racing cycles, cars, aircraft and even ships.

3   4   5

"We declare that the splendour of the world has been enriched with a new kind of beauty: the beauty of speed. A racing car whose body is decorated with great pipes like snakes with explosive breath (...), a howling car that seems to run on grapeshot is more beautiful than the Nike of Samothrace." In 1908, when Marinetti made this pronouncement in the Futurist Manifesto he saw speed as most powerfully symbolized by brutality. A quarter of a century later things were different; now society had acquired a sense the aesthetic refinement known as streamlining. Now the race against time had created a new formal language of its own. The process had started with submarines and continued with airships, then moved on to cars, railway trains and aeroplanes, and from there finally to home and office equipment. Streamlining always made the future imaginable, material and tangible; in streamlined garb what was 'coming' declared that it had 'come'. The astonishing feature is that this process of creating the future in the present went on for decades. Think of the extent to which the Lockheed 'Constellation' in about 1950 and the Citroën DS 19 in 1955 were symbols of their time!

That is history. But the fascination of this past lives on: it is easily remembered, and thus imaginable in the present day. The expressive force of streamlining is not exhausted. For many people 'streamlining' is simply synonymous with 'design'; with a given form that cannot be taken for granted; with sensuous creativity; with sculptural intensity; with the eroticism of objects; with 'vigorous motion' even when standing still. Effectively streamlining means the aesthetic of minimized drag. Could anyone deny that it produced extraordinarily powerful formal character? But a quality that gives character to objects takes it away from people: a 'streamlined' career is identified, and usually justly, with opportunism and lack of character. The opposite nature of these connotations is not a contradiction in itself. No-one would think of accusing an eroded mesa in the desert or water-smoothed pebbles on the beach of being characterless: modelling helps to give artefacts a visible profile, but for people it takes the profile away.

One of the aims of this book is to rehabilitate streamlining. For distinguished critics like Sigfried Giedion,[1] Max Bill[2] or even the 'Hochschule für Gestaltung' in Ulm it was almost a synonym for a vulgar 'made in Detroit' goods aesthetic: Giedion saw overblown formal language as its chief characteristic, and Bill found it wildly fractured. In the eyes of these authorities it had moved unrecognizably far away from scientific flow mechanics. Equating streamlining with decadent idioms in this way is no longer tenable in such abbreviated form.

The richness of this subject lies partly in the fact that there is not one single scientific formula for the most wind-resistant body. Even experts who make a scientific study of flow mechanics work against a background of certain selected premises. Streamlining cannot be deduced from an ideal theory but only induced from the constraints of each particular case. Qualitative description of a given flow is based on six fundamental mathematical equations. As they cannot be solved, hordes of scientists and engineers have tried to find partial solutions for flow problems.

Additional complexities are introduced by the fact that in most cases the shape of an object is not autonomous and is not there for its own sake. It almost always covers up a structure of internal functions and perceives itself as serving them. This is why an enormous variety of 'streamlined shapes' have come into the world under the same banner: torpedo-shaped racing cars, fish-like aircraft, 'tear-drop' cars, extensive cladding of locomotives and close-fitting skins for sportsmen.

One has only to compare two widely differing – though both are scientifically legitimate – approaches by men like Paul Jaray and Jean E. Andreau in order to gain an impression of the wide variety of results produced on a common basis of aerodynamics. The difference is not least an expression of different priorities.

Streamlining is a metaphor for progress, and as such has a surprising degree of formal diversity and ambiguity in terms of content. It does not absolutely require maximization of speed, but is looking to optimize effectiveness; to this extent it has remained entirely up to date. Today it can also be justified

6

7

3   Bob-sleigh, late forties.

4   Bob-sleigh, c. 1953.

5   Bob-sleigh, 1990.

6   Swimmer Dano Halsall.

7   High diver, c. 1990.

in terms of ecology and environmental politics. But as a stimulus it is a historical phenomenon that reached its first high point in the thirties and its second in the fifties.

Certainly streamlining did not become a formal topos until the 20th century, but its motifs go back considerably further. If the aim is faster and ever more homogenous transport (which it is a means of achieving), then the construction of the early railway lines in the 19th century is a facet of the same process. In comparison with the old roads running through the countryside, levelling the topography with viaducts and embankments and building long gentle curves introduced an inner correspondence with streamlining into the landscape. Liquefaction of movement is an elemental phenomenon of technical civilization and a mode of our existence. It is with us from motorways to skiing technique. The current conclusion: the mountain bike, where pedalling over tree roots and scree takes 'perpetual motion' (with no hint of self-irony) ad absurdum.

We have had these background elements continually in mind in the course of our work. In the context in which we see it, streamlining is an inherent tendency in Modernism, over and above stylistic matters, and a connecting element beyond formal similarity.

In this way the idea of streamlining could be extended to organizational processes, without straining it too much: timetables and syllabuses, business organization, stock control, logistics. We did not feel it appropriate to develop these connections in detail, but this aspect is important enough to warrant a mention: in the formal language(s) of 'streamlining' (its style or styles) it plays the same role as a fluid flowing around a streamlined body: it is the modelling medium.

There is another field that is not dealt with explicitly in this book: architecture, and this should therefore be mentioned here. In an extended sense twenties and thirties buildings are definitely streamlined. A building like Frank Lloyd Wright's offices for the Johnson Wax Corp. (1936–1939) is fundamentally different in formal terms from his previous cubic, angular structures. Undeniably the seductive power of gentle, continuous surfaces also seized this great master of rhythm. Building

complexes with rounded corners and gentle changes of direction are familiar to us from numerous cities. At the time this was the buildings' response to the demands of metropolitan traffic: they nestle up to the streams of traffic and by doing so illustrate these and the energies of the modern metropolis. The German architect Erich Mendelsohn placed architectural 'horizontalism' in a broad socio-historical and political context in 1923: "The vertical trust building creates the vacuum of use at its peak, and in its foundations the intolerable pressure of drudgery. Connecting such contradictory elements in series naturally creates revolutionary tensions and gradually yields to the horizontal tendency of parallel connection of elements in future production organisms."[3] He continued, referring directly to formal questions: "Human beings of our day can find compensation for the excitement of their rapid life only in the tension-free horizontal. It is only their desire for reality that makes them masters of their unrest, and their haste can be overcome only by the most perfect rapidity."[4] This statement is both poetic and intense, and has been refined by development – also by Mendelsohn himself, who incidentally got on well with a man like Norman Bel Geddes in terms of his formal temperament and view of the world.[5] Horizontality was 'tension-free' only in its elementary contrast with verticality; as soon as the public eye had learned to read the horizontal it could also perceive attempts to redynamize it with appropriate devices. Just as people always find new ways of hanging on to their haste (but have learned to mime being at peace while doing so: we have only to look at businessmen on a transatlantic flight by Concorde).

But is streamlining a historical phenomenon, or is it still with us as a creative force? Both are true to a certain extent. This is only apparently a contradiction. In the first place 'streamlining', as expounded in this book, is a historical phase that is now over. What streamlining used to be was strongly defined as a contrast with the standards of those times, and they were: cars with static form as a composition of individual volumes, squealing iron and creaking wood in sooty trains, flying structures of bizarre fragility, in constant danger of folding up at the wrong

8

9

10

moment. Then came streamlining, and with it formal compactness, static rigidity combined with low weight, smooth, spherically curved surfaces, bright light-weight metal and the kind of grace for which only the English have the right word: 'appeal'.

And today? This question continues to accompany us unasked – aircraft will never again be boxes braced with wire. The creative and technical leap of the years from 1925 to 1950 had a lasting effect, but its formally creative and imaginative significance for society have for a long time not been what they were; Modernism has become too much as a fact of everyday life for that, despite all flirtation with supposed post-industrialism. Certainly we have lost the punch, the irresistible penetrating power of progress. And furthermore, the change of paradigm is fundamental: progress has for a long time been second 'nature' to us, a shadow that follows us wherever we go.

Something that will also be a continuing theme is the question of minimizing energy consumption in transport. Aerodynamics and hydrodynamics derive from the same approach to problems as 'streamlining', but they are not identical with it, as to an extent they use different means to arrive at the same end. Perhaps, if one looks at modern cars, the idea is even undergoing a stylistic revival. It is probably a matter of taste whether one perceives the intended similarity as such. It seems to us that the charisma of historical 'streamlining' is not so readily transferable.

It is not easy to grasp the 'appeal' that we mentioned above, the way in which 'streamlining' expresses itself. Is it an aggressive form? No, at least not from the perspective of today, where the 'wedge' prevails. Streamlining is not the same as our impatient wedge shape: it demonstrates uniform movement, not choleric outbursts. To that extent, despite all its dynamism it has something harmonious and unaggressive about it, in precisely the spirit in which Mendelsohn was writing.

But its 'appeal' cannot be sufficiently explained by harmony. We have always been concerned with the simultaneity of 'harmony' and 'dynamics'. If the saying 'organic design' is ever anything more than a catch-phrase, then it is here, where func-

tions determined from 'inside' and 'outside' blend into a greater whole. (The dolphin's 'streamlining' is also rightly perceived by the public in this way: its shape emerged in a 'functional' way as a result of the modelling of internal and external purposes.)

Notable American designers used to say "streamlining is cleanlining". In fact there always is 'calm' in streamlining despite its dynamics; a form does not seem to have been assembled from individual components, but much more amalgamated to create a whole that cannot readily be taken apart again in one's head. This creation of homogeneous form from previously unconnected parts is streamlining's achievement in terms of design history. Elements were brought into line and shaped into a speedy whole. In our opinion the reason that the charisma of streamlining can still be felt today lies in the fusion of this formal 'calming' and the still powerful dynamic of its expression. This brings together matters that cannot be carefully weighed against each other here: professionalism and the art of seduction in the producers of 'streamlining', perhaps the public's wish to be seduced and – beyond ideological-critical targets – presumably in both cases a fundamental desire for 'concinnitas', artful harmony between the parts and the whole.

But today we can perceive a movement away from this harmony: 'restless' shapes are increasingly being sought; the coachwork of buses, which has to some extent developed aerodynamically, is being deconstructed with wedge-shaped decorative strips, motor cycles signal the rise of their lines towards the rear like layered cuts in a side of bacon. This is not by chance, ultimately it is all about attracting attention, and this relies on visible difference from what is customary. Against this background the decoration on a ski and an airliner are surprisingly closely related.

This new distinction between volumetric homogeneity and a surface that is deliberately made to look heterogeneous is a clear indication that the formerly coherent formal statement of streamlining has split into two components: physically verifiable shape offering the least possible wind resistance, and the 'form' in which it appears. Competitive sport is very well suited to explaining this. The shape of modern bob-sleighs has come closest to historical streamlining – but it has taken a very long time. Or take downhill ski racing: any skier who does not adopt the optimal aerodynamic crouch has no chance of a top place. And again: swimmers shave their heads to shoot through the water as quickly as possible. Streamlining as a mentality is probably more directly present in competitive sport than anywhere else. But once more things become complicated, as these three examples are intended to show:

Firstly: a nineties racing car is fundamentally different in appearance from a racing car built in 1950. Its problem is not so much excessive wind resistance as lift and the task of transmitting the power of the engine, which is scarcely controllable any longer, to the track. The fat tyres are aerodynamically highly disadvantageous, but indispensable. For this reason spoilers and special wings are mounted to create as much downward thrust as possible. There is a considerable difference from historical 'streamlining'. Its formal language united insights derived from biology and technology (the Franco-American designer Raymond Loewy saw the egg, which makes its way through the body of the hen, as the archetype of streamlining); aerodynamics and hydrodynamics were placed on a equal footing with streamlining. Today these things have developed separately, and so have their pictorial languages, as these examples reveal.

Secondly: the development of ski-jumping. The ideal in terms of shape has changed considerably to achieve the best possible performance: from arms stretched forwards to arms held close by the side, from skis held closed to skis held open, and recently to the V-style. The latter is aerodynamically the most efficient and thus superior in terms of performance, but deduction of points for style indicates that the earlier 'streamlined form' is still 'valid' (if the closed line of the tense, forward-thrusting body can be so called). Will the V-jump now become the new ideal for shape, and therefore for beauty? It has already often been the case that what is considered 'good' has amalgamated with the image of the 'beautiful'. Primacy in performance will soon mean that V-jumpers will not have to put

up with losing style points for much longer. Nevertheless we suggest that the closed jump will not be so readily dismissed as the ideal in terms of beauty. It is the best visual statement of the evening out of internal and external forces, and conveys the competence that lies in this ability most directly. That is to say: 'streamlining' contains more than awareness of its efficiency; it illustrates efficiency directly – although at the price that this illustration has in the course of time been transformed into a poetic image that can no longer produce quantified proof of its own correctness.

Thirdly: the formal development of passenger aircraft also casts light on the slow farewell to streamlining, which for us – in its wholly amiable translation from belief in progress to the 'shape of progress' – has become a clear indication of the relativity of our views and should therefore touch us in two ways: not only, uncritically and non-historically, as a nostalgic memory, but as a challenge to recognize intellectual and historical differences in comparison with earlier periods.

Aircraft: it might be possible to think that the dictates of high speed would favour the realization of pure streamlining. This is an error. The Lockheed 'Constellation' certainly brought a high point of 'streamlining' in aviation, but despite the fact that average journey speeds are twice as high passenger aircraft look different today. The fish-like shape of the fuselage with its successively changing cross-sections would no longer be economically viable today because of the enormous manufacturing costs. Thus passenger aircraft have had tubular fuselages for decades, which makes it easier to produce 'extended versions'. This happens at the expense of 'streamlining', but not at the expense of aerodynamic qualities. On the contrary: development of shapes is to a significant extent based on aerodynamic research. The new so-called 'supercritical' wings, i.e. reduced wing surface and a thicker fuselage, make passenger aircraft of our day look less elegant than the 1970 'Jumbo-Jet' for example. However, the decrease in visual stylishness is more than outweighed by demonstrable fuel savings, and perhaps even as far as speed is concerned. And so, in the light of current knowledge, aerodynamic shape and streamlining are no

longer one and the same thing, but the great effect of streamlining lay and lies precisely in the fact that this identity was
unquestioningly taken for granted. Streamlining is probably
still the most striking form in which aerodynamics is made visible. Contemporary aircraft must be far superior to the 'Constellation' in terms of aerodynamic quality. But there is scarcely
one that can compete with it in terms of elegance.

And so are the great days of streamlining over? The above
suggests that they are, but other things suggest that they are
not. Surely the railway revival – if it turns out to be a lasting
one – uses the same formal language as it did to embody the
future sixty years ago (TGV, ICE, Pendolino etc.)? And is there
not a stable core of the phenomenon of 'streamlining' within
in this continuing life?

We conclude these preliminary remarks with a reference to
the insuperable ambivalence of streamlining in terms of meaning that it lies within the two possible – though not simultane-
ously possible – answers to the question of the degree of effectiveness:

Is the aim higher speed with the same power – than could be
achieved without minimum wind resistance – or the same speed
with less power? This is one of the crucial questions with which
we see ourselves confronted. In the case of competitive sport
the answer is clear: it requires optimal performance. But ecology requires the minimum consumption of energy. The answer
cannot be expressed in a primary difference of formal language, it will show only in the sense previously allotted to use.
The decision for one purpose and against the other is one of
mentality and one of either-or; it is made before any imposi-
tion of form and outside the notion of 'streamlining' – as we shall
call shape with the least possible wind resistance, here and
throughout this book.

[1] S. Giedion: Mechanization takes Command, chapter on 'Streamlining and full mechanization' (Cambridge 1948) ed. New York 1969, pp. 607–611).

[2] Max Bill: Form. Eine Bilanz des Formschaffens um die Mitte des 20. Jahrhunderts, Basel 1952.

[3] E. Mendelsohn: Die internationale Übereinstimmung des neuen Baugedankens oder Dynamik und Funktion, in: Erich Mendelsohn: das Gesamtschaffen des Architekten, Berlin 1930, p. 23.

[4] E. Mendelsohn, loc. cit., p. 24 ff.

[5] Cf. correspondence between Erich Mendelsohn and Norman Bel Geddes at the University of Texas at Austin (Harry Ransom Humanities Research Center).

PAUL JARAY

1889-1974

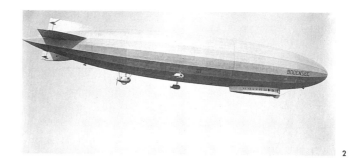

1889–1974 Paul Jaray grew up in Vienna. He knew he ultimately wanted to be an artist from an early age (painting, composition), decided not to bother about senior school leaving qualifications, but then went to the Maschinenbauschule in Vienna.

In 1909 he experienced an 'aeroplane' flight for the first time, in Vienna (Blériot), and struck up a friendship with the mechanic. From then on flying was a key issue for him. After a brief period as an assistant at the Technical College in Prague (Professor Dörfl) he became chief design engineer for the aircraft building firm 'Flugzeugbau Friedrichshafen'. His principal concern here was seaplanes. Jaray's decades of friendship with the Swiss pilot Robert Gsell (1889–1946) go back to these days. In 1915 (when Graf Zeppelin was still alive) Jaray moved

to 'Luftschiffbau Zeppelin', also in Friedrichshafen. Jaray's aim was to streamline the airships as effectively as possible. LZ Friedrichshafen's own wind tunnel was established under Jaray's direction (cf. p. 26). In his streamlining work he was concerned with unspectacular detail as well as getting large-scale form right: every brace, if it was considered essential, was streamlined, support-work was reduced to a minimum, and the shape of engine gondolas and rudders was optimized. Jaray was entirely responsible for the airship LZ-120 'Bodensee', and this was the model for the later LZ-127 'Graf Zeppelin', LZ-129 'Hindenburg' and LZ-130. Experiments in the wind tunnel gave Jaray the opportunity to grasp the difference, experimentally and theoretically, between a body with air flowing around it at ground level and a body with air

flowing around it on all sides. From this Jaray derived his important principles for a streamlined car, which made a decisive contribution to international recognition of the notion of 'streamlining' (cf. p. 186).

In 1923 Jaray moved with his family to Switzerland and opened a technical office in Brunnen (Canton Schwyz). He was engaged by the British government as an airship expert, but this was curtailed by the disastrous airship R 101 fire (1930), which signalled the end of British airship building.

In about 1927 Jaray, with Zurich businessman P. Susmann, founded the 'Stromlinien-Karosserie-Gesellschaft', which prepared numerous designs for streamlined bodywork (some of them for major manufacturers), and issued licences for streamlined bodywork built on Jaray's princi-

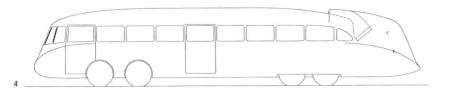

ples. There was no lack of publicity for 'stream-lined bodywork', but despite this the firm made no significant profit. The 'Jaray-Streamline-Cor-poration' was founded in New York in 1931, but it remained in existence only until 1938, and was likewise a commercial failure (licence income after a law suit against Chrysler: 5300 dollars). Even in the twenties Jaray's activities had shift-ed to radio technology to a significant extent; he lectured in Switzerland to promote 'radio', and also concerned himself with television, which was just starting to be a technical pos-sibility. In 1932 he founded the 'Alaphon, Radio-dienst und Radiobau AG' in Lucerne, which made its own sets, but also folded in 1938. In 1941 Jaray was appointed director of the tech-nical office of Farner AG (Grenchen), where he promoted the nosewheel undercarriage and in-

troduced it in small planes. The economic and political situation was against exploitation of Jaray's innovations in aircraft building. He set himself up as an independent engineer in the canton of Zurich in 1944 and addressed a wide variety of problems, like for example signalling or improved drawing equipment. But questions of handling airflow remained central: he designed an wind-driven power station in 1941; he patented an air compressor for railway carriages, and a device for handling exhaust gases in silencers etc. Clearly Professor Josef Ackeret saw how important he was, as he con-tinually invited him to lecture at the ETH. Jaray's scientific and technical estate is also at the ETH.

For Jaray see also p. 26, 28, 168ff., 198, 236ff., 256, 286, 312.

WILLIAM BUSHNELL STOUT

1880–1955

1 William B. Stout: three-engined all-metal aircraft, produced in large numbers as the Ford 'Tri-Motor', 1928. Photograph: Detroit Historical Department.

2 William B. Stout: 'Skycar', small aircraft with compression propeller and removable one-piece wing, first shown in 1930 at the Detroit Air Show; Stout's own machine, in which he flew himself for several years.

3 William B. Stout and Henry Ford with a Ford 'Tri-Motor' aircraft, about 1930. Photograph: Detroit Historical Department.

4 William B. Stout: 'Scarab' wide-bodied limousine, second version (1935), series of 100 planned, but fewer built. (Cf. p. 196).

5 William B. Stout: 'Railplane' railcar, developed 1932–1933 for Pullman, model. Photograph: Detroit Historical Department.

1880–1955 W.B.Stout was an intuitive practitioner pure and simple. He grew up in St. Paul/Minnesota (Mid-West), and experienced America's rough pioneering days in his childhood: no hint of the 'American way of life', of luxury and refinement or softness, but improvisation, 'do-it-yourself', 'trial and error'. As a child and young man Stout showed a flair for technical problems by inventing toys for himself and his friends (e.g. a water-powered gramophone). He entered the Mechanical Arts High School in 1897 (not a university, but a technical school that was the first in the Mid-West based on the 'manual training' method). Stout's love of mechanical toys led him to write handicraft instructions for local papers when he was still very young. He used this work to finance his first trip to Europe (1903), which took him to Great

Britain, Holland, Belgium, Germany and Switzerland. He came to Europe again in 1908, newly married, and with his wife on the pillion of a motor bike he had built himself. Stout published small articles on model aircraft in 'Dispatch' magazine from 1910; he founded the 'Illinois Model Airplane Club' (one of the first model aircraft clubs anywhere) in Chicago. He knew pioneer aviator Glenn Curtiss and the Wright brothers. Stout continued to be fascinated by flying throughout his life. As a dedicated design engineer he also approached other means of locomotion and technical problems (e.g. motor bikes, cars, railcars) with the prudence of an aviator whose maxim was lowest weight and the greatest possible rigidity.

In 1914 Stout moved to Detroit, the city that was on the point of becoming the centre of Ameri-

can car production. In 1917 he published his book 'Mechanical Toys' (second edition 1924), and wrote various articles about aircraft in 'Motor Age'. One of Stout's most important ideas was the 'thick wing', which could be developed as self-supporting because of its structural strength and which showed a high degree of lift. In 1922, very early, he built an aircraft entirely of Duralumin, an alloy stronger than aluminum. He intended to produce the aircraft for the Navy, but the prototype crashed. In order to be able to carry on Stout collected money (1000 dollars each) from Detroit businessmen like Henry Ford, to whom he promised one thing in writing: "You'll never see your money again! – but he actually did get the money together. He soon became friends – professionally at least – with Henry Ford. Other aircrafts by Stout

4

5

are the 'Air Sedan' and above all the 'Tri-Motor'
(1928), a light, three-engined all-metal aircraft
that became Stout's first commercial success.
Stout opened his own airline (Detroit-Cleveland)
with this model. He founded the 'Stout Engineering Company', which he financed by selling the
airline and production investments to Ford.
Stout is a typical American of his period in his
non-academic working methods; rather less typical is that he was not primarily interested in
earning money, but in inventing and realizing
things. In 1935 his extraordinary abilities brought
him the chairmanship of SAE, the 'Society of
Automotive Engineers', which he remained for
a number of years. Late in life he published his
amusing and informative memoirs 'So away I
went!' (Indianapolis/New York 1951).

For Stout see also p.136, 195,
212, 266.

NORMAN BEL GEDDES
1893–1958

1

2

1 Norman Bel Geddes: 'Locomotive No.1', fully shrouded steam locomotive, rendering (1931). Note the metal slatted blinds over the power units. (Cf.p.158).

2 Norman Bel Geddes: 'Ocean Liner', 1932 (according to other information as early as 1929), rendering. (Cf. p.256).

3 Norman Bel Geddes, c. 1935.

4 Norman Bel Geddes: design for a streamlined armoured vehicle ('Armored Car', 1940. The design was not chosen for the sake of higher speed, but to deflect bullets under attack.

5 Norman Bel Geddes 'Temple of Music', 1929, section (from 'Horizons').

6 Norman Bel Geddes: streamlined double-decker bus, model for 'Futurama', New York 1939. (Cf. p.212).

1, 2, 4, 6. Bel Geddes Collection, H.Ransom Humanities Research Center, University of Austin/Texas, by permission of Edith Lutyens Bel Geddes.

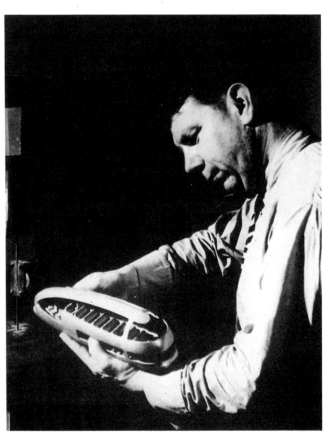

3

1893–1958 Norman Bel Geddes
Norman Bel Geddes is the visionary among the American design pioneers. Unlike Raymond Loewy or Henry Dreyfuss his principal contribution was not in work for industry but for the American theatre, in which he earned a reputation mainly as a set designer at an early stage. His work as a designer is the outstanding feature of his autobiographical fragment 'Miracle in the Evening' (New York 1960); as well as this he was a painter, illustrator, graphic designer, shopwindow designer, exhibition organizer, architect – and yes, an industrial designer and product planner. For all that he was first and foremost a highly professional 'communicator', and his publicity work made a considerable contribution to his significance in this respect. Bel Geddes caused a furore in 1932 with his book 'Horizons'.

Its title was a claim to visionary far-sightedness, and also alludes to a formal language typified by horizontals. The book appeared at the dawn of professional design in th United States. It would be worth investigating whether it gave the profession a voice for the first time or actually unleashed the design boom.
Bel Geddes' most constant source of work was the theatre. He was considered to be one of the most innovative forces in the field of stage design as early as the mid twenties; he knew great figures in the world of stage and film like Max Reinhardt, Nijinsky, Aline Barnsdall, Sergei Eisenstein, Carl Laemmle, Chaplin. In 1916 (according to information supplied by himself) he was the first to substitute spotlights mounted above the stage for footlights. His first exhibition of stage sets was held in New York in 1921;

he created a particular sensation with his model for 'Dante's Inferno' for a New York theatre. In 1923 he transformed the Century Theater into a Gothic cathedral for Max Reinhardt's production of 'The Miracle'. In 1925 he wrote 'Modern Theory of Design' (for the stage) for the 14th edition of 'Encyclopaedia Britannica'. He wrote screenplays and drew properties for Paramount films. The stage designs illustrated by Bel Geddes in 'Horizons' are outstanding for their symbolism and an expressively heightened naturalism.
He founded an industrial design studio in 1927. He designed a Graham Paige car intended still to be formally 'valid' even after five years' in production (not produced). 1928: a new style of shop-window decoration for Franklin Simon/ New York (colour coordination, interchangeable

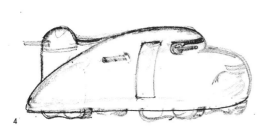

4

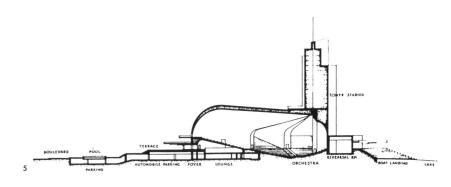

5

6

modules). He designed a mobile puppet theatre. In 1929 he became architectural adviser to the World Fair 'A Century of Progress', Chicago 1933. In 1930 he took part in the international architectural competition for the Ukrainian State Theatre in Kharkov, where his design was taken up. In 1939 Bel Geddes' 'Futurama', created for General Motors at the New York World Fair was a major draw for the public, a masterly production of urbanism and design using theatrical means (cf. the contribution by B. Hauss).

An episode that he described in his autobiographical fragment 'Miracle of the Evening' is typical of his way of thinking. Aline Barnsdall, the great innovator of the American theatre, for whom he worked as a set designer, wanted Frank Lloyd Wright to build her a theatre. Bel Geddes was involved in discussions about the project.

Geddes thought that Wright's ideas showed little expertise as far as the theatre was concerned. When Geddes asked Wright: "At what point will we see on your plans the locations for lighting and scenery equipment?" Wright is said to have answered: "First the essentials, the little things fall into place later" (Miracle ..., p.162). An answer that Bel Geddes, for whom the audience's perspective was of central significance in any job, absolutely did not agree with.

WINDTUNNELS AND SCIENCE

Experiments and buildings

1   The wind tunnel at 'Luftschiffbau Zeppelin GmbH', Friedrichshafen, 1904.

2   Aircraft manufacturer Hispano Suiza's wind tunnel building in Paris, built 1936.

3   Model of a Fiat G-91-Y fighter aircraft in the large wind tunnel, 1956.

4   Wind tunnel model for the 'Venom' fighter, 1960s.

5   Bernhard Russi in the wind tunnel, 1971/72.

6   Nose of an SLM locomotive in the wind tunnel, flow experiment, 1974.

7/10   Sucking-in experiment with a jet engine, about 1965.

8   Part of the façade of the 'Bank für Internationalen Zahlungsausgleich' BIZ, Basel. Architects Burckhardt und Partner, about 1972.

9   Ski-jumper Däscher in the wind tunnel, 1958.

3–10 by kind permission of the Eidgenössisches Flugzeugwerk Emmen.

3

4

5

6

7

8

9

10

Model of the Chrysler 'Trifon' proto-
type in the wind tunnel, 1932.
Photograph: Chrysler Historical
Foundation.

Model of a Deutsche Reichsbahn
express railcar train unit in the Luftschiffbau Zeppelin GmbH wind
tunnel, c. 1932. Photograph: LZ-Archiv,
Friedrichshafen.

AIRSHIP HANGARS WITH WIND-CONTROL DOORS

1921 Experiments by Paul Jaray

V.500/96

XV-c-45°

9

1 Paul Jaray: series of wind tunnel experiments on 'airship hangars with wind-control doors', conducted in April and May 1921 at 'Luftschiffbau Zeppelin GmbH', Friedrichshafen. Wind direction 0°, smooth interior and exterior walls, projecting roof, wind-control doors, windward doors closed.

2 Dito, but windward doors open.

3 Wind direction 0°, normal doors, severe turbulence.

4 Wind direction 0°, wind-control doors, calmer flow picture.

5 Wind direction 30°, exterior frame, smooth internal walls, wind-control doors.

6 Wind direction 30°, smooth interior and exterior walls, wind-control doors. Flow shown with small silk flags.

7/8 Wind direction 30°, smooth interior and exterior walls, projecting roof.

9/10 Wind direction 45°, smooth interior and exterior walls, projecting roof. Moving the Zeppelin into the hangar.

11 Streamlining image: hall with smooth interior and exterior walls, wind-control doors and projecting roof, wind direction 0°. Severe turbulence on the lee side with windward doors closed.

12 Steamlining image: the same hall with windward doors open, wind direction 30°: calm streamlining image, moving the airship into the hangar.

All photographs by kind permission of Zeppelin-Archiv, Luftschiffbau Zeppelin GmbH, Friedrichshafen.

1921 Experiments Accidents kept happening when airships were being moved in or out of their hangars because of unpredictable air movements in and around the hangar. Even light contact between airship and hangar could cause sever damage to the filigree structure. For this reason Paul Jaray, at the time chief engineer at the Luftschiffbau Zeppelin GmbH in Friedrichshafen, investigated air flow in the wind tunnel in April and May 1921, taking wind direction, the position of the airship and the position of the hangar doors into account. Jaray intended to use the airship hangar itself "to change the direction of the air flow, like the barrel of a gun". By doing this he distanced himself from projects aimed at protecting the airship from any moving air – an approach that he dismissed as pintless. He was trying to do precise-

ly the opposite, "to create an even air flow that could flow through the hangar as freely as possible". Jaray examined the problem from the point of view of three types of airship hangar: those with an external framework, an internal framework and those with sides that were smooth on the inside and the outside (covered). He preferred the latter option, considered an external framework practicable, but an internal framework incompatible with his stated intention.
The 'wind-control doors' were an important feature for Jaray: these were made up of several vertical elements that altered their prifle according to the wind direction, with the intention of controlling air flow in the hangar. The experiments revealed that even winds striking the hangar below 60 degrees to the longitudinal axis of the hall could be redirected in this way.

The series of experiments investigated the behaviour of the various types of hangars and gates at wind directions of 0°, 30°, 60° and 90° to the hangar axis. Air flow was illustrated by small silk flags. Flow strength was not investigated in the experiments, just its direction.
The experimental set-up was mounted on a plate that could be turned, in order to vary the wind direction. Hangar and airship were made of sheet metal (the former with a framework that could be inserted, in open or covered form). The photographs were taken vertically from measuring area. Size: the model Zeppelin was 90 cm long.
It seems that Paul Jaray first realized the possibility of the streamlined car when he confronted the problem under examination here. According to Jaray its shape depends on the question

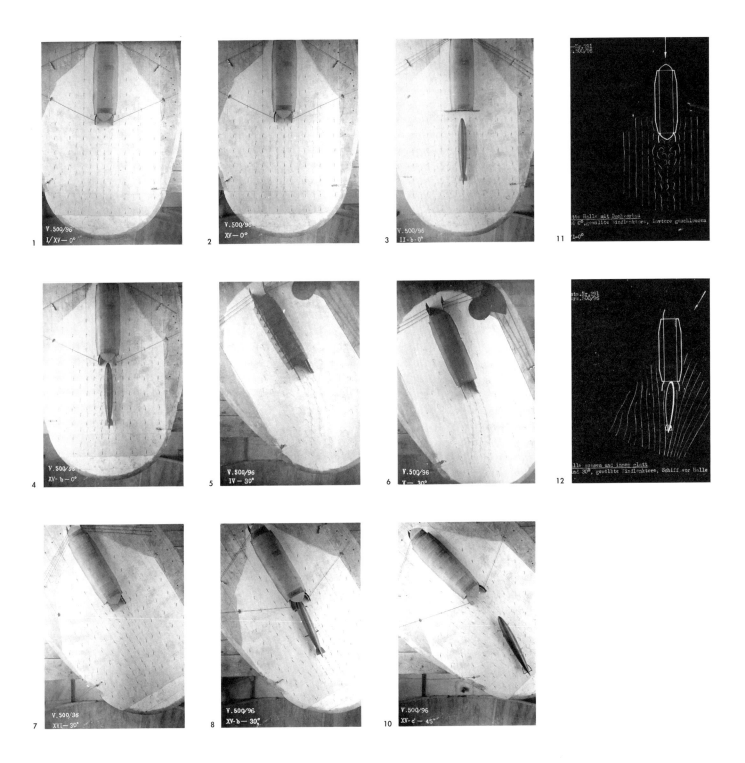

of the ideal streamlined form close to the ground (see p. 186). Consequently the experiment documented here had implications beyond the world of airships.

Paul Jaray's illustrated report on this elaborate series of tests fortunately survived in the LZ Friedrichshafen archieves. The sequence assembled here is a selection from a total of 64 photographs and the same number of schematic diagrams made from the photographs. Quite apart from their value as scientific evidence, the photographs have an almost artistic appeal to the contemporary eye.

1938/1939 R. Koenig-Fachsenfeld

Two exclusive sports cars were tested on German roads and motorways in 1938 and 1939: the 'Adler-Vollstromlinienwagen' and the 'V1 Volks-Sportwagen'.

The (exciting) bodywork for the 'Adler' car was by Paul Jaray and was built under the supervision of Freiherr Reinhard Koenig-Fachsenfeld in Cannstatt (in the Vetter bodywork plant). Koenig-Fachsenfeld represented Jaray and his interests in the German Reich. Jaray could not do this himself because of his 'non-Aryan' origins.

This was a bodywork on the chassis of the 2.5 litre 'Autobahn Adler', built with a view to racing in Le Mans. The intended driver, the racing driver von Guilleaume, also took part in the tests (top row). The 'V1 Volks-Sportwagen' was Koenig-Fachsenfeld's own design, conceived in

co-operation with racing driver Kurt C. Volkhart (cf. p.190). This design is also a remarkable achievement in formal respects. The car reached a top speed of 135 km/h with its 1.17 litre, 34 horsepower Ford four-cylinder engine set in front of the rear axle. The car is said to have reached an outstanding air resistance coefficient of $c_w = 2.0$ (bottom row).

A unique series of photographs of the test drives of both cars survived in the possession of Freiherr Koenig-Fachsenfeld (who died in March 1992 at the age of 93). They show (in contrast with the ideal world of the wind tunnels of the period) the flow pattern at a particular time under the real conditions of the outside world (changing winds, ground effect etc.) by the movement of the attached woollen threads.

Costruzione "Superleggera" eseguita in sottili tubi di acciaio saldati all'autogena. Sistema iniziato dalla "Carrozzeria Touring" nell'anno 1936. Brevetto N° 355450 F.B.A.

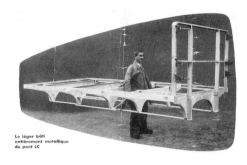

Le léger bâti entièrement métallique du pont LC

1 William Stout and a Pullman Corp. (?) employee lifting a bogie for the 'Railplane' light railcar (cf. p. 136), 1933. Photograph: Detroit Historical Department.

2 Two employees from 'Touring Superleggera' (Milan) lifting the tubular steel frame for an Alfa-Romeo sports car, c. 1940. T. Anselmi Collection.

3 Commercial vehicle loading ramp, aluminum, Saurer Arbon, 1935.

4 Airship LZ-129 under construction from lightweight metal sections, Luftschiffbau Zeppelin GmbH workshop, c. 1935. Interior view towards the bow point. Photograph: LZ Friedrichshafen.

5 Railplane supporting structure.

6 Two workers at the 'Airstream' factory (Jackson Center Ohio) factory lifting an aluminum shell, c. 1970.

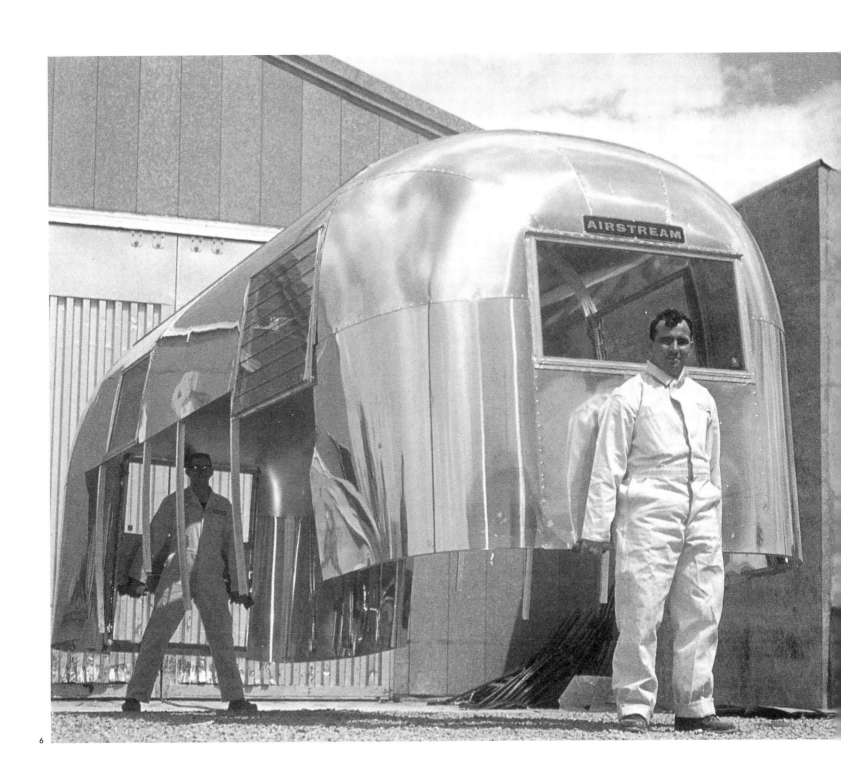

6

1

LZ 130
„Graf Zeppelin"

Mit dem Luftschiff über Länder und Meere zu fahren, ist die moderne Reisart. Das Zeppelin-Luftschiff LZ 130 bietet dem Überozeanreisenden vor allem: Zuverlässigkeit, schnelle und ruhige Fahrt, jede Annehmlichkeit und Bequemlichkeit. Die Eindrücke einer Zeppelinreise sind tief und vielgestaltig.

DEUTSCHE ZEPPELIN-REEDEREI G. M. B. H.

2

Leitwerkfläche
Fin

Höhenruder
Elevator

Längsträger
Longitudi...

Leitwerkfläche
Fin

Seitenruder
Ruder

Motorgondel
Engine car

D-LZ 130

NEW YORK
LAKEHURST

RECIFE
(PERNAMBUCO)

RIO DE JANEIRO

BUENOS AIRES

RÖMER
MÜNCHEN

LZ 130 wurde von dem Luftschiffbau Zeppelin, G. m. b. H. in Friedrichshafen a. B. erbaut. Seine Länge beträgt 245 m, bei einem größten Durchmesser von 41,2 m. Das Gerippe besteht nach der bewährten, bereits von Grafen Zeppelin angewandten Bauweise aus Längsträgern, Ringen und aus der Drahtverspannung. Die Außenhaut bildet ein starkes wasserdichtes Stoffgewebe. Das Traggas wird in 16 voneinander unabhängigen Gaszellen im Schiffskörper mitgeführt. Zum Vortrieb des Schiffes werden 4 Daimler-Benz-Dieselmotore von je 1000 PS Höchstleistung verwendet. Alle für die Schiffsführung erforderlichen Einrichtungen und Geräte sind in der unter dem Bug angeordneten Führergondel vereint.

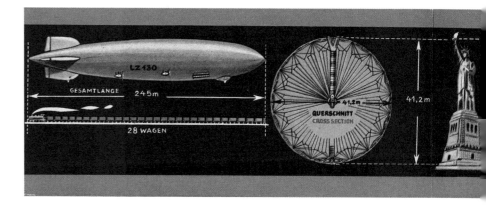

LZ 130

GESAMTLÄNGE 245 m

28 WAGEN

41,2 m

QUERSCHNITT
CROSS SECTION

41,2 m

LZ 130 „Graf Zeppelin"

Hilfsring
Intermediate ring

Hauptring
Main ring

Entlüftungshutzen
Ventilation hoods

Entlüftungsschacht
Ventilating shaft

Gaszelle
Gas cell

Achssteg
Axial corridor

Küche
Kitchen

Speisesaal
Dining room

Rauchzimmer und Bar
Smoking room and bar

Mannschaftsräume
Crew's quarters

Halle
Lounge

Kabinen
Cabins

Navigationsraum
Navigating room

Führergondel
Control car

Anker-Konus
Bow mooring cone

FRANKFURT a. M.
HALLE I
HALLE II
RHEIN-MAIN

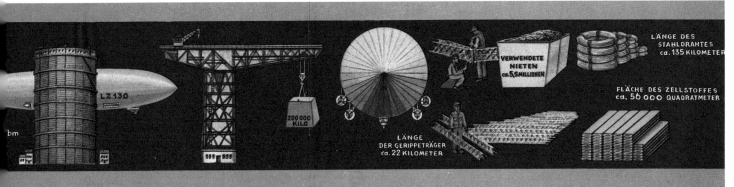

LZ 130

bm

200 000 KILO

VERWENDETE NIETEN ca. 5,5 MILLIONEN

LÄNGE DES STAHLDRAHTES ca. 135 KILOMETER

FLÄCHE DES ZELLSTOFFES ca. 56 000 QUADRATMETER

LÄNGE DER GERIPPETRÄGER ca. 22 KILOMETER

3

4

HUIT CYLINDRES / MOTEUR EN ARRIÈRE / REFROIDISSEMENT PAR AIR / 160 kms/h

5

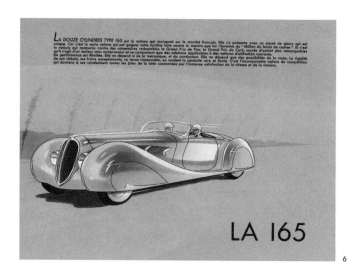

LA DOUZE CYLINDRES TYPE 165 est la voiture qui manquait sur le marché français. Elle s'y présente avec un passé de gloire qui est unique. Car c'est la seule voiture qui put gagner cette terrible lutte contre la montre que fut l'épreuve du "Million du fonds de course". Et c'est la voiture qui remporta contre des adversaires redoutables le Grand Prix de Pau, le Grand Prix de Cork, succès d'autant plus remarquables qu'il s'agit d'un moteur sans compresseur et ne comportant que des solutions applicables à des voitures d'utilisation courante. Sa performance est illimitée. Elle ne dépend ni de mécanique, ni du conducteur. Elle ne dépend que des possibilités de la route. La rigidité de son châssis, ses freins exceptionnels, sa tenue impeccable, en rendent la conduite sûre et facile. C'est l'incomparable voiture de compétition qui donnera à ses conducteurs toutes les joies de la lutte couronnées par l'immense satisfaction de la vitesse et de la victoire.

LA 165

8

9

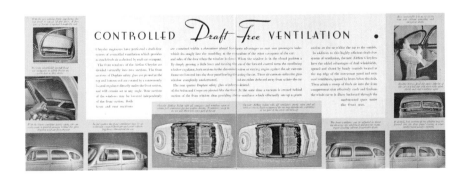

RECORD DU MONDE DE VITESSE SUR RAIL
196 KILOMÈTRES A L'HEURE
CHRONOMÉTRÉ ÉLECTRIQUEMENT SUR 10 KILOMÈTRES

FREINAGE A 150 Km/H.: ARRÊT EN 750 MÈTRES

AUTOMOTRICES RAPIDES

BUGATTI

VITESSE – CONFORT – SÉCURITÉ 10

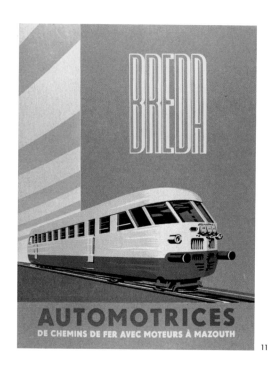

11

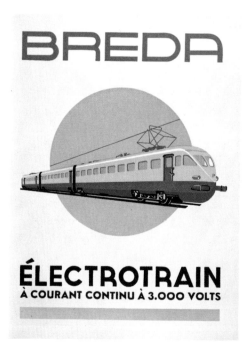

12

13

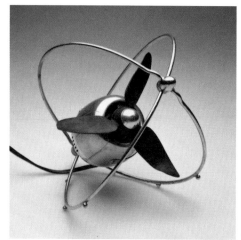

14

15

16

17

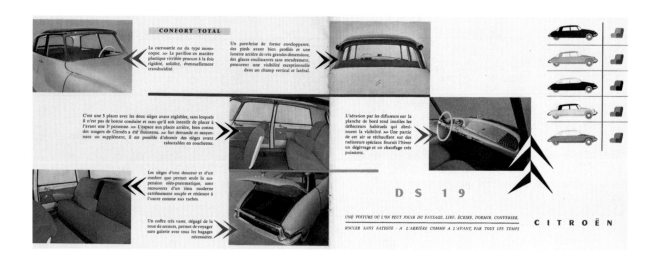

Pour vous cette voiture travaille toute seule...

La **DS 19** est le résultat d'un travail patient dans la recherche des solutions aux problèmes posés par l'utilisation d'une voiture. ≫ Rouler en voiture c'est être en sécurité, être bien, être "vite". ≫ De ces trois qualités on a souvent sacrifié l'une ou l'autre. ≫ A ce jour, il faut les mettre sur le même front, afin que le conducteur puisse emmener sa famille, ses amis, dans un confort suffisant pour qu'à l'arrivée, tous soient détendus, sans fatigue et, si c'est nécessaire, à l'heure. Ceci ne peut s'accomplir que:
≫ si la sécurité est assez poussée pour que personne n'ait la sensation de vitesse à tout prix,
≫ si les passagers, même ceux de l'arrière, peuvent allonger leurs jambes,
≫ si l'aération intérieure en quantité et en température est assurée,

en un mot, si tous les problèmes difficiles, grands et petits, posés par le transport rapide d'un lieu à un autre, sont résolus et ceci à la ville comme sur la route.

La lutte contre tous les éléments naturels qu'il faut vaincre pour bien rouler, depuis les cahots dus à la route jusqu'à la traîtrise d'un virage et la turbulence de l'air en mouvement, exigeait effort du conducteur et résignation des passagers. Maintenant, il vous suffit de diriger du bout des doigts, en pleine détente :
pour vous la **DS 19** travaille toute seule...

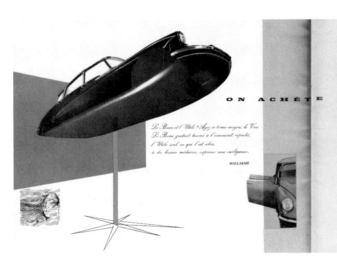

Fruit de l'étroite collaboration d'hommes de sciences et de techniciens spécialisés dans l'étude des formes et des couleurs, la ligne anticipée de la DS 19, solution apportée à des problèmes de tenue de route, de pénétration dans l'air, de confort, de sécurité, de visibilité, a atteint par ailleurs à cette beauté véritable qui est celle des volumes dictés par leur fonction et par les matériaux et les techniques qui président à leur élaboration.

ON ACHÈTE AVEC SES YEUX (Citroën)

Déjà consacrée par le Label Beauté France et par de nombreuses expositions d'Esthétique Industrielle, la carrosserie de la DS 19 devait en 1957 se voir décerner, pour la première fois dans l'histoire de l'automobile, la plus haute distinction de la célèbre Exposition Internationale d'Arts décoratifs : la **TRIENNALE DE MILAN**. Par cet honneur sans précédent, les plus grands esthéticiens entendaient signifier qu'avec cette voiture cesse l'aérodynamisme lourd des premiers temps. Il devient ailé, attribut de perfection il retrouve la fluidité des formes naturelles, les courbes lisses de la plante ou du galet. Une ère nouvelle s'ouvre, l'objet mécanique s'humanise, il s'offre à nouveau au plaisir des yeux, il scelle l'alliance de l'Art et des Sciences. Etre et non paraître, tel est le mot de passe de cette beauté technique. Abandonnant la vanité enfantine du lourd nickel et la gratuité vulgaire de l'ornement, elle offre l'équilibre de formes pures, harmonieusement mêlées à la visibilité de vastes pans d'air.

Le Beau et l'Utile ? Ayez ce bon sens, le Vrai
Le Beau gratuit tisme à l'arrangent séduit,
l'Utile seul, ce qui l'est obéi,
à de beaux méchants, espérez une intégrance.

MALLARMÉ

UNE SÉCURITÉ MAXIMUM

La sécurité, c'est avant tout l'absence de fatigue qui élimine les risques d'accident. A ce titre, le confort de la DS est un des éléments essentiels de la sécurité du véhicule. Mais il s'y ajoute naturellement

LA TENUE DE ROUTE

Jusqu'à l'apparition de la DS, la notion de confort s'était toujours trouvée en contradiction avec celle de la sécurité. Il avait toujours fallu choisir entre l'une ou l'autre : les constructeurs de voitures de course sacrifiant le confort à la tenue de route, les constructeurs de voitures de grand luxe, la tenue de route au confort. Pour la première fois dans l'histoire de la suspension, CITROEN a réussi cette synthèse impossible. S'inspirant à la célèbre technique de la Traction Avant qui seule accroche la voiture à la route, et que plus d'un million de véhicules ont dotée d'une réputation incontestée, l'hydropneumatique assure une adhérence parfaite des roues sur n'importe quel sol et porte à sa suprême expression la légendaire tenue de route CITROEN. Autre élément nouveau qui contribue à améliorer l'adhérence du véhicule : la voie des roues arrière est inférieure à celle des roues avant.

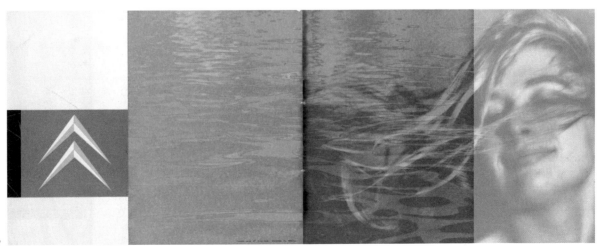

20

21

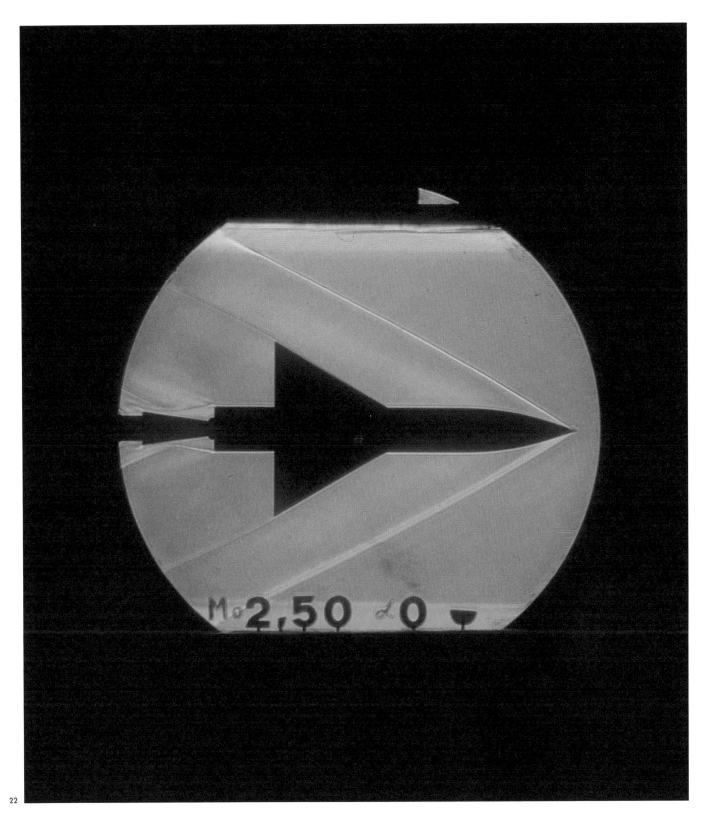

22

23

24

25

1   Goubet submarine on its way to the test site, Paris, 1890.

2   Zeppelin LZ-130 airship 'Graf Zeppelin', brochure, May 1939. (LZ-Archiv, Friedrichshafen).

3   Marque badge on radiator grille: Lincoln 'Zephyr', 1936. (Ford Historical Foundation).

4   Marque badge on title page of Tatra 77 brochure, 1934.

5   Title page of the Tatra 87 brochure, 1948.

6   Brochure for the French prestige marque 'Delahaye', Type 165, 12 cylinder, 1939.

7   Peugeot 402 – Andreau, 1936, title page of sales brochure.

8   Dodge brochure 1939.

9   Chrysler Airflow brochure 1934. (Chrysler Historical Foundation).

10   Bugatti Autorail, page from brochure, 1935. (E. Strebl Collection).

11/12 Two Breda, Milan brochures: left: diesel lightweight railcar ALN 56, lightweight electric express railcar train unit ETR 200.

Both publications printed 1939. (Archivio Storico Ernesto Breda).

13   DC-3 fleet aircraft (from 'Fortune', 1939).

14   Table fan, design by Ezio Pirati, Italy 1953. (M. Huwiler Collection).

15   Vacherin-Constantin watch advertisement, with the Lockheed 'Constellation' (from 'Du', 1947).

16   Breda ETR 300 'Arlecchino' express railcar train unit, c. 1952; exterior with the 'Belvedere' for passengers; interior of the 'Belvedere'. Design Gio Ponti. (Archivio Storico Ernesto Breda).

17   'Trans Europe Express' RAE 1051-1-55, Swiss version 1960, exterior and restaurant car (Schweizerische Industrie-Gesellschaft SIG company brochure, 1961).

18   Citroën DS 19, first brochure, 1955.

19   Citroën DS 19, 1959 brochure.

20   Chevrolet Impala 1959.

21   'Dreamcar' General Motors Firebird III, 1959.

22   View of a body in the ultrasonic speed range with visible displacement cones, c. 1985. (Eidgenössisches Flugzeugwerk Emmen).

23   Model of the 'Hermes' space shuttle (Dassault, France) in the Eidgenössisches Flugzeugwerk Emmen wind tunnel.

24   High-speed racing skier in the Eidgenössisches Flugzeugwerk Emmen wind tunnel, c. 1990.

25   'Esoro' world champion solar vehicle (Esoro, Zurich) in the Eidgenössisches Flugzeugwerk Emmen wind tunnel.

26   Elettrotreno Rapido Fiat ETR 450 'Pendolino', rendering, 1988 company brochure.

FLYING TRAINS

The development of streamlining on the railways

Sabine Bohle-Heintzenberg

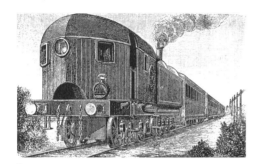

1

2

Almost as soon as the railway was invented the idea of flying was associated with it. But at the same time there was something eerie and suspect about it because according to ideas current at the time flying, man's dream throughout the millennia and the epitome of speed, suggested supernatural powers. For this reason the breathtaking tempo of the railway, its well-nigh unimaginable speed – although in the early days it was little more than 30 miles an hour – was at first a source of fear and terror rather than fascination. Heinrich Heine was seized by an 'eerie horror' when thinking of the railway; because he felt that it assaulted "even the elemental notions of time and space".[1] It was associated with sorcery and even the work of the devil, and many people believed that the breakneck speed of the railway could make people ill, and perhaps even drive them to delirium.

Hans Christian Andersen summed up his experiences with the railway impressively after a journey through the Duchy of Anhalt-Köthen in 'A Poet's Bazaar' in 1842: "Oh, what a great feat of the mind this invention is! One feels as powerful as a magician in the olden days! We harness our magic horse to the carriage and space disappears; we fly like the clouds in a storm, and imitate migrating birds! Our wild horse snorts and blows, and black smoke billows out of its nostrils. Mephistopheles could not fly any faster with Faust on his cloak! In our time natural resources have made us as powerful as the Middle Ages believed only the devil could be, our sharpness of mind has overtaken him and before he knows where he is we're past him."[2]

Belief in magic and sorcery disappeared with technical progress, and confidence in the railway increased, so that precisely its best quality, speed that at the time was not exceeded by any other vehicle, gradually started to exercise a certain fascination. The desire for speed was promoted by increasingly refined technology, stimulated by the competition slowly building up from cars and aeroplanes, and ultimately also controlled by deliberate propaganda. About a hundred years of rail experience finally led to utter intoxication with speed, and this found its most visible expression in streamlining.

Even shortly before the turn of the century the first hesitant attempts were made to increase the speed of trains by using streamlined coverings. France led the way, because her trains, especially in the Rhône valley, constantly had to struggle with the Mistral blowing from the south. French engineers thought they had created the best aerodynamic shape for the locomotive by covering individual parts like funnel and dome and introducing a wedge-shaped driver's cab that came to a point, and a similar shape for the end wall of the smoke arch.

Coverings like this were called wind-cutters in specialist language, as they were intended to cut through the air like a knife. They were considered highly progressive, but the streamlined driver's cab placed in front of the boiler, as proposed by French designer Jean Jacques Heilmann for his steam-electric locomotive 'Fusée' in 1892, seemed absolutely revolutionary. An arrangement of this kind, then thought to be extremely curious, questioned classic locomotive design for the first time.[3]

The streamlined driver's cab placed at the front also found supporters in Germany in 1904 in an experimental locomotive, the so-called Wittfeld locomotive, designed by Wittfeld and Kuhn and built by the firm of Henschel & Sohn in Kassel for the Königliche Preussische Staatsbahnen. This locomotive, unflatteringly christened the 'furniture van' because of its box-like covering was a response to Siemens & Halske and AEG's three-phase railcar, which set a world record with a top speed of 210.2 kph on the Marienfelde–Zossen run in 1903. The Wittfeld locomotive with its top speed of 144 kph was hardly comparable with this, but it was quite remarkable for a steam-powered vehicle. For this reason, and because of its unusual appearance it also attracted a lot of attention at the St. Louis World Fair in 1904.

But as the railway still led the field without competition there was no real need for faster locomotives, and so railway experts took very little interest in this question at first. Railway engineers were largely a conservative breed, and anyway thought streamlining was almost a betrayal of the time-honoured steam engine – an attitude that was to alter very little even considerably later on.

3

Thus significant stimuli were scarcely to be expected from this source. In fact they came from a very different direction, and included some fundamentally new and sensational ideas. August Scherl (1849–1921), one of the large Berlin newspaper publishers alongside Ullstein, "a personality always wandering on the fringes of madness",[4] and indubitably somewhat eccentric, caused general astonishment in 1909 when he published an express railway project[5] that set completely new standards and was well ahead of its time.

Scherl felt that the future of rapid rail traffic lay in a monorail that could travel at speeds of up to 200 kph, would run overhead through towns, and would also operate outside towns, without junctions. The trains, which Scherl felt had hitherto been nothing more than post-coaches running on rails, were to be like hotels, with dining room, lounge, writing room, smoking room and even a library for longer journeys. He planned a train with three cars as a complete unit. "The cars are connected in such a way that free movement is possible throughout the length of the train. The two end coaches are sharpened to guarantee that the train cuts through the air as well as possible. Sharpening of this kind has already more than proved its worth in the electrical express vehicles on the Zossen experimental railway and seems indispensable on trains intended to run at 200 kph."[6]

With this Scherl, who was at the same time a great patron of 'aviatics', or flying, which was then beginning to make progress,[7] had taken a crucial step in the direction of streamlining, without special technical background knowledge, without any experience in the design sector, and without wind tunnel calculations,[8] which would have eaten up his entire fortune. Everything that happened in the next 25 years – the power unit made up of several cars, the locomotive with a slender nose and shaped like a parabola, torpedo or even a wedge – may have been better thought through and sounder in scientific terms, may have been more perfect and more elegant, but always goes back to Scherl as far as ideas are concerned. Scherl's locomotive's extremely pointed nose, compared with which the 'sharpening' of the Zossen express car was merely a hesitant experiment, is reminiscent of plans by the Reverend Samuel R. Calthrop, who patented a design for an 'air-resisting train', which was pointed at the front like a torpedo. Scherl certainly did not know this remarkable design, which makes the identical features all the more astonishing. In the notes on his patent Calthrop compares his train with an 'aerial ship',[9] an airship. This makes his brilliant idea, which fundamentally also contains the notion of flying, almost visionary in character: he is talking about a vehicle that did not exist in this form at the time, but was to be of crucial significance for the development of the streamlined train 50 years later. And the name of one man is inextricably linked with this development, that of Franz Kruckenberg.

The Rail Zeppelin

Franz Kruckenberg (1882–1965) trained as an shipbuilding engineer in Berlin and Danzig. He worked with his teacher Johannes Schütte in the newly-founded 'Luftfahrzeugbau Schütte-Lanz' company in Mannheim from 1909, and was chief design engineer and director of this firm from 1915–1918; it built airships, in competition with the Zeppelin factory in Ludwigshafen. Immediately after the First World War it was forbidden to build aircraft and airships in Germany under the requirements of the Versailles Treaty of 28 June 1919, and so Kruckenberg had to look for other work. He founded the 'Gesellschaft für Verkehrstechnik' in Heidelberg in 1924, and worked on plans for a suspension railway. The design provided for a streamlined, propeller-driven vehicle intended to run freely suspended on a single rail.

All that Kruckenberg had done here was to take the airship out of the air and hang it on a rail. At first the shape of this vehicle was almost identical with the airship as well, but varied in a number of ways in his later designs. As an experienced builder of airships Kruckenberg had been quick to recognize the difference between the free-flying vehicle with air flowing around it on all sides and a vehicle in 'guided flight',[10] that

4

5

was subject to considerable side thrust, and had started experiments to solve this aerodynamic problem with model experiments in the Göttingen wind tunnel[11] as early as 1924. On the basis of his discoveries there the rounded front was temporarily replaced with a cone-shaped nose. The final 1927/28 version had a very individual rounded front with a cockpit sloping diagonally upwards, of the kind still to be found in aircraft and trains today – of course without the pointed roof necessary for suspending the vehicle.

But as the suspension railway, for which two routes – the Havelflugbahn from Berlin–Charlottenburg to Potsdam and a Düsseldorf–Essen line – were already planned – turned out to be much too expensive because of its costly track, Kruckenberg abandoned these plans in 1928. To give his express train a chance at all he had to transfer it to existing rails, i.e. to the Reichsbahn rail network. To this end he founded the 'Flugbahn-Gesellschaft' in April 1928. After much searching he was allotted an 8 kilometre section of track near Burgwedel east of Hanover as an experimental line. Fritz von Opel had conducted his sensational experiments with a rocket-propelled railcar in summer 1928. These were successful at first, but then had to be abandoned because of several accidents involving explosions.[12]

For his first experiments Kruckenberg used a propeller-driven car commissioned by the 'Deutsche Versuchsanstalt für Luftfahrt' (DVL) in Adlershof near Berlin to a design by Carl Geissen in 1916.[13] Apart from its propeller drive this unusual, strikingly bulky vehicle had little to do with aerodynamics. However, this car, much too heavy and squat, was entirely suitable for testing propeller drive on rails and for taking measurements. In addition to this, model tests in the Göttingen wind tunnel provided the necessary information about the external shape of the planned new vehicle.

In autumn 1930 Kruckenberg was able to introduce his own creation to the public. This had come into being in cooperation with Curt Stedefeld, his fellow worker from the Schütte-Lanz period, and was a propeller-driven express railcar which was to go down in railway history as the 'Rail Zeppelin'. It caused a world-wide sensation on 21.6.1931 with its speed record of 230 kph. This record was not broken until 23 years later, by the French in 1955.

The secret of the Rail Zeppelin lay first and foremost in its aerodynamically sound design, paired with lightweight construction. Both were fundamental prerequisites for minimizing wind resistance. With a view to the fact that wind resistance increases with the square of the speed, it was the streamlined shape that was the deciding factor. Propeller drive was chosen by Kruckenberg only because at the time there was no more efficient and above all lighter power transmission device. Additionally the track, signalling system and brakes had all to be specifically adapted for high speeds.[14]

The advantages of lightweight construction and streamlining for express travel were already adequately known,[15] but had never really been demonstrated by practical experiments. Carl Geissen, builder of the DVL propeller car, had once again emphatically pointed out these advantages in his 1921 essay 'Airscrew drive and lightweight construction for railway vehicles',[16] and in this context had also introduced his three-part, lightweight construction railcar with propeller drive at both ends, planned as early as 1919. This train – although never built – with its combination of aerodynamically pointed car ends and propeller drive was an absolute innovation. Its influence on Kruckenberg's Rail Zeppelin is unmistakable.

Externally Kruckenberg's Rail Zeppelin looked like a smooth, streamlined body with a low centre of gravity. In contrast with the Geissen design it was asymmetrical, i.e. it had only one propeller, at the back, and could thus travel in one direction only. Similarly to the Geissen design this propeller was attached above the low-slung fuselage section, which tapered towards the bottom; it was however not vertical, but inclined slightly upwards, to avoid any potential lift. For the front Kruckenberg chose a paraboloid shape with the cockpit set back, a design that cropped up again in aircraft as well, especially in the United States (e.g. in the 1936 Douglas DC-3). This individual shape for the front, which seemed very futuristic at the time, survived – somewhat shortened by compression – in Krucken-

6

4   Franz Kruckenberg, GVT
express suspension railway, design
1927. Reproduction of a demonstration picture from the Franz Kruckenberg estate. A. B. Gottwaldt Collection.

5   Deutsche Versuchsanstalt für
Luftfahrt, Berlin Adlershof, propeller-
driven vehicle, 1916. Used by
Kruckenberg for experiments. From:
A. B. Gottwaldt, Schienenzeppelin
(Augsburg 1972).

6   Franz Kruckenberg and the
Rail Zeppelin (photo-montage).
A. B. Gottwaldt Collection.

berg's two railcar-unit trains designed for the Deutsche Bundesbahn in 1953, 'Senat' and 'Komet', and was adopted by the
Trans-Europa-Express (TEE), among others, in 1957. This shape
for the front with set-back cockpit is also a characteristic of
high-speed trains in France (TGV) and Japan (Shinkansen).

The 26 m long body of the car consisted of a bending and tor-
sion-resistant skeleton in perforated steel girders and tubular
steel. This structure corresponded with the skeleton building
method for rigid airships, of the kind that Kruckenberg had
built at Schütte-Lanz – although in wood, not lightweight
metal, as at the Zeppelin factory. And just like this kind of airship the Rail Zeppelin was covered with an outer skin of fire-
proof impregnated sailcloth painted silver. Beaten sheet-alumi-
num shells were used only for the rounded front of the car. To
reduce wind resistance the doors and continuous strips of windows were flush with the outer skin. Steps, door handles,
hinges etc. were also placed under the outer skin for the same
reason, and could be folded out when needed. The wheels
protruded only 30 cm from the completely smooth underside
of the vehicle.

The interior was furnished like a Pullman car, with tubular
steel furniture as an attractive feature. As the interior of the
car was only 2.5 m wide there was only one seat on each side
of the central aisle. Thus the total number of seats, 24, subdi-
vided into a smoking and a non-smoking compartment, was
very low, but with a different arrangement could easily have
been extended to 40 to 50 seats. The double-glazed windows
could not be opened, for aerodynamic reasons. The cars were
ventilated by two rows of holes in the ceiling. Illumination was
provided by continuous tubular strip lights. Because of its
enormous speed, with which the accompanying vehicles could
scarcely keep up on the occasion of the legendary record run
in June 1931,[17] the Rail Zeppelin caused a world-wide sensation. But its extravagant appearance also exerted great fascination. The American Norman Bel Geddes, one of the pioneers
of industrial design, allotted a fitting amount of space to the
Rail Zeppelin in his sensational book 'Horizons', a passionate
declaration of belief in streamlining, in 1932.[18] Raymond Loewy

was also stimulated by Geddes to design his 'propeller-driven
rail car'.[19] But the far-sighted Geddes judged the Rail Zeppelin
absolutely accurately when he acknowledged its significance
for the future in terms of its streamlining, lightweight construction and low centre of gravity, but did not see any real future
for the propeller drive. For him the Rail Zepp was an interesting 'experimental project'.[20] Geddes was right with his proph-
ecy, relating at first only to the USA. In Europe there was a
much more receptive attitude to the propeller car at first. A
vehicle of this type was still under consideration for the French
Chemins de Fer du Nord in 1937.[21] Kurt Wiesinger, Professor
at the ETH Zurich, worked particularly intensively on this subject, and his projects, none of which was realized, are comparable with Kruckenberg's. Wiesinger even publicly claimed
to be the 'spiritual father' of the Rail Zeppelin, but was compelled to withdraw this assertion after several trials.[22]

Despite apparently favourable conditions the Deutsche Reichsbahn-Gesellschaft treated the Rail Zeppelin with extreme scep-
ticism – principally because of its unusual propeller drive,[23]
which had been declared unsafe. Kruckenberg therefore decided to replace the propeller with a Föttinger speed transformer
with wheel drive. This was installed immediately behind the
front of the car, whose shape otherwise remained the same.
The BMW aircraft engine selected by Kruckenberg to drive the
propeller continued to be the main power source.

But the BMW motor combined with the Föttinger speed transformer was a compromise solution – no real substitute for the
Maybach diesel engine with direct-current generator that was
originally considered, whose development Kruckenberg had
proposed as early as 1929, but had then dropped after deciding on propeller drive.[24] This decision had fateful consequences for Kruckenberg. The Reichsbahn-Gesellschaft, with which
Kruckenberg had co-operated closely in good faith because
the Rail Zeppelin was intended to be integrated into their network, had pursued his ideas further in the mean time and was
now working on its own plans for an express railcar in antici-
pation of the new Maybach engine, and without Kruckenberg's
knowledge. These plans came to fruition in 1932 in the 'Flie-

7

gender Hamburger', internationally acclaimed as a great technical success.

Kruckenberg was not able to compete against the 'Fliegender Hamburger' until 1938, with his shiny-silver three-sectioned express railcar type 'Kruckenberg'. This railcar, built in Köln-Deutz by the Vereinigte Westdeutsche Wagenfabriken AG, with its strikingly streamlined front of highly technoid appearance, was made using monocoque construction,[25] but this car never went into full service because of the outbreak of war.

Although the fate of the once so forward-looking Rail Zeppelin was finally sealed when it was scrapped in March 1939 Kruckenberg never quite dropped the idea of propeller drive. He had been working on plans for a new propeller-driven railplane ever since 1937, when he had almost finished developing the 'Kruckenberg' express railcar. This was intended to run on special tracks, and to be far larger than the Rail Zeppelin.[26] The drawings for this model show the new vehicle in an impressive perspective suggesting power and self-confidence.

Although it was not granted to Kruckenberg ever to experience the Rail Zeppelin or one of its successors in regular service he had set completely new standards with his projects in both formal and technical respects. In fact it is possible to say that without Kruckenberg and his Rail Zeppelin the 'Fliegender Hamburger' as it appeared in 1933 could never have existed.

The 'Fliegender Hamburger'

On 15 May 1933, only a few months after the Nazi 'seizure of power', the 'Fliegender Hamburger' started on the Berlin-Hamburg route as the first high-speed railcar in the world in regular service. It covered the 287 kilometres in 2 hours and 18 minutes. As a small flexible train unit that thanks to its lightweight construction had good acceleration and rapid braking, and thus theoretically allowed trains to run in quick succession, the 'Fliegender Hamburger' did not just complement heavy steam locomotives. Its high speed and elegant exterior rapidly

became an attraction, the epitome of comfortable travel, and it offered a feasible alternative to cars and planes – both of which were now heavily in competition with the railway.

Essential elements of the Rail Zeppelin like lightweight construction and streamlining were adopted for the new high-speed railcar. Weaknesses of the Rail Zeppelin were avoided, especially the disadvantages that Kruckenberg had already identified: difficulty in travelling backwards, and very limited space. To achieve equally good wind resistance in both directions of travel the 'Fliegender Hamburger' was conceived as a two-part symmetrical car unit, with one of the newly developed 410 horsepower Maybach diesel engines with Siemens direct-current generator at each end. The good aerodynamic shape had been developed by experiments in the Luftschiffbau Zeppelin GmbH wind tunnel in Friedrichshafen.

The car was built by the Waggon- und Maschinebau AG (Wumag) in Görlitz, which already had experience in lightweight construction. The car body was made up of a skeleton of light welded steel sections. The sides were clad with thin sheet metal,[27] and the curved roof with special drill on a plywood reinforcement. The 'Fliegender Hamburger's' characteristic appearance was derived from the ends of the car, which were very strongly rounded in ground plan, with the car roof sloping slightly downwards a the front, and picked out in a lighter colour. Sheet metal aprons at the sides, drawn deeply under the car body, were intended to prevent unnecessary air turbulence. The emergency buffers with which the car was equipped for reasons of safety – although conceived as an independent unit without any possibility of couplings – were flattened and finlike in shape looking more like the stubby wings of the Rumpler teardrop car than the buffer plates on steam locomotives. Windows and doors closed flush with the outer skin, in a similar way to the Rail Zeppelin. The two halves of the car were joined tightly together by a bellows and were supported on a common bogie (Jacobs type) that also contained the electric motors. The external paintwork in purple and ivory, combined with the aluminum-coloured roof and the sheet-metal aprons made the car look extremely solid, yet light.

7   Carl Geissen: Deutsche Versuchsanstalt für Luftfahrt, propeller-driven railcar, 1919. From: Glaser's Annalen (1931).

The interior of the car, with its wood-covered walls and heavy upholstered seats, despite the lively geometrical patterning reminiscent of modern sprayed decoration, made a far more conventional impression than the Rail Zeppelin. However, the 'Fliegender Hamburger' with its 98 seats and small kitchen also had clear advantages. Passenger comfort was further improved in subsequent years. The new version of the 'Fliegender Hamburger', the 1935 'Hamburg' type, with its pompously upholstered seats aimed at making a prestigious impression, was nevertheless more comfortable. The number of seats available was later greatly increased by building larger car units, starting with the three-part 'Leipzig' type railcar (1935) and 'Köln' (1938) to the four-part 'Berlin' type railcar (1938) with separate dining area.[28]

The external shape was also slightly changed. The shape of the front had been improved as early as the new 'Hamburg' type in 1935 as a result of new wind tunnel experiments in Friedrichshafen[29] conducted for a Belgian car. The shape now became a little more slender by abandoning the individual, downward slope on the roof, the windows were enlarged both in the driver's cab and the passenger area and the side aprons were drawn even more deeply under the car. The rubber buffers that were such a characteristic of the prototype 'Fliegender Hamburger' were now dropped, because automatic coupling for double traction had been built in.

The 'Fliegender Hamburger' made such an impact abroad that diesel-electric trains were soon running there as well. The French Chemins de Fer du Nord TAR (Train Automoteur Rapide) and the first electric railcars for Dutch railways, both also using Maybach engines, and in operation from 1934, are strongly influenced by the 'Fliegender Hamburger' in formal and structural terms.[30] Diesel-electric trains for Belgian railways and the Danish state railway, which had been in service since 1935, can scarcely deny their indebtedness to the German model.

Diesel electric railcars were also a sensational success in the United States,[31] at first in the form of the famous 'Burlington Zephyr', which operated on the Chicago-Denver run from May 1934. Like the 'Fliegender Hamburger' the 'Zephyr' became a symbol of speed – not least thanks to its silver-coloured cladding in welded stainless steel, a convincing demonstration of lightweight construction. The shovel nose, obliquely inclined, reminiscent of an Etruscan helmet and tested in the Massachusetts Institute of Technology wind tunnel, had very little in common with the 'Fliegender Hamburger', but its shape was so convincing that it became a model for the first generation of streamlined locomotives in the USA.[32] (For streamlining in the USA cf. essay by Barbara Hauss in this book.)

The 'Fliegender Hamburger's' international success came at an all too convenient time for the new rulers of Nazi Germany. It would be hard to imagine better propaganda. The Nazis were quick to exploit the functional nature of the aerodynamic design, the streamlining, supported by serious scientists and engineers in terms of pure calculation or by research and experimental try-outs, and rapidly acquiring fashionable status in the USA. Using the notion of 'Biotechnik', which concealed a comprehensive design programme, propaganda was made for technology's dependence on nature,[33] and an intellectual edifice was constructed in which only Nordic men and women, closely linked with nature and rooted in their homeland, were conceded the ability to biologically sound technical thinking.[34] It was said that the most convincing external manifestation of this was in flowing curved lines, streamlining.[35]

The steam locomotive in streamlined form

The Nazis sold streamlining as something specifically German, and not the least of its uses was as propaganda by the Reichsbahn under the pressure of international competition, and so the idea of putting steam locomotives into a streamlined costume as well thus immediately suggested itself, with almost remorseless logic. Also included in this programme were the so-called 'Schnellreisewagen', an express bus service that the Reichsbahn ran on the autobahn system.[36] Their shape was based on the most recent aerodynamic research, which had been carried out in the context of developing the Volkswagen.

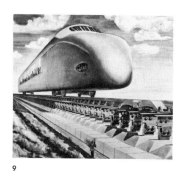

8 9 10

This, the 'Strength through Joy' car was more or less a political response to the first experiments with streamlined cars in
the USA,[37] and the Nazis built it up into a symbol epitomizing
organic form.

But the use of streamlining for steam locomotives had other
reasons as well. One was that the Reichsbahn urgently needed to improve its image, as it had suffered significant losses
since 1932 as a result of the world economic crisis. A second
reason was the intention of guaranteeing the railway's indepen-
dence from imports by recourse to domestic energy sources
(coal instead of oil) – a remarkably far-sighted political decision, given Hitler's ultimate intentions.

The Class 05 locomotive, a special streamlined version of the
standard locomotive,[38] built by Borsig in Berlin and completed
in spring 1935, was the first result of this policy. It had been
preceded by numerous experiments with partially streamlined
Class 03 locomotives, and various experiments with models in
the Göttingen wind tunnel.[39] The result of this was that for the
Class 05 locomotive all the typical elements of a steam locomotive like boiler, chimney and driving wheels were covered
with a smooth streamlined shell reaching down almost to the
rails, with additional windshields on the funnel. This shell was
riveted and welded together from sheet steel, and sat on a
structure supported by a rather conventional bar-frame locomotive. Shutters and flaps built into the shell were intended to
make the locomotive easier to service.[40] There is no doubt that
the Borsig locomotive, designed by Borsig's head of engineering design, Adolf H. Wolff, was unique in its extreme uniformity and homogeneity. The slightly bevelled front section, rounded at the top and bottom, the striking decorative stripe picking
out the central periphery and the sensational wine-red paint
all helped to give it an attractive, almost elegant appeal. The
first Borsig locomotive of this class, number 05001, was proudly introduced in summer 1935 at the '100 Years of German
Railways' exhibition in Nuremberg. After the Second World
War it returned to Nuremberg, as an exhibit in the Transport
Museum.[42] The sister locomotive 05002, completed only a few
weeks after 05001, enjoyed a triumphant success on 11 May

1936. It set a new world record for steam locomotives of
200.4 kph, on the Berlin-Hamburg run. There could hardly be
a better demonstration of this streamlined locomotive's mature
concept.[43]

The Class 06 locomotive built in 1939 by Friedrich Krupp AG
in Essen, at the time the largest steam locomotive in Europe,
was closely based on the successful Borsig locomotive in formal terms. The megalomaniac Third Reich wanted this mammoth locomotive to be one of its visual monuments. It was
intended to document the superiority of German technology,
but in the last resort it was unable to compete with the
Pennsylvania Railroad's gigantic S-1 streamlined locomotive,
designed by Raymond Loewy, at the time the largest locomotive in the world and one of the main attractions at the New
York World Fair of 1939, especially as it had major structural
faults. Details of the streamlined covering also show that Germany was entirely dependent on foreign ideas when it was
striving to reach an international standard. Thus the Krupp
locomotive's driving wheels remained uncovered, clearly a
borrowing from American models. The three parallel coloured
decorative stripes are reminiscent of the typical 'speed lines'
on streamlined American locomotives.

From 1939 the Class 01.10 streamlined locomotive, built in a
large series by the Berliner Maschinenbau Act. Ges., formally
L. Schwartzkopff, was a heavy Pacific locomotive and the lighter Class 03.10 locomotive built in parallel by Borsig, Krupp
and Kraus-Maffei also saw the gradual introduction of open
driving wheels, or the locomotive was delivered ex-works with
cut-out driving wheel apron, a practice followed by Borsig
and then even more consistently by Krupp. The shape the streamlined shell had now acquired, with strongly prominent flanks,
curving vigorously downwards at the front, and further emphasized by coloured bands was characteristic of the uniform
appearance of most German streamlined locomotives built
after 1939.

In parallel with Borsig, Henschel & Sohn AG in Kassel, with
the Weymann & Co coach factory, worked from 1933 on a
train that was originally intended as a simple counterpart to

11

the 'Fliegender Hamburger', but then combined the advantages of the railcar with those of the steam locomotive. Henschel's original 1933 concept was based on a two-coach train with a locomotive and tender, whose funnel-shaped end was intended to fit over the point of the double coach it was to pull. The locomotive's streamlined, rounded nose corresponded with the end of the train, creating a train unit visually related to the 'Fliegender Hamburger'. As this design – if one disregards the use of domestic energy sources – offered no advantages over the railcar, the concept was thoroughly worked over once again. The Henschel-Wegmann train, completed in 1935, then appeared with four lightweight coaches and an approximately symmetrically designed tender locomotive that could travel in either direction without being turned. With just under 200 seats, an additional dining-car and kitchen and an observation car at the end of the train on the American model, the Henschel-Wegmann train offered considerably more comfort than the 'Fliegender Hamburger'. The locomotive, designed by Georg Heise, Henschel's chief design engineer, known as number 61001, with its blunt front section and flanks sloping diagonally forwards or backwards was surprisingly similar to the Pennsylvania Railroad's GG-1 electric locomotive, whose design had been modified in 1934 by Raymond Loewy with a new colour scheme underlining the streamlined shape. Like the GG-1 the Henschel loco had a double cabin, i.e. two driver's cabs, making it possible to travel in both directions. Only the asymmetrical placing of the cabin, caused by the placing of the boiler, distinguished the Henschel loco from the GG-1, and showed that a steam locomotive was hidden under its streamlined shell. This asymmetrical quality, further emphasized by the diagonal slope of the flanks, which was picked out by the paintwork, created an unusual dynamic that was continued through the length of the train, thanks to the uniform colour scheme. Even before the Henschel-Wegmann unit went into regular service on the Berlin–Dresden route, this attractive train, striking in its delicate colour combination of violet, ivory-white and silver, was used as Pullman car for state visits.

Less attractive in terms of colour, but no less successful, was the Henschel locomotive used by the Lübeck-Büchen railway for the Hamburg–Lübeck suburban service. Its principal role was to carry the largest possible number of people to the Baltic at the greatest possible speed. This Henschel locomotive, also called 'Mickey Mouse' because of its mouse-grey paintwork, was similar to the 61001 loco in shape, but smaller and not as elegant, pulled a unit made up of two double-decker coaches. "Great store was set by simple, tasteful and comfortable interior furnishings, design by Frau Architekt Bertsch of Berlin. Leather-upholstered steel seats were used in the 3rd class, the 2nd class has comfortable seats, and is clad in walnut on the side walls and maple on the ceilings."[44]

Hitler's megalomaniac plans

The double-decker train with streamlined locomotive to carry large numbers of people immediately evokes associations. If one considers subsequent history, then this train seems almost like a dress rehearsal for an enterprise on a scale that only the Nazis could dream up. Since autumn 1941, i.e. after the initial success of the Russian campaign, Hitler had been considering a broad-gauge railway,[45] which he at first attempted – to distract from his actual aims – to associate with his megalomaniac urban development plans. The cities of Berlin, Hamburg, Nuremberg, Munich and Linz were to be dominated by gigantic monumental buildings, and connected by an equally enormous 4 m gauge railway with 6 m wide double-decker coaches. In reality however the railway – and this became all the more urgent the more the collapse loomed – was intended for economic opening up and settlement of the eastern area, especially the Ukraine and the Donets basin as the future granary of Europe. Planning was pushed forward on Hitler's express orders and continued almost undiminished into the last days of the war.[46] There was no discussion about the necessity and economic viability of a mammoth railway of this kind; the engineers responsible never offered any criticism as their

12   13

lives were safer at the drawing board than at the front. Albert Speer remembered Hitler's plans in his 'Spandauer Tagebücher': "Hitler occasionally explained a modern 4 m gauge railway system to Minister of Transport Dorpmüller, using sketches that he had made himself. He thought that this would permit a usable width of six metres, so that proper, attractive sleeping compartment, almost bedrooms, would be possible on both sides of a central corridor. He fixed the height of the cars at four and a half to five metres, making possible double-decker cars with a compartment height of two to two and a half metres. These are the proportions of a residential building, and obviously this was how Hitler imagined the eastern railway system. It was intended to be spacious, because whole families would have to live there together for days on end: "But the dining car will have only one floor. It will then be six metres wide, thirty metres long and five metres high. Now that would be a fine banqueting chamber even in a palace, as Minister Speer will confirm."[47]

The plan was to equip these trains with heavy furniture, thick plush, wood-panelled walls and chandeliers in the dining room, appropriately to the conservative tastes of the Nazi regime. Various special cars, including bath cars with lounges, cinema cars and double-decker observation cars at the streamlined end of the train were intended to provide increased comfort on the long journey to the East. By summer 1943 a total of 33 locomotive designs with all kinds of power systems – from steam to electric to gas turbine and various hybrid forms – had been developed and submitted in a five-volume report by a wide range of locomotive factories like Borsig, Henschel, Berliner Maschinebau Act. Ges. (Schwartzkopff), Krupp, the Wiener Lokomotivfabrik AG Wien-Floridsdorf, the Reichsbahn central offices in Berlin and Munich and the electrical firms Siemens and BBC.[48] These designs were based on the "requirements for construction principle for locomotives and coaches for broad gauge main line trains", a memorandum prepared by Günther Wiens for secretary of state Ganzenmüller in November 1942.[49] This memorandum laid down that the locomotives, intended to reach speeds of 250 kph, should all be

streamlined, but left a great deal of variation for the shape of the front. The optimal shape for locomotive and final car was to be determined by wind tunnel experiments in Professor Kamm's Kraftfahrforschungsinstitut in Stuttgart.[50]

After Hitler had given the go-ahead for thinking on this almost inconceivable scale there seemed to be no limits any more. For example the Zeppelin GmbH airship building in Friedrichshafen, stimulated by its role as expert adviser to the Reichsbahn office in Munich, but presumably also as well because the days of the airship were numbered anyway, submitted its study for building a 'Large-scale propeller-driven railcar' in October 1942.[51] This open-plan rail Zeppelin outdid all previous projects: it was 90 m long, 12.5 m high and 12.5 m wide, with room for 650 passengers and 50 crew, also 213 beds (188 for passengers and 35 for crew), distributed over a total of four decks.[52] It makes Kruckenberg's 1937 design for a propeller driven car, seemingly gigantic at the time, look rather more than modest with its length of 40 m and room for 96 passengers.

One is more inclined to think of Norman Bel Geddes and his design, as early as 1929, for Air Liner Number 4, a giant flying boat with a wing-span of 47.1 m and 9 decks (including café, bar, hairdressing salon and solarium), which exceeded all previous dimensions.[53] In the USA, however, the land of unlimited possibilities and almost boundless belief in technology designs like Geddes' were intended to bolster hope; they were utopias intended to help people through the depression period and herald a better future, but gigantic projects like this in the hands of the Nazis became pure political instruments. Like monumental architecture they were part of the Nazis' intimidatory tactics. There is scarcely any better commentary on these excesses than the words of Heinrich Heine, who was seized by profound distress at the thought of the railway as early as 1843: "the thinker is seized by eerie horror of the kind that we always feel when something monstrous, something absolutely unheard-of happens, with unforeseeable and unpredictable consequences".[54]

14

12   Deutsche Reichsbahn streamlined steam locomotive 06001, built
1939 by Krupp. Photograph: H. Maey.
A. B. Gottwaldt Collection.

13   Type 03.10 streamlined steam
locomotive with open driving wheels,
built by Krupp, 1939. A. B. Gottwaldt
Collection.

14   Steam locomotive for the
Henschel-Wegmann train, 1936.
A. B. Gottwaldt Collection.

Further excesses were prevented by the end of the war. Confrontation with a dreadful reality led to great sobriety. For the time being there was no demand for speed records. The only goal was survival, for the railways as well. The few locomotives that were still intact had to be deployed as economically as possible. For steam locomotives this meant above all liberating them from their expensive streamlined shell, still suspect to most railway engineers. Their great days were over anyway. The future of the railway lay much more in modern power possibilities, in new technologies that went better with aerodynamic design. Modern high-speed trains – the Shinkansen, the TGV and the ICE – are products of this development. Kruckenberg had done a great deal of preliminary work towards them with his Rail Zeppelin.

15

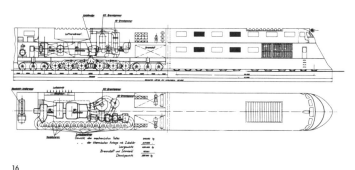

16

[1] Heinrich Heine on 5 May 1843 in Paris on the occasion of the opening of the Paris–Orléans and Paris–Rouen railway, in: Heine, Heinrich: Sämtliche Werke. N.F. vol. 3. Vermischte Schriften. III. Lutezia, part 2, LVII, Amsterdam 1858, p. 77 f.

[2] Andersen, Hans Christian: Eines Dichters Basar, Leipzig 1973, p. 25.

[3] Spielmann, Karl: Jean Jacques Heilmann und die dampfelektrische Lokomotive, in: Lok-Magazin, no. 18, June 1955, p. 15 ff.

[4] Kiaulehn, Walther: Berlin. Schicksal einer Weltstadt, Munich 1958, p. 489.

[5] Scherl, August: Ein neues Schnellbahnsystem, Berlin 1909.

[6] Scherl, loc. cit., p. 53.

[7] With his newspaper, the 'Berliner Lokal-Anzeiger', Scherl had also been involved in financing foreign flying demonstrations on the Tempelhofer Feld near Berlin in 1909; French aviator Armand Zipfel had been to Berlin with his Voisin biplane in January/February 1909 at the expense of the Scherl-Verlag, and American Orville Wright with the first motorized aeroplane in the world. Cf. also Erman, Hans: August Scherl, Dämonie und Erfolg in wilhelminischer Zeit, Berlin 1954, p. 242 ff.

[8] Scherl proved the practicability of his gyroscopically stabilized monorail by large-scale tests. Cf. Kruckenberg, Franz: Fernschnellbahn und Verkehrshaus, Heidelberg 1959, p. 31. On 10 November 1909 Scherl introduced a model of his monorail controlled by his son Richard to the public in the Ausstellungshallen am Zoo Berlin. Cf. Erman, loc. cit, p. 252 and ill. following p. 256.

[9] Quoted from Bush, Donald J.: The Streamlined Decade, 4th ed., New York 1988, p. 56.

[10] Kruckenberg, loc. cit., p. 25.

[11] The 'Göttinger Windkanal' was established by Ludwig Prandtl in 1907. It was the first wind tunnel in Germany. From it emerged the Aerodynamische Versuchsanstalt Göttingen, which merged with the Deutsche Versuchsanstalt für Luft- und Raumfahrt e.V. to form the Deutsche Forschungs- und Versuchsanstalt für Luft- und Raumfahrt (DFVLR) in 1969. Models tested in the Göttingen wind tunnel included the Rumpler-Tropfenwagen, the Volkswagen, racing cars and the Borsig Class 05 steam locomotive.

[12] Jäger, Kurt: Schienenwagen mit Raketenantrieb, in: Lok-Magazin, no. 93, Nov.–Dez. 1978, p. 467 ff.

[13] Otto Steinitz had promoted the production of this propeller-driven car as early as 1903. It was intended to be used for danger-free measurements for new aircraft. The first test run by an aircraft on the DVL car took place in November 1916 on a length of the Zossen–Jüterborg military railway south of Berlin. Cf. Gottwaldt, Alfred B.: Die Vorläufer des Schienenzeppelins. Kleine Geschichte der Propellerwagen in Deutschland, in: Lok-Magazin. no. 79. July/Aug. 1976, p. 267.

[14] Kruckenberg developed a completely new welding technique in cooperation with AEG for the manufacture of smooth, continuously welded rails. Cf. Kruckenberg, loc. cit., p. 37.

[15] Use of light metals in large quantities and thus application of the lightweight building technique for transport purposes did not become possible until economically viable aluminum manufacture developed in the 1890s.

[16] Geissen, Carl: Luftschraubenantrieb und Leichtbau von Eisenbahnfahrzeugen, in: Annalen für Gewerbe und Bauwesen, vol. 88, 1921, p. 53 ff.

[17] Cf. Münchner Neueste Nachrichten of 22 June 1931, quoted from: aluminum. Das Metall der Moderne. Gestalt, Gebrauch, Geschichte. Ed. by Werner Schäfke et. al., Cologne 1991, p. 60.

[18] Geddes, Norman Bel: Horizons, Boston 1932, p. 32 ff.

[19] Illustrated in: Bush, loc. cit., p. 58/9, ill. 43.

[20] Geddes, loc. cit., p. 34.

[21] Cf. Mühl, Albert: Die Verbrennungstriebwagen der französischen Eisenbahngesellschaften, in: Lok-Magazin, no. 121, July/Aug. 1983, p. 277.

[22] Wiesinger claims that he had planned a propeller-driven all-terrain railway as early as 1909. Cf. Glasers Annalen, 1931, p. 114. He refers here to his essay 'Das Schnellbahnproblem' in the 'Technische Rundschau' of the 'Berliner Tageblatt' of 5.8.1914; but there is not a syllable about propeller drive to be found. In other publications as well Wiesinger liked to refer retrospectively to designs that he claimed were very early, but without establishing a date. For the dispute between Kruckenberg and Wiesinger cf. Feldhaus, Franz Maria: Vom Dampfross zum Schnellwagen. Eine kritische Studie, Hanover 1932. This study suggests that Wiesinger manipulated his design dates. No date is confirmed by documentation, none of his designs shows structural detail, none was realized. It is also typical of Wiesingers approach that after an earlier judgment by the Berliner Landgericht II dated 19 December 1932 in favour of Kruckenberg he was again forbidden, in a second judgment by the Kammergericht dated 12 June 1933, to continue to assert in the press that: "the Kammergericht, in the dispute about the intellectual property regarding the propeller-driven express train (Rail Zeppelin) and regarding the railplane concept, decided for Wiesinger against Dipl. Ing. Kruckenberg". Judgment of the 31. Zivilsenat of the Kammergericht in Berlin. Archiv des Museums für Verkehr und Technik Berlin. Feldhaus Collection, document 6840.

[23] This fear was completely unfounded. Experiments had shown that even a newspaper spread out on the platform showed only slight movement when the Rail Zeppelin passed through at full speed.

[24] Kruckenberg had suggested building an engine unit of this kind, consisting of diesel engine, generator and electric traction motor, to the Maybach factory in Friedrichshafen in 1929. He had already worked for them as an airship engineer.

[25] It was possible to build the shell only because of the introduction of the new material Dural or Duralumin, an aluminum alloy developed in the 'Centralstelle für wissenschaftlich technische Untersuchungen GmbH' in Neu-Babelsberg near Berlin under Alfred Wilm in

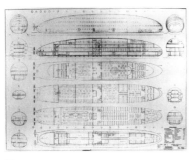

17

15   Lübeck-Büchen double-decker train by Henschel, 1936. Photograph: Henschel.

16   Locomotive for the 3 metre broad-gauge railway, c. 1942/3. Design by BBC for a gas-turbine express locomotive with a top speed of 250 kph and an anticipated performance of 25 000 hp. A. B. Gottwaldt Collection.

17   Design by Luftschiffbau Zeppelin GmbH for a large-scale propeller-driven railcar. Four decks, 650 seats, c. 1941. (Luftschiffbau Zeppelin GmbH).

1906, introduced at the International Aviation Fair in Frankfurt am Main in 1909 and used by Graf Zeppelin for his airships from 1914, and at the same time by Dornier, then by Junkers for aircraft building from 1917. Kruckenberg had not used this material for his Rail Zeppelin on grounds of cost. The 'Kruckenberg' express railcar shell was produced using a special spot-welding process developed by the Flugbahngesellschaft with AEG.

[26] Kruckenberg, loc. cit., p. 60 ff.

[27] Under the window parapet the sheet metal was 2 mm thick, above it 1.5 mm, in later versions 2.5 mm and 2 mm respectively.

[28] Breuer, M.: Neue vierteilige, dieselelektrische Schnelltriebwagen der deutschen Reichsbahn, in: Organ für die Fortschritte des Eisenbahnwesens, vol. 92, 1937, p. 421 ff.; Zielke G.: Die dreiteiligen Schnelltriebwagen Bauart Köln der Deutschen Reichsbahn, in: Organ für die Fortschritte des Eisenbahnwesens, vol. 93, 1938, p. 421 ff.

[29] Gottwaldt, A. B.: Schienenzeppelin. Franz Kruckenberg und die Reichsbahn-Schnelltriebwagen der Vorkriegszeit, 1929–1939, Augsburg 1972, p. 54; Breuer, M.: Schnelltriebwagen der Deutschen Reichsbahn, in: Zeitschrift des Vereins deutscher Ingenieure, vol. 79, 1935, p. 111.

[30] The French had even considered buying the 'Fliegender Hamburger'. Cf. Mühl, loc. cit., p. 275.

[31] The 'City of Salina', built by the Union Pacific Railroad with the Pullmann Car and Manufacturing Company and introduced to the public in February 1934, and thus in principle the first streamlined train in the USA, did not go into regular service until 1935.

[32] This shape is also found especially in steam locomotives, thus for example 'Commodore Vanderbildt' by Norman F. Zapf for the New York Central Railway (1934) and 'Hiawatha' by Otto Kuhler for the Milwaukee Railway (1935). This kind of streamlining was called the bathtub shape because of the bevelled nose and above all because of the shallow arch-shaped cut-out above the driving wheels.

[33] Giessler, Alf: Gesetzmässigkeit bindet Technik und Natur, in: Deutsche Technik, vol. 5, 1937, p. 215 ff.

[34] Giessler, Alf: Der nordische Mensch und die Technik, in: Deutsche Technik, vol. 5, 1937, p. 53 ff.

[35] Schultze, Ernst: Die Angleichung der Verkehrsmittel an die Formen der Natur, in: Deutsche Technik, vol. 5, 1937, p. 162 ff.

[36] Schröder: Reichsbahnschnellreisewagen für die Autobahnen, in: Verkehrstechnische Woche, vol. 30, 1936, p. 530 ff.

[37] As well as Norman Bel Geddes' teardrop car designs (1931), what is meant especially here are the 'Dymaxion Cars', experimental streamlined cars by Buckminster Fuller (cf. p. 194).

[38] After the regional railways were taken over by the Deutsche Reichsbahn in 1920 it was decided that so-called standard locomotives should be built. The first standard locomotive was completed in 1925.

[39] The Göttingen wind tunnel experiments began in spring 1933. Previously small-scale experiments had been carried out in the Technische Hochschule in Berlin-Charlottenburg. Nordmann, H.: Versuchsergebnisse mit Stromlinien-Dampflokomotiven, in: Zeitschrift des Vereins deutscher Ingenieure, vol. 79, 1935, p. 1226 ff.; Normann, H.: Versuche mit Dampflokomotiven für hohe Geschwindigkeiten, in: Verkehrstechnische Woche, vol. 30, 1936, p. 546 ff.; Beil, William: Die Entwicklung der Stromlinienlokomotiven der deutschen Reichsbahn, in: Die Lokomotive, vol. 37, 1940, p. 35 ff.

[40] For this reason and because of the danger of overheating the driving wheels were left uncovered as a matter of principle abroad, especially in the USA.

[41] Maedell, Karl-Ernst: Adolf Wolff und die Borsig-Projekte der Jahre 1931–1945, in: Lok-Magazin, no. 50, Oct. 1971, p. 819 ff.

[42] The streamlined cladding was first removed after the Second World War, then later partially replaced for the purposes of the Museum.

[43] A later variant, the 1937 05003 locomotive, had the driver's cab at the front – recognizable from the position of the windows – because it was coal-dust fired, but this proved unsuitable in practice.

[44] Mauck, Paul: Doppelstöckige Stromlinienzüge der Lübeck-Büchener Eisenbahn, in: Deutsche Technik, vol. 4, 1936, p. 287.

[45] The idea of a 4 metre broad gauge railway had been touched upon by Hitler in a conversation with Kruckenberg in the Reichskanzlei as early as summer 1934. Cf. Kruckenberg, loc. cit., p. 64.

[46] Special departments were set up in Kiev and Rostov on Don in 1943, in order to make a start on laying out the track for the termini. Cf. Joachimsthaler, A.: Gigantomanie auf Rädern. Die Breitspurbahn Adolf Hitlers in: Zug der Zeit – Zeit der Züge. Deutsche Eisenbahn 1935–1985, vol. 2, Berlin 1985, p. 712.

[47] Speer, Albert: Spandauer Tagebücher, 4th ed., Berlin 1975, p. 239.

[48] Cf. Joachimsthaler, Anton: Die Breitspurbahn Hitlers. Freiburg im Breisgau 1981, p. 113 ff.

[49] Joachimsthaler, Die Breitspurbahn Hitlers, loc. cit., p. 95 ff.

[50] Joachimsthaler, Die Breitspurbahn Hitlers, loc. cit., p. 107.

[51] Luftschiffbau Zeppelin GmbH Freiburg, archive. Document experiment 600/299. This study, not related to a contract, dates from 30 October 1942. It emerges from the report that it was dealing only with first thoughts about this subject, to be followed by further investigations.

[52] The seating design and arangements were intended to correspond approximately to that of the airship LZ-129 'Hindenburg' of 1936. The LZ-129's interior design was by architect Fritz August Breuhaus, with Cäsar Pinnau and graphic designer Otto Arpke.

[53] Geddes, Horizons, loc. cit., p. 109.

[54] Heine, loc. cit, p. 77.

AERODYNAMICS THE ITALIAN WAY

Angelo Tito Anselmi

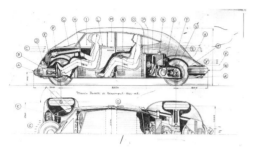

1

2

Italy was perhaps less fortunate than Germany, in that it lacked a school of scientific aerodynamics comparable to that which took shape around Ferdinand von Zeppelin; nevertheless, it managed to produce a highly developed aircraft industry, a fact that is particularly remarkable when seen in relation to Italy's limited economic and political importance. And one thing is beyond any doubt: Italians have always loved car races.

Italy's poverty, compounded by stiff taxation proportional to engine displacement, also encouraged interest in aerodynamics. Italian automobile engines were invariably small, if not tiny. Whoever entertained the notion of entering the Mille Miglia in a Topolino Sport (30 horsepower in the meanest versions) had to be concerned with optimal air penetration in order to coax just a bit more speed out of his vehicle.

Another, peculiarly Italian paradox was the abundance of engineers among automotive journalists at a time when car design was bereft of engineering competence. While the cars were being designed by attorneys such as Cavalli at Fiat, skilled draftsmen like Merosi and even foremen such as Jano, both with Alfa, they were described and critiqued in the press by trained engineers like Giovanni Canestrini or Giovanni Lurani, who rationalised the theory behind their designs and explained it to the public. The rationale in those days was 'aerodynamics': a magazine such as 'Motor Italia' came down squarely on the side of 'aerodinamismo' and a renewal of form, with the help of Gino Cabutti's explanatory talents and the contributions of top-level freelance designers such as Fedele Bianco and Mario Revelli de Beaumont.

Why do we put 'aerodynamics' in quotation marks? Because we know that it was more a question of visual style than fluid dynamics. In Italy during the thirties, despite all the favorable influences mentioned above, empirical aerodynamics was 'de rigueur' for sports use but was not a serious option when it came to making luxury cars.

Even in the second half of the decade, the new style encountered fierce resistance which it overcame only through costly compromise. In a country such as Italy, where the automobile is a matter not only of reason but of the heart as well, the clas-

sical style (inherited, in the words of Gianni Agnelli, "from the thinkers of ancient Greece") put up a valiant fight. There is little doubt that the visual landscape was and probably still is to an extent dominated by an orthodoxy of taste. This arises less from the salutary contemplation of Italy's monuments (however invisible they may become in the long run through familiarity) than from antiquated teaching in matters of aesthetics. As late as in the fifties, the School of Architecture in Milan included in its curriculum the subject of 'monument drawing'. Even in classes on Drawing from Nature, students were expected to copy Corinthian capitals. Small wonder, then, that design was in those days more a dissident view than a true profession.

In the early thirties, the 'aerodynamic' mode of thought, suffering from Italy's autarchic isolation and the relative weakness of the mass media at the time, had difficulty in overcoming tradition as a weak and still unfamiliar opponent of what I would term the 'Vitruvian' school of coachbuilding. The term is justified in that all involved in the traditional view, be they coachbuilders or clients, must have been unwitting prisoners of the classical mold. How else can we account for the extraordinary durability of certain motifs, such as the horizontal belt line of car bodies? But how is one to break the rules without making some enemies?

The conflict between tradition and innovation was more stridently felt in Italy than elsewhere, but it also found a uniquely elegant compromise solution. Great coachbuilders such as Touring and Pininfarina invented a 'poetic' aerodynamic vocabulary by mediating between racetrack-inspired shapes and bourgeois tastes.

In the process, of course, much was lost in the way of true aerodynamic efficiency (no doubt to the chagrin of the very same coachbuilders, who were busy improving airflow for racing). Even more would be lost if 'aerodynamic' intentions were to become a mere fashion or, even worse, a stylistic vernacular: if aerodynamic design were reduced to a calligraphic exercise on the basic egg shape – an exercise as meaningless as placing a row of Ionian columns on the fassade of a power station. But the best studios did not make the fundamental mis-

1   Mario Revelli di Beaumont: design for a unitary vehicle, 1933.

2   Emilio Castagna: design for a streamlined car, 1934 (not built).

3   Fiat Tipo 'Zero' (Brooklands), 1913.

4   Fiat S76 record attempt car, cubic capacity 28.3 litres, achieved 213 kph.

3

4

take of turning the aerodynamic form into an everyday banality. It may be in order here to turn back for a moment to the early years of the century to recall the background of stifling middle class mediocrity from which automobile design was struggling to emerge, a situation not dissimilar to the present one. Architecture was undergoing an eclectic phase, with elements of a Gothic revival. Furniture design was stuck in a sort of late Biedermeier, and things tended to slip further in time when going from rich to poor.

Today, of course, the mass media give us immediate access to everything, and it is difficult for us to imagine just how slow the diffusion of images was sixty years ago. Not only was image production technically difficult, but censorship and self-censorship also played a role. Pictures from abroad were considered subversive material. It is difficult to overestimate the resilience and immutability of the aesthetic culture of order and harmony, not just among consumers, but also in the places where new cars were being designed.

Cars in those days were metaphors on wheels, not means to an end: part royal carriage, part house, part Mephistophelean swirl. True, scientific aerodynamics is at odds with this cluster of symbols, and equally incompatible with the Vitruvian notions of structure. No radical change of scene took place then, and in some ways, it still hasn't taken place today.

Aerodynamic styling was by no means confined to automobiles, however. Since the beginning of the century, it was at least implicitly existent and had two important and venerable examples to refer to: the design of artillery projectiles and clipper ships (not to mention the field of ichthyology. In Gozzani's Italy, Agello set his speed records, aerodynamic railcars (the 'Littorine') entered line service, and some reasonably aerodynamic (and sublimely beautiful) cars did get built. A new order was slowly learning to live with the old one.

Let me illustrate the slowness of this process. The concept of one-box designs, first advocated by Mario Revelli de Beaumont in the long years between 1933 and 1940, took all of fifty years to become acceptable as an élite product, in the Renault Espace, the Pontiac Trans Sport and the Toyota Previa. It seems

that a time span sufficient to redraw the map of the world is too short to alter popular taste.

In addition, one has to reckon with the Italian passion for subtlety and elegance at any cost. German experts in aerodynamics may play with their exact, ugly shapes, but Italy must live up to its role as the Land of Beauty. Despite all of this, many creative miracles did take place in Italy, which is all the more remarkable for the kitsch context in which they appeared – something that would delight (or appall, as the case may be) a specialist such as Alberto Arbasino. What is truly miraculous is the complete isolation in which great creations were produced, in an environment saturated by official Italian culture of the twenties and thirties, that is to say the epitome of 'squareness' in every sense. The influence of Europe's artistic avant-garde was hardly felt within this secluded atmosphere.

What kind of educational background was available to coachbuilders? A crucial role was played by professional schools, the great channel of educational amelioration at the turn of the century. Apprentice coachbuilders attended evening classes in arts and crafts, in which the 'art' chiefly consisted of academic drawing, thought to be useful as a practical means of expressing ideas on paper as well as a stimulus to creativity. The latter part was more in the nature of wishful thinking.

Students and teachers in professional schools were, then, experienced both in drafting and in elementary mathematics, which they used for communicative purposes and to perform very rough checks on structural aspects of a design. In practice, the apprentice coachbuilder was in a position akin to that of a musician able to count to four but unaware of musical notation or harmonic theory. Projective geometry was of little use as a tool, and still less as an end in itself, which it became through the customary perversity of traditional schooling.

Worse still, students and teachers were firm believers in the notion, drummed into them as part of a minimum understanding of the 'humanities', that the practice, or at any rate the interest in, ornamental design was of value in itself. These values, models and styles I have above characterised as 'Vitruvian'. May Vitruvius forgive me for invoking his name in the

5
6
7

context of those horrendous albums with reproductions of ornamental designs on the left page, which the student was supposed to replicate on the opposite page.

Students and teachers, of course, but also active coachbuilders all suffered from a sort of time-warp with regard to their aesthetic points of reference, as if they were stuck in the past. Moreover, their view of the past was rhetorical, monumental and more or less static. An example, not directly related to the topic of aerodynamics, will suffice to illustrate this point.

Not until 1912 did official Fiat car bodies, among the most modern in Italy at the turn of the century, show any sign of the 'Art Nouveau' style. Even if one charitably assumes that the early manifestations of this tendency (Arthur Lasemby working in London in 1875, the Art Nouveau gallery opening in Paris in 1895) had gone unnoticed, Italy could not have been unaware of its own Exhibition of Modern Decorative Art held in Turin in 1902. It included a much-talked-about Scottish section with the famous 'Rose Boudoir' designed by Charles Rennie Mackintosh's group.

It seems that coachbuilders were running ten years late. And mind that this was not a small provincial workshop, but an international firm in the flower of its early cosmopolitan influence and social prestige. An example, this, of the fact that Italy's coachbuilding culture needed to develop a language and expressive guidelines all by itself.

Towards an Industrial Automobile

The liberation of the automobile from the design rules of the horse-drawn carriage was, of course, a necessary prerequisite for its industrialisation, but it must be recognised that this was a slow process, unfinished even today in some ways. Early steps were slowed down by a variety of factors, of which we will name a few:

1 The necessity for a change in construction techniques, which required new tooling and space. Let us recall what seems

today an unlikely fact: at the turn of the century, coachbuilders were upstarts without any specialised tooling, while builders of horse-drawn coaches were large, traditional concerns with a full complement of specialised tools, including those needed for repetitive work.

2 The industrially-built car body found itself unable to attain either the quality of detailing and materials or the prestige of the true coachbuilt automobile. As a result, the latter survived as a luxury product well into the fifties and is far from extinct even today.

3 Insofar as they mostly built chassis, the automobile factories at the beginning of the century had little know-how other than mechanical, and even that had its origins in earlier vocations such as light arms and textile equipment. This enabled the great coachbuilding firms to present themselves as builders of car bodies, or at any rate, to design and build prototypes which were later replicated by automobile manufacturers proper. These, in turn, made up for their lack of early experience by buying out small coachbuilding firms or hiring skilled workmen and foremen away from the larger ones.

4 The truly independent designer found it very hard to make his mark and, in any event, did not appear until the latter half of the twenties. Even then, only one or two names made it to the top in each generation, for instance in Turin: Mario Revelli, Fedele Bianco and Giovanni Michelotti. A much more frequent occurrence was for a full-time employee or junior member of the industrialist's family to fill the role of art director or designer, as was the case with Emilio Castagna.

Obviously, all these factors contributed to delay and conservatism, because the system engendered the separation of creative minds and innovations in production technology. The turning point came with a simultaneous change of style and of technology: aerodynamic styling, functional or conceptual, and stamped body panels.

There began a highly fruitful dialogue between those who believed in the formal and craft aspects of the old school and

5   Fiat 34–45 hp, 6 cylinders.
Note the curved windscreen.

6   Carrozzeria Touring Superleggera: Fiat 508 C 1100 MM (Mille
Miglia), 1938.

7   Pinin Farina: Lancia Aprilla
Coupé Aerodinamico, 1937. One only
manufactured, here as exhibited at the
1937 Milan Motor Show.

8   Pinin Farina: Alfa Romeo,
Type 6 C 2300 Pescara, 1935. Cars
from Carrosserie Pourtout (Paris) would
be comparable: Talbot Lago SS or
Bentley 'Embiricos', both c. 1938/39.

9   Carrozzeria Touring Superleggera: Alfa Romeo 8 C 2900 B
Speciale. One only manufactured,
intended for the 1938 Le Mans
24 hour race.

8

9

the innovators. The latter often belonged to the very same tradition, not infrequently being junior members of a traditional
coachbuilding family (Pinin Farina vs Giovanni Farina) or
junior partners able to go their own way. Though they were
doomed in the long term by innovation, the great coachbuilding firms found some comfort in the fact that they still could
take new ideas, soften and dilute them, and channel them pain-
lessly into the social ritual. Thus they turned into a fashion what
originally was an aesthetic, structural and social revolution. It
is not by accident, given their high profile, that the best remembered aerodynamic innovations seem to be attributable to one
or the other of the great firms (Castagna, from as far back as
1913). But it would have been difficult for these firms, which
had over the years become focal points of the Italian coachbuilding tradition, to break the rules of 'savoir faire' which they
had drafted and which made them purveyors of the establish-
ment.

The transformation was made possible by way of the luxury
sports car, less bound by the rules of etiquette. And it took
place within the frequently provocative context of high fashion, which had become a part of the cycle of obsolescence: a
successful innovation displaced the rules of the previous orthodoxy by declaring them archaic.

This happened first within, and later outside the great coachbuilding firms, particularly when the large companies began
to reproduce by budding off new firms like Pininfarina, Touring
and Zagato. In the working groups led by these men, who were
literally "as old as the automobile", there emerged a new culture, increasingly free but never entirely forgetful of the good
aesthetic manners required by their refined and rich clientèle.

Towards a Streamlined Automobile

The long road to the fully integrated car body shape as exem-
plified by the designs of the late forties began in reality a few
years before the turn of the century, precisely because of the
aerodynamic idea.

A simple shuttle shape was already in evidence in the record-
breaking electric car 'Jamais contente' built from lightweight
alloys by Carrosserie Rothschild for Camille Jenatzy. Plowshare and inverted hull shapes frequently appeared in record
attempts and in the speed races of the early years of the century. In some of his cars, Amédée Bollée Fils even tried to give
plowshare shapes to the large frontal radiators, while his 'tor-
pilleur' of 1899 sported what seems to be the first sloping windscreen in history.

During this first period, however, the striving for efficiency did
not go beyond the purely functional use of shapes thought, for
one reason or another, to be particularly suited to the penetration of fluids. The concern with efficiency not only failed to
create a new stylistic metaphor, as it was to do later in the thirties, but was also unable to attract users of normal cars, which
continued to look like horse-drawn carriages.

After 1910, aerodynamics was confined to exceptional sports
cars. Etiquette rigorously proscribed any breach of the traditional borders between the formal automobile ('town car' or
'opera coupé') and the sports or casual car, the roadster. But
even with this form of car body, which was to become increasingly popular, it was not until 1912 that we see an obvious
case of a touring car intended for sale to normal customers
with features obviously borrowed from a record-breaking car
(i.e. a 'dream car,' in some sense of the word).

Between 1912 and 1913, Fiat entrusted the Turin coachbuilding
firm Locati and Viarengo with the design of a new type of
roadster for a small group of Zero-type chassis with high-per-
formance mechanicals. The rounded radiator hinted at the
large record-breaking car type S 76 300 HP built by Fiat in
1911 at the behest of the Russian prince Boris Soukhanoff. In
the S 76, the high, narrow and rounded radiator was a striking visual element. The period also saw attempts, particularly
in Turin with Fiat and Garavini, to use rounded forms in bodies
built for enclosed cars. This required the use of highly expensive curved windscreens. But all this exploration was to stop
with the advent of the Great War.

10 11

Aerodynamics and Aerodynamic Styling

From the early thirties, the aerodynamic suggestion became an 'a priori' need, extended to all types of car bodies. But normal and even sports cars gained little in the way of true aerodynamics, while cosmetic touches abounded, more pleasing to the eye than to a stream of air. Windscreens acquired a few degrees' tilt, bonnets sprouted fairings to hide the radiator, and the tail of convertible cars flattened out. The 'bateau' shape, no less efficient, fell from favour.

There remained, however, the irksome problem of the vortices generated by the large wing-like front fenders. Only in 1934 did the first egg-shaped wheel fairings appear, designed to give each individual wheel a better overall profile. The schematic arrangement of a car at this point was made up of five elliptical shapes: four for the wheels, one for the body proper. They were connected to one another by more or less curved volumes, thus starting a long process which gradually led to the 'monolithic' car. The latter remained for the moment a 'dream car', impractical and far beyond the bounds of good taste, approached only by sports cars and the more audacious production models.

In the years 1932–1936, popular tourers remained stuck with the solution of the front fender connected with the running board, though by this time the wheel arch was frequently covered by a fairing lid to give an impression of greater aerodynamic efficiency. As for the body of the car, the vertical windscreen was going out of style and the greenhouse was becoming rounder. The term 'aerodynamic' became a discussion point or a sales argument intended to justify styling changes with little effect on performance, but arising instead from the increasingly widespread use of deep stamped body panels. This was the case for the emblematic redesign of the Fiat 508 Balilla for 1934.

At the same time, news and ample information about the achievements of Paul Jaray, Wolfgang B. Klemperer, Wunibald Kamm and Emil August Everling reached Italy. They were given generous coverage by an enthusiastic and a trifle snobbish press, with Motor Italia at the forefront, whose able editorial team enjoyed privileged relationships with great coachbuilders as well as independent stylists. It must be kept in mind, however, that while much space was dedicated to the subject in its pages, Motor Italia remained an elitist periodical with less than 2000 copies sold.

The major contribution to making these disconcerting shapes acceptable to the general public came from Pinin Farina, Touring and Viotti. They reproduced them in attenuated form in a new kind of car: the small sports berlinetta derived from a production chassis and modified to enter the longest endurance races such as the famous Mille Miglia and the Le Mans 24 Hours. Their presence in crowd-pulling races such as these, compounded with the uncertainty of the races' outcome, did more to publicise this new 'species' than any written words. For this was, without a doubt, a new breed: Touring's Alfa Romeos in particular predicted almost prophetically the classic 'granturismo' of the postwar years.

This sleek, efficient approach to car design, however timely and well-founded, was nonetheless a minor phenomenon. The same period saw the emergence, first among the 'one-off' creations of small coachbuilders and later in production cars, of an 'aerodynamic style' of mostly symbolic value, in reality completely indifferent to scientific aerodynamics. The emphatic prows, thrusting curves and rear overhangs of some 'one-off' creations became truly monstrous, particularly when attached to medium-sized and medium-powered cars (small Fiats trying to be big Delahayes) in true Walter Mitty style. The resulting hybrids were overloaded in every sense of the word. Such a tendency was bound to collapse upon itself. In any case, the Second World War put an end to all this.

The end of the thirties, particularly the extraordinary years 1938–1939, saw the emergence of truly revolutionary automobiles (witness for instance the Fiat 508C MM built for the 1938 Mille Miglia), but these failed to influence popular taste other than by way of contrast. The uninformed eye was tempted to see these deliberately stark forms as simply unfinished. Others were superficially decorated in complete contradiction to the underlying theme.

12

10   Mario Revelli di Beaumont: bodywork for the Alfa Romeo 8 C 2300, built by Carrozzeria Viotto, 1938.

11   Carrozzeria Zagato: special bodywork for the Fiat 500 Topolino ('Siata'), Mille Miglia 1938. Photograph C. Milanta.

12   Carrozzeria Touring Superleggera: Alfa Romeo 6 C 2500 SS (Tipo 256), with driver Ercole Baratto, Brescia 1940.

A far subtler and more useful mediation was provided by the parallel work undertaken by the great coachbuilders on vehicles intended for a wider audience. We thus discover how influential the 'aerodynamic style' of Pinin Farina and Touring Superleggera has been when compared to their more extreme research efforts. The progress of true aerodynamics in Italy was rather slow, as witnessed by the fact that as late as the fifties, cars like the Ferrari sport for the Le Mans 24 Hours were liable to lift off at high speeds due to excessive lift generated by the body. If we really want to be censorious, let us mention a similar mistake made in the seventies, the Montreal coupé designed by Bertone for Alfa Romeo.

This being said, the styling results are plain for all to see: sometimes sublime, always controlled and civilised for daily use. It may be that Auguste Perret's famous quip applies here as well: "On devient ingénieur, mais on naît architecte." ("One becomes an engineer, but one is born an architect.")

Translation: Luca Turin

Barbara Hauss-Fitton

1

2

The 1930s – a period that has acquired the epithet 'the streamlined decade' in American design history – commenced and concluded with a world's fair in two major U.S. cities.[1] Chicago's 'A Century of Progress' (1933/34) and New York's 'The World of Tomorrow' (1939/40) shared the common goal of bringing new hope and optimism to a society shaken by economic distress, social uncertainty, and international instability. This hope was largely generated by a fresh, unsullied belief in technological progress and its potential for improving social conditions. Initially a result of scientific research and its applications, the streamlined form eventually became a symbol of all that was associated with the thirties' vision of an ideal modern society: shared prosperity, mobility, social harmony, and international cooperation.

A Century of Progress 1933/34: Streamlining as Science

The 100th anniversary of Chicago's incorporation as a village in 1833 provided the initial impetus for 'A Century of Progress'. In just one hundred years, the 'Windy City' had grown from a small, swampy settlement into the fourth largest city in the world, a transportation hub with 33 railroads, a major Great Lakes harbor, and a growing airport. After the city was virtually razed by the Great Fire of 1871, Chicago became the birthplace of the modern skyscraper, rising like a phoenix from the ashes. When the stock market crash sent the nascent Fair project into a tailspin in 1929, Fair planners evoked the lesson of the Great Fire: "The forces of progress sweep on. They are the forces of science, linked with the forces of industry."[2] Just as technological progress had been a source of renewal after the fire, transforming disaster into opportunity, it would inevitably triumph over the present economic slump.

The Theme

This conviction provided the thematic focus of the fair. The organizing committee exhorted exhibitors to create dynamic displays that would convey the industrial applications of new scientific discoveries to the public. The notion that the resulting products would bring unprecedented benefits to both the individual and society was by no means restricted to the manufacturers and merchants of the new consumer goods. The 'Official Guide Book of the Fair' informs the visitor that he will observe "the fundamentals of science, and then [see] their step-by-step progress to the finished product that contributes so much to his well-being, and comfort, and health."[3] The most impressive example of this exhibition concept was Chevrolet's 'Model Automobile Factory' in the General Motors Pavilion, a huge assembly hall with synchronized production lines that turned out eighteen new automobiles every day.

The courageous decision of local businessmen to proceed with plans for the Fair in spite of the precarious economic situation paid off. Although 'A Century of Progress' was financed without government subsidies, it was not only a popular success, but a financial one as well. More than 38.6 million people visited the fairgrounds on Lake Michigan between opening day, May 27, 1933, and October 31, 1934, when the gates closed for the last time.[4] (The success of the 1933 Fair had persuaded organizers to extend it for an additional season.) The public responded enthusiastically to the promise of a better future communicated through a wide array of displays; whether they perceived the Fair as a means of overcoming the Depression, or as a temporary respite from its daily miseries, remains moot. A presidentially appointed Research Committee on Social Trends observed in 1933 that "streamlined products seemed to most people to be better-looking and more appropriate to modern times."[5] However, that does not mean that they were ubiquitous at the beginning of the thirties. A survey of both the products introduced at the 1933 Fair and contemporary reactions to them indicates that streamlined forms were exceptional, and that they attracted a great deal of attention as technological novelties. The principles of streamlining were almost

3

1   Pierce-Arrow: 'Silver Arrow',
1933, front view.

2   'A new Way to Travel', brochure
on the De Soto 'Airflow' published for
the World Fair, 1934. Photograph:
Chicago Historical Society, Chicago.

3   'A Century of Progress' exhibition, Chicago 1933/34, in the foreground a Goodyear blimp, in the
background the General Motors pavilion. D. Phillips Collection.

exclusively applied to means of transportation: automobiles, trains, ships, and aircraft. Manufacturers cited greater speed and efficiency as justification for unconventional shapes and details. Americans regarded the improved performance of the single vehicle – and above all, its greater capacity for speed – as proof that progress could not be halted, and that it would eventually transcend the present crisis. It is in this context that Norman Bel Geddes' proclamation is best understood: "... speed is the cry of our era, and greater speed one of the goals of tomorrow." Although such unbounded faith in the positive potential of physical mobility may seem naive today, it was the catalyst for many developments that came to define present-day society.

Automobiles

In 1933, the leading automobile and train manufacturers were caught up in a heated competition to complete their first streamlined models. All of the streamlined automobiles shown during the first season of the Chicago World's Fair were hand-made prototypes. Foremost among them, and seldom mentioned since, was Pierce-Arrow's 'Silver Arrow'. Philip Wright had developed the initial design for the 'Silver Arrow' during a 'Car of the Future' contest conducted by Harley Earl among his young staff in General Motor's Art and Colour Section. When Wright left GM, he took his pioneering design for a 147-inch Pierce-Arrow chassis to Roy Faulkner, a vice-president at Pierce. The project was then transferred to Studebaker, Pierce-Arrow's parent company, where five prototypes were developed and constructed under highly secretive conditions beginning in 1932.[7]

Studebaker's chief body engineer, James Hughes, modified Wright's model to fit a 139-inch wheelbase chassis and added various details. However, he retained the most notable characteristic of the original design, namely the continuation of the high front fender line with its integrated headlamps past the doors and down into the tail. The resulting space between the fender and front door served as a spare wheel compartment.

The all-steel, 'step-down' body design, shrouded rear baggage compartment, enclosed running boards, concealed horn and door hinges, and recessed door handles were features that justified the claim: "Pierce-Arrow gives you in 1933 the car of 1940!"[8] A contemporary critic agreed, calling the 'Silver Arrow' "one of the sensational things of the Exposition."[9]

In 1934, the second year of the Chicago Fair, Chrysler proudly introduced the 'Airflow', the first American-made production car whose entire design was based on the principles of streamlining. The similarities between the world's fair brochures of the 'Silver Arrow' and the 'Airflow' are striking. Both emphasize the role of wind-tunnel experiments in producing "a modern aero-dynamic car" ('Airflow') with "scientifically accurate stream-lining" ('Silver Arrow'). Both show diagrams demonstrating the wind resistance of the conventional scow-shaped automobile as compared to a streamlined profile. And both make a great effort to convince the general public that the car's unusual appearance is "a concrete vision of the automobile of the future" ('Silver Arrow'), rather than a faddish aberation. Pierce-Arrow's text reads in places like an apology:

"Your first reaction to the Silver Arrow design is almost certain to be strong and definite ... strongly favorable or strongly unfavorable. But it is designed for permanency. It will wear well. The more you see it, the more at home with it you will feel."[10]

In view of the fact that the 'Silver Arrow', a luxury car with a sales price of 10000 dollars at the height of the Great Depression, and the more modestly priced 'Airflow' were presented to the public with similar sales strategies, it is evident that both companies were uncertain as to how their new streamlined designs would be received.[11] While it was the price and, more importantly, the financial troubles at Studebaker that prevented the 'Silver Arrow' from becoming a viable production car, some critics suggest that the 'Airflow's' limited success was due to its uninspiring appearance, the result of an overly stringent adherence to streamline principles.[12] Yet in spite of the fact that neither car was successful on the market, they did indeed change the entire trend of car design. Ten years down the road,

4   5

basic features of the 'Airflow' and 'Silver Arrow' had become standard elements on most production cars: an all-steel frame and body, the forward relocation of the engine and passengers, the lowering of the body in relation to the frame, and a unified outer shell.

Another streamlined automobile attracted considerable attention at the Chicago World's Fair: Richard Buckminster Fuller's 'Dymaxion Car'. 'Dymaxion Car Number One' elicited negative headlines when the driver was killed and a potential buyer injured in an accident outside the gates of the '33 Fair. 'Dymaxion Car Number Three" was exhibited during the second season in front of George Fred Keck and Leland Atwood's Crystal House. The car was also included as an example of the modern automobile in the finale of 'Wings of a Century', a grandiose open-air staging of the history of transportation.[13] Yet in spite of the conviction of several leading designers that the teardrop form would eventually dominate automobile design, the 'Dymaxion Car' remained an eccentric experiment.[14] Today, one can only begin to get a sense of the stunning impression the first streamlined automobiles must have made on the average person when one compares them with contemporary models. The cars exhibited in Chicago by General Motors, Ford and Chrysler were, with few exceptions, direct descendants of the 'horseless carriage'. Some had streamlined details such as teardrop-shaped headlights, a V-type windshield and radiator grille, and rounded windows. Cadillac's 1933 World's Fair V-16 Fastback Coupe (forerunner of the 1934 452-D Series Fleetwood fastback) even sported an all-steel roof that flowed into the tail, teardrop fenders, an integrated rear luggage compartment, and concealed spare wheel.[15] However, the streamlining on most standard models was a matter of cosmetic enhancement, rather than the manifestation of a completely new approach to automobile engineering and design.

Railroads

The participation of at least 15 railroad companies in 'A Century of Progress' is one indication of their prominent position in the realm of transportation at the beginning of the thirties. Again, the main attractions during the 1933 Fair had very little to do with streamlining; the railroads' exhibition brochures emphasized the size and power of their locomotives, and the luxurious appointments and air-conditioning of their cars. The Pullman Car and Manufacturing Company of Chicago and the Milwaukee Road were two exceptions. Pullman showed its first streamlined sleeper, the 'George M. Pullman', and an aluminum observation car.[18] The Milwaukee Road proudly unveiled its 'Progress Coach', a lightweight passenger car, pointing out its "sleek, streamlined appearance – the complete absence of window sills, belt rails and roof projections."[19]

The second season of 'A Century of Progress' brought two epoch-making trains to Chicago. In February of 1934, the Union Pacific Railroad's M-10 000 ('City of Salina') rolled out of Pullman's construction yards, giving it the distinction of becoming America's first fully streamlined lightweight high-speed train. Following a transcontinental test run and promotional tour, the M 10 000 went on display at the Fair. Just two months later, the Chicago, Burlington & Quincy Railroad's 'Zephyr' (built by the E. G. Budd Co. in Philadelphia) was delivered and made a non-stop trip from Denver to Chicago, where it, too, was admired by hundreds of thousands of Fair visitors.[20] To a public accustomed to the long black barrels of conventional steam locomotives – studded with lights, smokestacks, handrails and sundry other protrusions – the uninterrupted forms of the M-10 000 and Burlington 'Zephyr' must have been astonishing in their sleek simplicity. As in the case of the new streamlined automobiles, Union Pacific pointed out the scientific sources of the M-10 000's design and the influence it would have on the future:

"Its ultra-modern design and tradition-smashing type of construction is a tribute to the inventive genius of the leaders in the automotive, aeronautical and railway engineering fields. Recognized authorities in the aeronautical industry directed the wind tunnel tests which developed the design for this first fully streamlined train. Scientific studies proved that the use of an aluminum alloy was practical. ... The entire train ... offers

4   'A Century of Progress', view across the exhibition site from the suspension railway mast. D. Pillips Collection.

5   'A Century of Progress', 'Rocket Car' suspension public.

a graphic view into the future of railroad transportation."[21] In case visitors might be inclined to view the M-10000 as an impractical oddity, the brochure states clearly: "This train is not an experiment." ... "It is truly 'Tomorrow's train – Today.'" The first streamlined objects, while attracting great attention, also posed a genuine visual challenge to contemporary society. The development and marketing of streamlined products at the beginning of the 1930s was a risk, and the pioneers of this movement sought to win over the public by emphasizing the scientific validation of their products.

Aircraft

Contrary to what one might expect, the word 'streamlined' was rarely invoked in connection with airplanes and ships at the Chicago World's Fair. Even the cruise of the German dirigible 'Graf Zeppelin' over the fairgrounds on October 26, 1933, failed to provoke any mention of streamlining. Only Boeing's new 247 monoplane (which prompted the development of Douglas Aircraft's DC-2 and DC-3) was praised for its streamlining in United Air Lines' literature and touted (paradoxically) as a "modern flying Pullman" in the 'Official World's Fair Weekly'.[22]

Architecture

In comparison to the smooth sculptural shapes and plethora of airplane motifs that characterized the architecture at the 1939 New York World's Fair, Chicago's exhibition architecture had very little to do with streamlining. Its perpendicular planes and jagged silhouettes, described in the 'Guide Book' as an "architectural scheme of utilitarian modernity," earned it the nickname "Zig-Zag Moderne" among critics.[23] Among the most interesting ideas for Fair buildings were Norman Bel Geddes' unrealized restaurant designs. Each of the three proposals explored the relationship between architectural mass and water or air as a fluid element a 'Revolving Restaurant' with three staggered disks perched upon a 278-ft. shaft; an 'Aquar-

ium Restaurant' as part of a dam with a waterfall flowing over it; and an 'Island Dance Restaurant' consisting of four islands in the center of a lagoon.[24] Not until the New York World's Fair was Bel Geddes able to present his dramatic visions of futuristic architectural environments to a large audience.

One searches in vain for superficial or merely fashionable examples of streamlining at 'A Century of Progress'. The daring technical construction of the 'Sky Ride', an Amusement Zone attraction that transported sightseers in cable cars between two 628-ft.-high (190 m) steel pylons, was such that the streamlining of its aluminum and glass 'Rocket Cars' seemed appropriate, even though they moved at just 6 mph (10 km/h).[25] During the early thirties, the scientific earnestness of streamlined products and the unfamiliarity of their forms prevented them from being exploited for purely commercial aims. That, like much else, was about to change.

The World of Tomorrow 1939/40:
Streamlining as Style

So profound were the historical, political, and thematic changes that took place between the initial planning stages of the New York World's Fair and its culmination five years later that, in retrospect, one feels as if one is looking at a last, fleeting vision of a society subsequently forced to exchange its hopeful idealism for the harsh realities of a new era.

The manifold social and economic problems that had followed the stock market crash still weighed heavily on America in the mid-thirties. Probably inspired by the success of 'A Century of Progress' during the worst years of the Depression, a group of New York businessmen founded the New York World's Fair Corporation in the spring of 1935, believing that the project would make the greater metropolitan area more attractive and provide it with new economic incentives.

6   7

The Theme

The organizers initially chose the 150th anniversary of George Washington's inauguration as the first President of the United States for the main theme of the Fair. However, under the guidance of Walter Dorwin Teague and Robert Kohn, the thematic focus eventually shifted towards social idealism and public edification. The Theme Committee outlined its goals in the Official Guide Book:

"The New York World's Fair is ... to show the way toward the improvement of all the factors contributing to human welfare. ... The Fair will show the most promising developments of production, service and social factors of the present day ... [and] the interdependence of every contributing form of life and work."[26]

This rather long-winded explanation was summarized in the slogans: "Building the World of Tomorrow With the Tools of Today" and "The Interdependence of Men and Nations." The organizers decided to erect a Theme Center in order to communicate these ideals to the public. With its simple geometric structures and unbroken white surfaces, the Theme Center, built by the New York firm Harrison & Fouilhoux, became the trademark of the Fair. The exhibit space was located in the 'Perisphere', a spherical structure 180 feet in diameter. Next to it stood the 'Trylon', a tapering triangular tower 610 feet tall. Visitors entered the exhibit by means of two escalators located in a bridge between the 'Perisphere' and 'Trylon'. After the show, they exited across the bridge and descended back to ground level on a spiraling, open-air ramp called the 'Helicline'.

Planners wanted the display in the Theme Center to appeal to fairgoers of every cast. Psychologists recommended the creation of a "great spectacle" in order to communicate the social message of the main exhibit "to 60 000 000 sightseers bent on making whoopee."[27] It was only natural that this job be entrusted to industrial designers, some of whom had begun their careers in the theater and were capable of applying their experience in set design to the creation of dramatic exhibits. As a result, the New York World's Fair became a 'designer's

fair' nonpareil: Teague, Norman Bel Geddes, Raymond Loewy, Henry Dreyfuss, Donald Deskey, Russell Wright, Gilbert Rohde, Egmont Arens, George Sakier – the list of men responsible for the Fair's main exhibits reads like a compilation of the most influential designers of the '30s and '40s. Both commercial and civic exhibitors had something to sell to the crowds, be it a new product or a social idea, and both employed the abilities of industrial designers for this purpose.

Democracity

Henry Dreyfuss was asked to create the 'World of Tomorrow' in the Theme Center. He envisioned a perfectly functioning, futuristic metropolis in which the work of every citizen would contribute to the common good. After entering the 'Perisphere', the visitors were led onto a two-tiered balcony that revolved slowly around the expansive central space, where a miniature model city was spread out before them. During the six-minute multi-media performance, they observed a 24-hour day in the life of 'Democracity'.

First a voice explained the different parts of 'Democracity', an area covering the equivalent of 11 000 square miles and consisting of an urban business center and cultural district, surrounding residential towns, smaller industrial cities, and farms. Great attention was devoted to transportation systems connecting outlying areas with a multi-purpose terminal in the metropolitan center. The traffic of the future, as Dreyfuss conceived it, provided for the separation of pedestrians and motor traffic, the convergence of air, land, and sea transportation at a terminus, an express underground connection between terminus and business district, and the prioritization of rail and shipping for freight transport. The presentation ended with a spectacular slide show which filled the dome of the 'Perisphere'. Ten synchronized projectors created the illusion of workers "marching in triumph" to the accompaniment of heroic music and inspiring commentary.[28]

It is no coincidence that traffic systems composed a major facet of the Theme Center exhibit. The positive potential ascribed to

6   Norman Bel Geddes: 'Futurama', General Motors pavilion at the 1939 New York World Fair, exterior. Photograph: H. Ransom Humanities Research Center University of Austin/ Texas, by permission of Edith Lutyens Bel Geddes.

7   Norman Bel Geddes: 'Futurama', interior. Model of the city of 1960 built for General Motors. Visitors were around the whole model on a spiral path by a conveyor device, which meant that they could remain seated. Photograph: H. Ransom Humanities Research Center, University of Austin/ Texas, by permission of Edith Lutyens Bel Geddes.

mobility was as great in 1939 as it had been in 1933, when the ever-increasing speed of new vehicles was regarded as proof of unwavering progress. What had changed was a shift in emphasis from the single vehicle – the source of individual mobility – to entire traffic systems, which would create a mobile society.

Transportation Focal Exhibit

In addition to the Theme Center, the Fair Corporation sponsored a number of focal exhibits in the different zones of the fairgrounds. For the focal exhibit of the Transportation Zone, Raymond Loewy also combined a multi-media show with a diorama. The presentation began with a series of moving pictures projected onto a huge map of the world. Strings of lights compared the distance that one could travel in a week on foot, or with historical means of transportation, as opposed to the distance covered by "the swift automobile, the stream-lined train, the Zeppelin, and the modern plane that can encircle the globe, 25000 miles in less than one week." An animated diorama then showed visitors what transportation might be like in the World of Tomorrow. Futuristic ships, trains, and automobiles carried travelers to a 'rocketport', where a passenger rocket was preparing to take off to London on a trip through the stratosphere. After "a moment of awesome silence ... a flash, a muffled explosion ...," the miniature rocket shot through a hole in the ceiling and disappeared.[29] Following the show, the visitor passed by drawings and models of the vehicles of the future as Loewy envisioned them: a teardrop automobile "with a far smaller motor than that of today, movable seats, and extreme aerodynamic streamline"; a taxi with just three wheels and short wheelbase "to meet increasing traffic problems"; busses and airplanes with comfortable sleeping quarters; and an oceanliner "fully enclosed so as to be waterproof."[30]

Ford Pavilion

Like the exhibits in the Theme Center and Transportation Zone, the Ford Motor Company's 'Road of Tomorrow' addressed the problem of future traffic systems. A chauffeured ride in a new Ford, Mercury, or Lincoln on the 'Road of Tomorrow', which rose on a spiral ramp and circled for more than half a mile around the Ford Pavilion, demonstrated the advantages of elevated highways (and of a new automobile) to the visitor: "... On such roads there will be no intersecting streets, no traffic light delays. They can separate local and express traffic, or separate all motorized traffic from pedestrians. They provide for a complete physical separation of opposing streams of traffic.
The spiral type of ramp ... shows how traffic can be lifted to the express level in the heart of a city without wasting space."[31]
When one considers the major attractions in the Transportation Zone, one might have the impression that automakers were no longer interested in streamlining. That, however, was not the case; a shift in the 'applications' of streamline principles had taken place. In 1939, the word 'streamline' was no longer used primarily to describe the scientifically derived form of an individual object, but rather – insofar as it referred to a single product at all – an aesthetic element of design. Advertising texts for Studebaker, De Soto, and Ford Mercury did not praise the streamlining of their cars for technical reasons, but because it represented "beautiful styling."[32] In addition, the meaning of streamlining was extended to denote the general elimination of anything obstructive, inefficient, or superfluous. In this context, the term could be applied both to singular products and complex systems.

Futurama

Nowhere was the expanded notion of streamlining more evident than in the work of Norman Bel Geddes. His 'Futurama' exhibit for General Motors is a quintessential example of the development that took place between 1933 and 1939. After pursuing radical designs for streamlined automobiles, trains, ships, aircraft, and buildings during the early thirties, Bel Geddes increasingly recognized the pertinence and potential of a streamlined society. His attention shifted from teardrop-shaped automobiles and exotic airliners to efficient traffic systems and large-scale city planning. GM's 'Futurama' gave him the opportunity to translate his vision of motorized America in 1960 into a vast working model that became the most popular attraction at the New York Fair.

The main theme of the GM exhibit was "highway progress and possible trends in motor transportation facilities of the future."[33] As the visitors entered the building, they stepped into a dimly lit lobby with a huge map of the United States showing the present transportation system and a traffic network as it might exist in the year 1960. They then took a seat in a 'moving chair-train' equipped with an integrated audio system. As the chair-train moved one third of a mile (540 meters) around a huge panoramic model, the synchronized sound system explained each scene. Subtle variations in scale, an astonishing attention to detail, and animated effects such as active smokestacks, moving cars and trains, and flowing rivers completed the illusion of flying hundreds of miles across the 'World of Tomorrow'.

The presentation concluded with a brilliant surprise. Near the end of the ride, ninety blocks of the metropolis of the future passed by, a city whose citizens enjoyed the amenities of express boulevards, feeder streets, and elevated sidewalks. The enlarged final scene gave the rider a detailed view of a single street intersection and its buildings. Suddenly the chair turned, and the visitor found himself at a full-size reconstruction of the same intersection, right in the middle of the General Motors Pavilion.[34]

A number of Bel Geddes' ideas for future traffic systems were not unique; both the Ford exhibit (Teague) and 'Democracity' (Loewy) demonstrated similar concepts. However, nothing rivaled the scope and creative genius of 'Futurama'. Control towers regulated traffic traveling at up to 100 mph (170 km/h) on seven-lane, single-direction highways. High-speed entrance ramps took the place of cloverleaf intersections. Tube lighting

was built into the curbs to provide even, continuous illumination at night. The theoretical engineering of cantilevered mountain highways and daring suspension bridges received as much attention as the design of teardrop-shaped automobiles and streamlined trains. Even today, the 'Futurama' would live up to its name.

The major reason for the numerous comprehensive exhibits dealing with traffic systems was the recent realization that "the motor vehicle is already operating well below its capacity to serve."[35] The uneven flow of vehicles on expressways and traffic backups in cities were problems that could not be solved by increasing the performance of the individual automobile. By 1939, streamlining made sense only in a larger context.

Railroads

At the time of the New York World's Fair, the automobile was in the process of achieving lasting predominance over the railroad as the preferred means of personal transportation. The major eastern railroad companies were still strong enough to sponsor the largest pavilion at the Fair, accompanied by impressive track exhibits. But they failed to offer their own vision of what automobile manufacturers were so imaginatively displaying, namely "a statement of the future shape of the American landscape."[36] Not the railroad, but the highway played the leading role in this new landscape.

During the short time between the introduction of the first streamlined cars by Pullman and Budd in 1933 and the end of the decade, the word 'streamliner' had become synonymous with the modern train. As this automatic association strengthened, explicit references to streamlining in advertising literature declined. Pullman's brochure for 'The World of Tomorrow' mentions the streamlining of its five new cars just once – as if it were almost redundant. Instead, the booklet points out the modern lightweight construction, comfortable appointments, and attractive interiors of the cars.[37]

The most impressive railroad displays at the New York Fair were the track exhibits and the open-air pageant 'Railroads on Parade'.[38] Visitors could get a close look at Henry Dreyfuss' Hudson-type steam locomotive for the New York Central Railroad's 'Twentieth Century Limited', the Pennsylvania Railroad's 'Broadway Limited' with Raymond Loewy's 'Engine 3768', and – as a special thriller – Loewy's S-1 locomotive for the Pennsylvania Railroad, which ran continuously at 60 mph atop a roller bed. This assemblage of the most remarkable streamlined locomotives and cars of the thirties marked what was perhaps the last great moment of the passenger train in America.

Architecture

Streamlining had an increasing influence on design in areas that had little or nothing to do with it from a scientific perspective. The exhibition buildings at the New York Fair represented a broad spectrum of 'streamline architecture', some earnest and effective, others merely frivolous. Among the most convincing were the Ford Pavilion and the General Motors complex, both designed by Albert Kahn. Their rounded, sculptural forms and uninterrupted surfaces made subtle reference to streamline principles. The Long Island Railroad's new train station and a pedestrian bridge across from the Administration Building earned praise for their daring engineering; gracefully curved roof planes echoed the repeated arches of exposed steel beams. The less a building had to do with transportation, the more it flaunted popular motifs borrowed from the aircraft industry. The principal feature of the Firestone Building was a gigantic fin which resembled the tail of an airplane. The dairy conglomerate Sealtest adopted the same symbol – tripling it for effect. Swift & Company, a leading producer of frankfurters, also joined the airplane trend with a building by Skidmore & Owings that looked like "a gleaming super-airliner", according to the Official Guide Book.[39]

In comparison to the use of the word 'streamlining' at 'A Century of Progress' in 1933, when it connoted all of the seriousness of scientific pursuit, the New York Fair contributed to the semantic generalization and inflationary usage of the term. Pullman no longer talked about streamlining, but one could find "streamlined festivity" in the Amusement Zone, go on "a streamlined 'Trip Around the World'" in the children's park, and even purchase a "modern streamlined book of 'tomorrow'" as a souvenir.[40]

These examples bear witness to a major development that had taken place during the 'streamlined decade'. The person who was seriously interested in applying the principles of streamlining in 1939 did so primarily from the vantage point of future social planning. In the area of vehicular transportation, where streamlining had become a permanent aspect of design, it was most often mentioned as a stylistic attribute. Over the course of just a few years, the public had not only become accustomed to legitimately streamlined products, but had also accepted the superficial transferral of these forms to objects that had nothing to do with motion.

By 1939, the dream of a future in which individuals and nations would live and work together in harmony, utilizing technological progress to the benefit of all, was fading fast. The idealistic themes of 'The World of Tomorrow' no longer seemed appropriate in 1940; they were supplanted by the mottos "For Peace and Freedom" and "See America First". Both the fighting in Europe and the financial losses of the Fair during the first season brought about a change in the entire tenor of the exhibition. A new administration lowered the entrance fee, played down the thematic context of the focal exhibits, and extolled entertainment and patriotism at the expense of social ideals. The Soviet Pavilion, one of the most frequented buildings during the 1939 fair, was torn down. Posters featuring an average middle-class citizen and the phrase "Makes You Proud to Be an American" replaced the futuristic placards of the first year. When the New York World's Fair finally closed its gates on October 27, 1940, a new era had begun – and in its wake, the hope inspired by progress and symbolized by the streamlined form slowly ebbed away.

[1] Cf. Donald J. Bush, The Streamlined Decade (New York: George Braziller, 1975), pp. 2–33; Arthur J. Pulos, American Design Ethic: A History of Industrial Design to 1940 (Cambridge, Mass./London: MIT Press, 1983), p. 393.

[2] Official Guide Book of the Fair (Chicago: Cuneo Press, 1934), 2nd ed., p. 10.

[3] Ibid., p. 38.

[4] Facts of the Fair, Herald and Examiner, Chicago, Nov. 1, 1934; Gene Morgan, Curtain Rose on 1933 Fair 10 Years Ago, Daily News, Chicago, May 27, 1943.

[5] Pulos, op. cit., p. 336.

[6] Norman Bel Geddes, Horizons (Boston: Little Brown, 1932), p. 24.

[7] Paul J. Auman, The Silver Arrow Project, Automobile Quarterly, VI, No. 3 (Winter 1968), p. 266–271.

[8] Pierce-Arrow Looks Ahead (Buffalo: Pierce-Arrow Motor Car Co., Jan. 1933) (pamphlet).

[9] Joseph C. Folsom, The House of Tomorrow, Official World's Fair Weekly, I, No. 22, Sept. 24, 1933, 34.

[10] Cf. Pierce-Arrow Looks Ahead, op. cit. A New Way to Travel (Chrysler Corporation, 1934), (pamphlet).

[11] One major difference in sales strategies was the attention given to the 'Silver Arrow's' speed and luxurious interior, while Chrysler emphasized the smooth ride and safety of the 'Airflow'.

[12] Bush, op. cit., p. 121 f.

[13] Ibid., p. 108. A photograph shows the 'Dymaxion' Car outside the Crystal House, David Phillips Collection.

[14] Among them were Raymond Loewy and Norman Bel Geddes, who were still designing teardrop-shaped autos at the end of the thirties.

[15] General Motors: The First 75 Years of Transportation Products (Princeton, N.J./Detroit: Automobile Quarterly, Inc., 1983), pp. 72–75.

[16] The two prototypes were built by Pullman and Brill at the request of the Chicago Surface Lines. Pullman car 4001, which looked much like today's streetcars, had an all-aluminum body, fully rounded outer shell, and flush doors and windows. Brill car 7001 was designed by Otto Kuhler and also impressed CSL with its speed and smooth ride, as well as increased passenger comfort. Both cars were completed in 1934 and put into service at the Fair. The PCC car was developed by the Presidents' Conference Committee of the American Electric Railway Association and built by Pullman and the St. Louis Car Company. See Alan R. Lind, Chicago Surface Lines: An Illustrated History (Park Forest, IL: Transport History Press, 1979), 3rd ed., p. 36 f. Also: Bush, op. cit., p. 96 f.

[17] Motor Busses, Resembling Large Dachshunds, Will Transport Visitors at World's Fair, Daily News, Chicago, April 8, 1932.

[18] Ralph L. Barger, A Century of Pullman Cars (Sykesville, MD: Greenberg Publ., 1988), I, p. 313. – Official Story and Encyclopedia: A Century of Progress (Chicago, n.d.), p. 221.

[19] Presenting the Progress Coach: One of the Milwaukee Road's Contributions to A Century of Progress in Transportation (n.d.) (brochure).

[20] Streamlining America (Dearborn: Henry Ford Museum, 1986), p. 15.

[21] Progress – Union Pacific (Chicago, 1934) (pamphlet).

[22] United Air Lines (1933), pamphlet. – Official World's Fair Weekly, I, No. 17 (August 20, 1933), p. 5 f.

[23] Official Guide Book 1934, op. cit., p. 20. – Bush, op. cit., p. 169.

[24] Bush, op. cit., p. 23. – Pulos, op. cit., p. 347 and 350.

[25] Sky Ride (pamphlet). The Sky Ride was the most successful attraction in the Amusement Zone. It was designed by the New York firm Robinson and Steinman, who made a name for themselves with their designs for suspension bridges (Mackinac Bridge, George Washington Bridge).

[26] Official Guide Book: New York World's Fair 1939 (New York: Exposition Publ., 1939), p. 41.

[27] World of Tomorrow: New York World's Fair 1939, chapter: "The Theme ...," p. 4 (bound typescript compiled by the Planning Committee, dated Dec. 16, 1938).

[28] Larry Zim, Mel Lerner and Herbert Rolfes, The World of Tomorrow: The 1939 New York World's Fair (New York/etc.: Harper & Row, 1988), p. 55. – Gilbert Seldes, Your World of Tomorrow (New York: Rogers-Kellogg-Stillson, Inc., 1939), souvenir booklet. – Helen A. Harrison, "The Fair Perceived: Color and Light as Elements in Design and Planning," Dawn of a New Day. The New York World's Fair, 1939/40 (New York/London: The Queens Museum, 1980), p. 50.

[29] Official Guide Book 1939, op. cit., p. 199 f.

[30] World of Tomorrow (typescript), op. cit., chapter: "Transportation in the World of Tomorrow," p. 2 f. – Official Guide Book 1939, op. cit., p. 199 f.

[31] The Ford Exposition (n.d.) (pamphlet).

[32] Examples of this marketing strategy: "Styled For Beauty? Yes! ... De Soto's streamline style provides more room ...": De Soto (Chrysler Motors Corp., n.d.). – "This deft arrangement keeps the sweeping Studebaker streamlines unmarred": Studebaker Commander and President for 1940. – "There is smart new beauty in its streamlined styling ...": New Mercury 8 (Ford, 1940) (all pamphlets).

[33] Futurama (1940; pamphlet).

[34] An engaging contemporary commentary by Edmund Gilligan, a newspaper reporter for The Sun, is reprinted in: Zim et al., op. cit., p. 43 f.

[35] General Motors Highways and Horizons (1939; pamphlet)

[36] Joseph P. Cusker, "The World of Tomorrow: Science, Culture and Community at the New World's Fair," Dawn of a New Day, op.cit., p.14.

[37] Pullman, n.d. (pamphlet).

[38] Railroads on Parade was the counterpart to Chicago's theatrical open-air pageant Wings of a Century. Both shows were produced by Edward Hungerford.

[39] Official Guide Book 1939, op.cit., p.115.

[40] Ibid., pp.49, 55, and 250. – World of Tomorrow (typescript), op.cit., chapter: "The Children's World," p.4.

Locations of the primary sources cited in the Notes:
Chicago Historical Society: 2, 4, 9, 10b, 17, 19b, 20, 22, 26, 29b
David Phillips Collection: 13, 23a
Harrah's Automotive Library, National Automobile Museum, Reno, NV: 8
New-York Historical Society: 27, 32, 33, 34, 36, 38
New York Public Library/Annex: 28

1   Kaplan blade wheel for Birsfelden power station. Photograph: Escher-Wyss.

2   Armoured surge chamber for Lavey power station. Photograph: Escher-Wyss.

3   Slide projector for cinema advertising. Manufacturer: G. Andreoli, (Lucerne), c.1945. Photograph: F.-X. Jaggy, MfGZ.

4   Engine test run for the Dornier DO-X flying boat, c.1928. Potograph: Flug- und Fahrzeugwerk Altenrhein.

5/6   Junkers G38 under construction, Dessau 1929–1930. High-capacity aircraft with passenger space in the wing roots. Stadtarchiv Dessau.

7   Airship LZ-129 'Hindenburg', engine gondola with mechanics, 1936. Photograph: LZ-Archiv, Friedrichshafen.

8   Airship LZ-127 'Graf Zeppelin', model in the Luftschiffbau Zeppelin GmbH wind tunnel, c.1927. Photograph: LZ-Archiv, Friedrichshafen.

9   New York World Fair 1939: Futurama, City of Tomorrow; model and staging by Norman Bel Geddes, photograph by Margaret Bourke-White. Photograph: Bel Geddes Collection, H. Ransom Humanities Research Center, University of Austin/ Texas, by permission of Edith Lutyens Bel Geddes.

10   General Electric F 40 steam iron, USA, c.1948. Presumably designed by Henry Dreyfuss. Photograph: F.-X. Jaggy, MfGZ.

11   Illinois Central Railroad: 'Green Diamond' in Chicago, 1936. D. Phillips Collection.

12   Wooden frame for the Tatra 'Type 77' private car, 1934. Photograph: Tatra-Museum, Kopřivnice/ Czech Republic.

13   Corrado Millanta: detail of the Alfa Romeo 2900 Touring, 1937 Milan Motor Show. Archivio Corrado Millanta.

14   Corrado Millanta: detail of Delahaye at the 1937 Mille Miglia. Archivio Corrado Millanta.

15   'Master rider' Ernst Henne on a BMW in the Luftschiff Zeppelin GmbH wind tunnel, c.1930. Photograph: LZ-Archiv, Friedrichshafen.

16   Auto-Union record car, c.1938. ETH-Bibliothek, Wissenschaftshistorische Sammlungen.

17   Record run by racing cyclist Berthet in the 'Aérodyne', c.1930 (direction of travel from left to right).

18   Raymond Loewy: Pennsylvania Railroad K4S locomotive, 1936. Photograph: Ivan Dmitri (from R. Loewy: The Locomotive, New York/London, 1937).

19   'Theos' thermos flask, Switzerland, c.1930. Photograph: M. Perez, MfGZ.

20   ETAT railway two-part electric suburban railcar with stainless steel shell, 1937.

21   Assembly shop with various DC-2s under construction, Santa Monica 1934. Sammlung U. Haller.

22   Two 'Concorde' supersonic passenger aircraft. Photograph: Air France.

23   Three DC3 piston-engined aircraft at an American airport. D. Phillips Collection.

24   'France' passenger steamer under construction. From '303 – Arts, Recherches et Créations', Nantes.

25   'France' passenger steamer under construction: fitting the smoke deflector on the rear funnel, 1961. From '303 – Arts, Recherches et Créations', Nantes.

26   'System Rowenta' toaster, Rotel (Switzerland), c.1960. Photograph: M. Perez, MfGZ.

27   'Airstream' caravan with riveted aluminum bodywork, c.1950. Photograph: Airstream. Jackson Center, Ohio/USA.

1

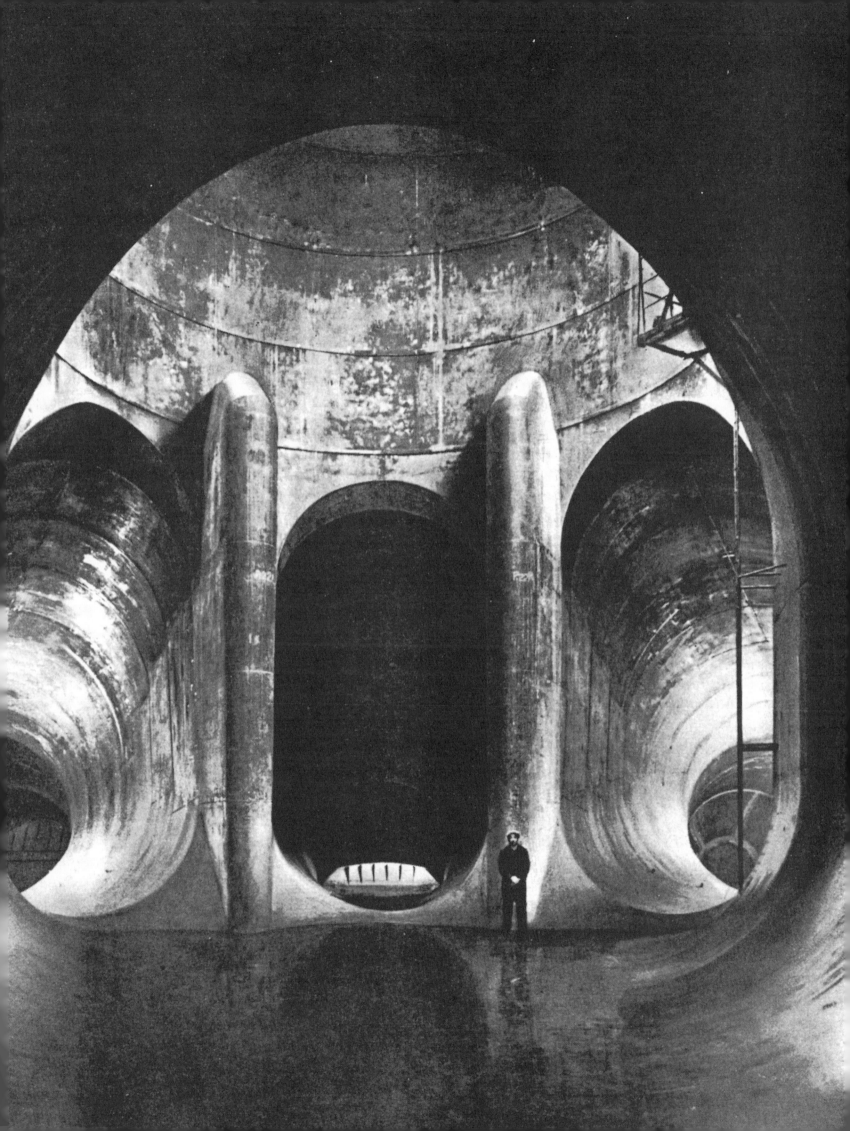

3

8

10

11

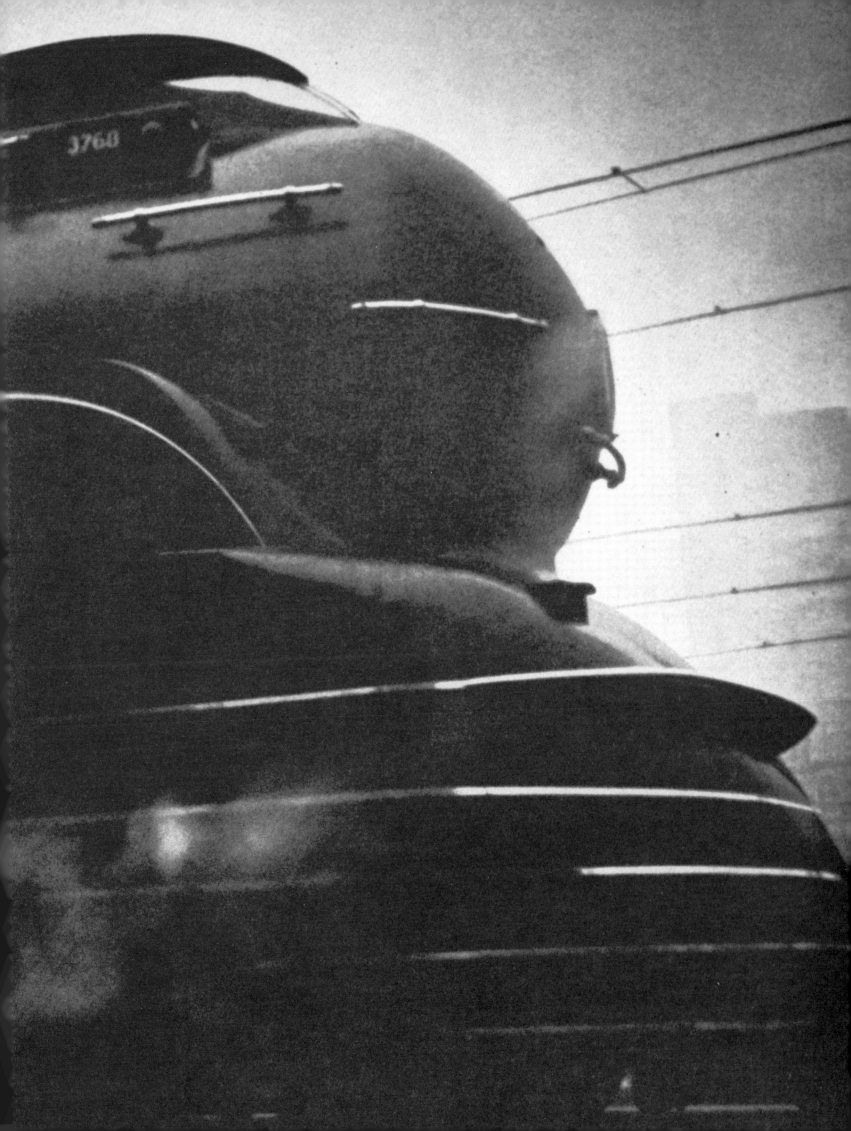

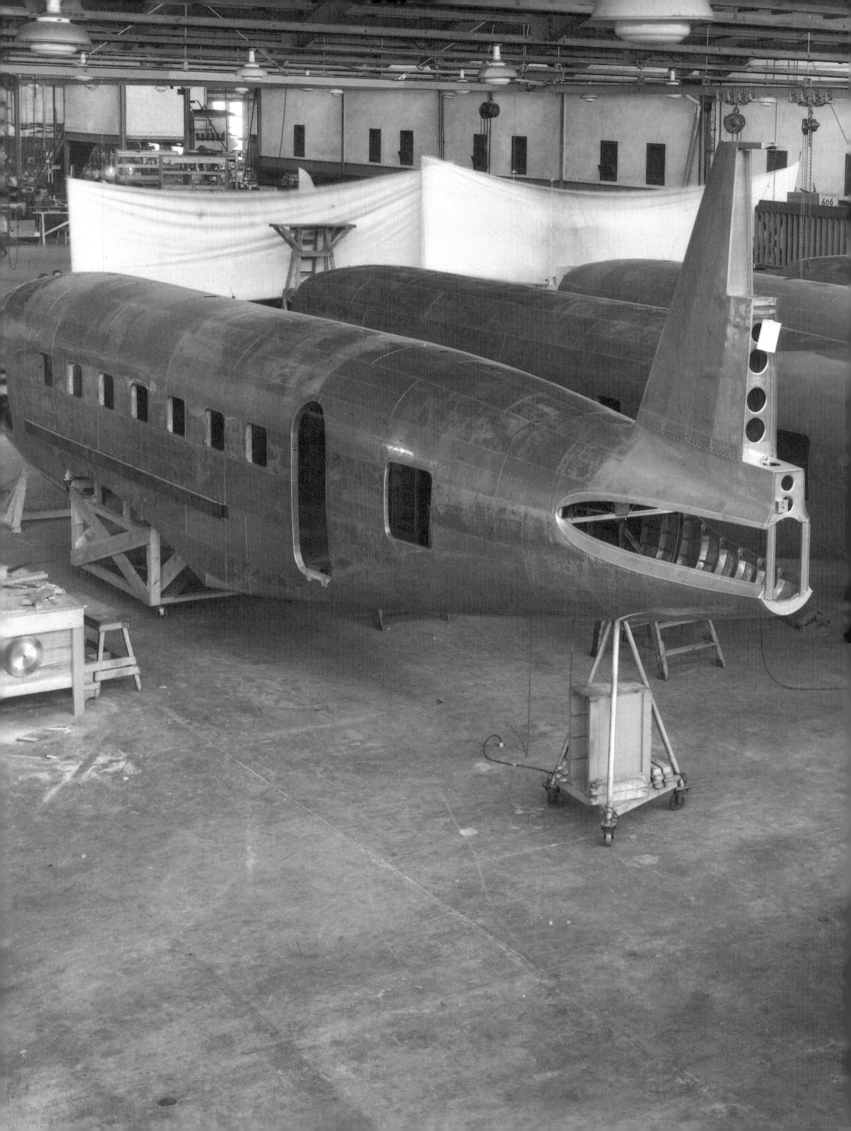

5685
DC-2
2-20-34

24

25

KALEIDOSCOPE

A kind of catalogue

Franz Engler and Claude Lichtenstein

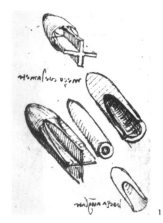

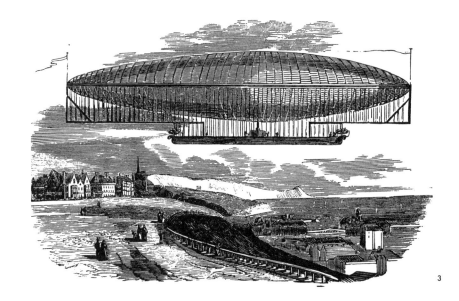

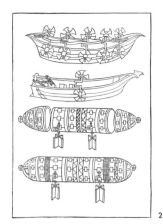

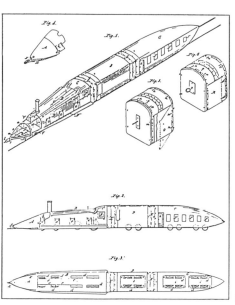

1   Leonardo da Vinci: designs for projectiles with stabilizing wings, c.1500 (from Gibbs-Smith: 'Leonardo da Vinci's Inventions').

2   Robert Valturio: designs for submersibles, 1532 (from 'De re militari').

3   James Nye: 3 airship using the recoil principle, USA 1852.

4/5   Reverend Samuel R. Calthrop: 'Air resisting train', patent drawing and graphic representation, USA 1865.

6   Illustration for Jules Verne's 'Journey to the Moon', 1865.

7   Submarine after Goubet in a contemporary woodcut, c.1890.

6

7

Rigid airships built using the Zeppelin system take lightweight construction to its extreme. The LZ-129, which is documented here, had a volume of over 200 000 m³ but weighed only 80 tons empty, in other words 400 grams per cubic metre of structural volume. Optimum streamlined shape was essential to achieve maximum range, given the engine performance and the high level of surface friction drag (due to size). But insuperable limitations were placed on running Zeppelins economically. Streamlined form was the perfect image of their dream; the airship's contribution to streamlining can scarcely be overestimated.

ZEPPELIN AIRSHIPS

1936 LZ-129 Hindenburg

1 Model of the LZ-127 in the wind tunnel, Friedrichshafen, c. 1927.

2 Riveted parts for the LZ-129, c. 1935.

3 Gondola floor for the LZ-129.

4 LZ-129, assembling the ring elements, diameter of the largest ring 41 m, c. 1935.

1

3

4

1900 Zeppelin Graf Ferdinand Zeppelin (1838–1917) invented the rigid airship. Their structure (light metal frame with gas containers) seemed to suggest that they would scarcely be subjected to size limitations – unlike the blimps. As the years went by they became more and more divorced from reality than anything that had moved through the air until then. Zeppelin's first rigid airship, the LZ-1 (Luftschiff Zeppelin 1) travelled in 1900 (airships did not 'fly', they 'travelled'). It was a long cylinder with two pointed ends, at that time without stabilizing fins. In subsequent decades 'Luftschiffbau Zeppelin GmbH's' creations persistently increased in volume. Research on the optimum streamlined shape was conducted from 1912 to 1921, including a significant amount of work by Paul Jaray (cf. p. 16). It was concerned with detail and the

overall shape. On the first point: it emerged that the envelope offered less resistance with longitudinally sewn strips of fabric than with seams running round the vessel in rings. On the overall shape: the rival firm of Schütte-Lanz (Mannheim) had already built airships in the spindle shape that had now become typical, using a remarkable structure of lozenge-shaped ash members. The spindle shape, with an aspect ratio of about 6:1 (length to greatest diameter), emerged as the most favourable in terms of the proportion of cross-section and volume or air resistance and carrying power.

1936 LZ-129 Hindenburg The LZ-129 ('Hindenburg') was the largest airship to go into public service (the even larger LZ-130 was completed but used only for survey flights

and was soon recycled i.e. scrapped to reclaim the materials for war preparations). The 'Hindenburg' became legendary when it exploded at the mooring mast on 6 May 1937 (helium was manufactured only in the United States at that time; the American state banned its export to Germany in the climate of approaching risk of war, which meant that airships were compelled to continue to use highly explosive hydrogen). Thus the enormously expensive LZ-129 was in existence only for a year, during which it undertook 60 voyages, principally to North and South America. These were journeys for the 'haute volée': a journey across the Atlantic cost many times more than a worker's monthly wages.

The LZ-129 was 248 m long and had a maximum diameter of 41 m. The airship had a structural volume of about 250 000 m³ and weighed

80 tons empty, 140 tons with a full load of fuel and about 200 tons with payload. Unlike blimps, rigid airships were not dirigible balloons, but carried interior gas tanks that provided buoyancy. As well as this there was an empty space between tanks and framework or envelope, and a catwalk suspended on the longitudinal centre line for the crew. The LZ-129's gas tanks had a capacity of 190 000 m³. The four diesel engines produced a total of 4400 hp and gave the airship a top speed of 135 kph. It would not have been possible to improve upon this significantly, even with higher engine performance, because of the enormous surface area and the surface friction drag associated with it.

Passengers occupied 400 m² of space in the lower part of the gondola, distributed over two floors. The successful Berlin architect Fritz August Breuhaus-De Groot was responsible for the interior design of the passenger section. Something anathematized on the ground as 'Bauhaus' style by the regime was a necessity in the air because of the weight factor; even the piano was built of special lightweight metal. Although Breuhaus was interested in Modernism only in an indirect and stylistic sense, the LZ-129 passenger area with overhanging lines of windows through which the journey could be followed must have been one of the exciting spaces of the century. In 1929 newspaper magnate William Randolph Hearst wanted to send a submarine under the pack ice to the North Pole and have the LZ-127 ('Graf Zeppelin', at the time the largest airship in the world) travel to the North Pole by air; the two craft were to greet each other through a hole in the pack-ice. Nothing became of this eccentric plan, as the submarine that had been especially bought and converted turned out to be unsuitable. The Berlin publisher Ullstein bought the project from Hearst for a very reasonable price. This led to the LZ-127's famous Arctic journey, which took place in July 1931 under the direction of Hugo Eckener, director of Luftschiffbau-Zeppelin GmbH. Arthur Koestler, then just 26 years old, was on board as exclusive correspondent, and he described the exciting expedition in his memoirs in 1950. Arthur Koestler: "The passenger gondola, as it was so poetically called, was attached below the hull, near the bow. It contained the bridge and the passenger cabins, which were furnished with all the luxury of a modern ocean-going liner. At the end of the gondola was a door that was usually kept closed. From it a dark corridor led to a land

5   View into the interior of the keel fin. The silk covering has not yet been painted, which is why the space is light.

6   LZ-1299, view of the still uncovered tail fin.

7   Painting the airship's envelope, a surface area of about 20000 m².

5

6

7

of mystery: into the belly of the whale. And it really was the most fantastic place that you could possibly think of.

Darkness reigned in the whole of the interior, whose dimensions were greater than those of a cathedral, except that they were elongated in the shape of a cigar, it smelt like bitter almonds and there was a dull grinding sound as though invisible bats were lazily flapping their wings. The smell came from the hydrogen cyanide that was mixed with the fuel and the noise from the balloon envelopes, the floating whale's most important organs, its air bladders as it were, as it was their enormous buoyancy that carried the gigantic structure through the skies. These balloons were arranged in two rows along the whole of the interior and hung down like enormous pears, each about 15 m in diameter. Under

normal air pressure, when the airship was on the ground, they hung slack, with loose, wrinkled skin, like old witches' breasts; but when the airship climbed into thinner air they became tight and firm and filled the belly of the whale with a noise like a thousand whips being cracked. Between the rows of balloons, suspended freely in the air and in complete darkness a dangerously narrow catwalk hung at a height of 20 metres; the gas cells were serviced from here, by the light of miners' lamps, because of the enormous danger of explosion.

Although it was permissible to use this catwalk only when accompanied by a ship's officer I often wandered about on it, which was always a profoundly exciting experience. In the surrounding darkness, amidst the soporifically bitter almond smell the trembling of the body of

the ship and the grinding and banging of the balloon envelopes was overwhelming. I was surrounded by a framework labyrinth of girders and spars, cables and ribs, a jungle of steel and aluminum, while only a few hundred metres below extended the nameless white desert of the deep North."

Arthur Koestler, Frühe Empörung,
vol. 1, Vienna, Munich, Zurich 1970,
p. 295 f.

11

10

12

13

8–10 'De-hangaring' in Friedrichshafen for the maiden voyage,
17.3.1936.

11   Captain's gondola from the outside, view of the front landing gear.

12   LZ-129, inside the captain's gondola: ship's wheel and chains.

13   LZ-129 outside the airship hangar, engine gondolas with closed air
cooling vents.

9

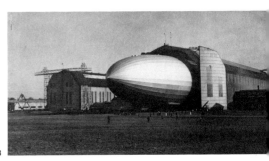

8

14

14 LZ-129, a downward view, a precious privilege for the very few. Passenger lounge, designed by architect Fritz August Breuhaus. Weight restrictions: lightweight metal furniture despite official scorn for Modernism.

15 Shadow of the LZ-127 on stacks of timber near Archangelsk; photograph by the 1931 polar expedition.

All photographs: Luftschiffbau Zeppelin GmbH, Friedrichshafen.

15

Streamlining came to the railway via railcars.
The reason for their development (in numerous
industrial countries at the same time) was
the need to use branch lines more rationally.
The new breed of petrol-, diesel- or electri-
cally-powered rail vehicles led to the development of express railcar unit trains for rapid
and comfortable long-distance journeys
that were economically viable for the railway
companies.

EARLY RAILCARS

1893 F.U. Adams

1908 McKeen

1920 MAK railcar (Kiel)

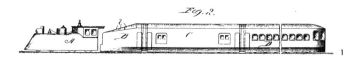

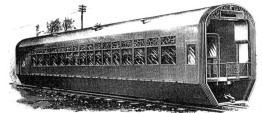

1   Frederick Upton Adams: patent drawing for the 'Windsplitter' train, 1893. Fully covered, low locomotive, tender in a rising wedge shape, cars closed on the under-side, closed galleries between the cars. (From Reed, 1975.)

2   F. U. Adams: cutaway drawing of a 'Windsplitter' car: side aprons reaching down to the rails, bellows at the point where the cars join, closed windows, pressure fan on the roof.

One train (without locomotive, was built for the 'Baltimore and Ohio Railroad' and ran between Baltimore and Ohio from 1900. (From Reed, 1975.)

3   Mc Keen Railway Motor Car (Omaha, Nebraska): petrol-driven railcar with pointed nose and bullseye windows, designed 1905, 150 built for the Union Pacific Railroad (from 1908). Licensees in the German Reich. D. Phillips Collection.

4/5   Railcar units by 'Deutsche Werke AG', Kiel yard, Type 1a, 61 seats, 14 standing passengers, 66 kph, 1920. Photographs: Krupp.

5

4

FRANZ KRUCKENBERG

1930 Rail Zeppelin

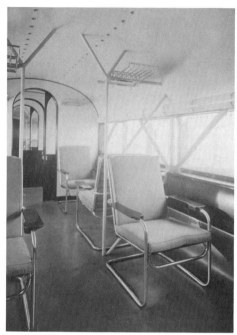

1930 Rail Zeppelin Franz Kruckenberg (1882–1965) was a qualified engineer employed from 1909 to 1924 as chief design engineer for airship builders Schütte-Lanz (Mannheim). There he met Curt Stedefeld, with whom he collaborated closely. When Schütte-Lanz closed (1924) Kruckenberg founded the 'Gesellschaft für Verkehrstechnik' in Heidelberg, and in 1928 the 'Flughafen GmbH'. His aim was to develop a propeller-driven suspension railway, but for financial reasons he and Stedefeld had to prove the capabilities of propeller drive with a conventional rail vehicle on existing Deutsche Reichsbahn track. Kruckenberg's first sketch of the 'flying train' dates from June 1929; in November 1929 he had a detailed project ready for testing in the aerodynamic research institution in Göttingen. The vehicle was built in spring

and summer 1930, and the first test run was on 25 September 1930.

The car was a welded perforated girder/tubular structure covered with sailcloth. The front was covered with a beaten aluminum shell. The vehicle was extraordinarily low: 2.8 m at the highest point of the roof ('Fliegender Hamburger': 3.7 m). It had only two axles, which could be swivelled in a makeshift fashion (axle base 19.6 m). The BMW aircraft engine was inclined upwards at an angle of 7 degrees to create downward thrust. The wooden propeller could be reversed for travelling backwards. The single vehicle built soon became known to the workers as the 'Rail Zeppelin'. The nickname soon caught on: the shape, with its low air resistance, was associated with airships and not aeroplanes. Airships were enormously popular at

the time, particularly because of the Atlantic flights.

The vehicle achieved a speed of 180 kph on its first test run on a straight stretch between Hanover and Celle. The car reached speeds of 230 kph on a spectacular record run from Hamburg to Berlin-Spandau on 21 June 1931 (257 km in 98 minutes). Despite these successes, and although the public was literally spellbound by the 'Rail Zeppelin', the Deutsche Reichsbahn never developed it any further and it never went into regular service. The Reichsbahn was sceptical about the propeller drive for safety reasons, and was now working – independently of Kruckenberg – on the express railcar unit train that went into regular service as the 'Fliegender Hamburger'.

1   The 'Rail Zeppelin' before covering: lightweight metal frame and ash timbers, 1930. Axle base 19.6 m, internal width 2.5 m, overall height 2.8 m.

2   Interior view with tubular steel furniture.

3   Franz Kruckenberg with the 'Rail Zeppelin' (photomontage).

4   The Rail Zeppelin passing through Berlin-Spandau, 1931.

5   'Kruckenberg' express three-part railcar in the Westwagen assembly shop in Cologne, 1938. This train never went into service before the war but had a considerable influence in design terms on the Deutsche Bundesbahn's 1957 'TEE' VT 11.5 and 1963 SVT 18.16.

1–5: A. B. Gottwaldt Collection.

5

Die Reichsbahn (1930), p. 1139 ff.
Schweizerische Bauzeitung: SBZ (1930/2), p. 321 f., SBZ (1931/2), p. 26, SBZ (1939/2), p. 312.

VALDNER

c.1925 Monorail suspension railway

BÄSELER

1932 Panoramic car

WIESINGER

1939 Ultra-fast train

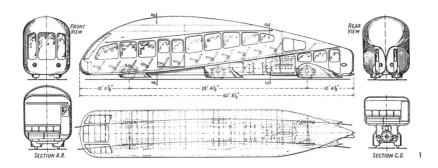

1939 Ultra-fast train The Swabian engineer Kurt Wiesinger worked on propeller-driven express suspension railways from the early years of the century. He was a professor in the mechanical engineering department at the ETH Zurich from 1912, where he did research into the problem of express trains that could not be derailed. He thought that the greatest possible level of relaxation during a journey was achieved by the smallest number of changes of speed; his (somewhat unusual) conclusion from this insight ran like this: "Ideally a journey can consist of only the starting and braking periods provided that the highest speeds reached are not restricted for other reasons. Acceleration at 0.5 m/s² and the same deceleration would produce journey times of 26 minutes on the approximately 300 km Berlin–Hamburg route and about

50 minutes for the approximately 1000 km from Berlin to Paris." (K. Wiesinger: Aus dem Leben eines Ingenieurs und Erfinders, typescript, p. 173 f. Verkehrshaus Luzern library.)
In the late thirties he introduced a plan for an ultra-fast train running across Switzerland, intended to cover the east-west main line in just an hour, with a top speed of 300 kph. Its characteristic feature was wheels set at an angle, intended to permit high speeds on bends and make derailment a complete impossibility.
Wiesinger set up a test plant at Zurich's main station and ran the model in front of large audiences for several days. At a later stage he continued his experiments during several winters at the Dolder swimming pool.

Bäseler: The Railway Gazette: RG (7. 7. 1933), p. 2; Schweizerische Bauzeitung (1933/1), p. 147.

Wiesinger: RG (5. 5. 1933), p. 615 f., RG (12. 7. 1935), p. 62, RG (4. 3. 1938), p. 413.

1   Panoramic car, Deutsche Reichs-bahn design, engineer Bäseler. Vehicle with front view for road and rail, 180 kph, (not built).

2   K. Wiesinger: test track at the Zurich-Dolder swimming pool, c. 1939. Photograph: Verkehrshaus Luzern.

3   K. Wiesinger: ultra-fast derailment-proof train, test model 2.5 m long, 1939. Photograph, Verkehrshaus Luzern.

4   K. Wiesinger: test track between two lecture theatres in the old mechanical engineering laboratory at ETH Zurich, 1929. Photograph: Verkehrshaus Luzern.

5   Monorail suspension railway project by the Russian engineer Valdner, two cars effectively yoked together with the rail between them, 300 kph; c. 1925 (not built in full scale).

5

1–5   Railcar fronts for the 'Fliegender Hamburger', model version for the wind tunnel, 1932. The chronological sequence cannot be ascertained. The criteria were probably not just minimum air resistance but also the driver's view ahead. Version 5 corresponds largely to the shape built. Photographs: MTU Friedrichshafen.

6   'Fliegender Hamburger', general view. Photograph: MTU Friedrichshafen.

7   'Typ Hamburg' express railcar, 1935 version, larger front windows.

8   'Fliegender Hamburger', front section with low upper edge to the windows.

1931 Fliegender Hamburger The composite train that became famous as the Fliegender Hamburger is a very significant development in historical terms; it had a direct influence on American railcar train units like the 'Burlington Zephyr', the 'Railplane' or the 'City of Salina' (see below). This railcar was the project in competition with the 'Rail Zeppelin'. It was commissioned by the Deutsche Reichsbahn in February 1931, developed by and built by WUMAG (Waggon- und Maschinenbau Aktiengesellschaft Görlitz) and delivered in late 1932. The Nazis may have exploited it later for propaganda purposes, but it was not their creation. The two-part composite train rests on two bogies, and so the central link has a common bogie (Jacobs bogie). The two 410 hp Maybach diesel engines, each placed on an end bogie, pro-

duced electric current for the actual traction motor on the centre bogie (diesel-electric drive). The 42 m long unit weighed 77.5 tons empty and could travel at 160 kph, which was the maximum practicable speed on the tracks of the time. Speeds of this kind were completely new. The passengers could read the speed from speedometers over the doors at all times.

What the popular name 'Fliegender Hamburger' expressed was supported by the design. The shape was developed in the wind tunnel at the Zeppelin works in Friedrichshafen. Photographs of various versions of the railcar front have survived, evidence of the search for the ideal shape. A striking feature of the version built is the way in which the roof is drawn low over the driver's cab – the train literally crouches under the wind. The ground plan of the front was more strongly

wedge-shaped than usual; it follows a parabolic curve, not an arc of a circle, like the 'Zephyr', for example (cf. p.136). The train was carefully developed in detail as well. The integral headlights with covering glass and the side aprons are further evidence of the search for an ideal shape.

5

8

7

Schweizerische Bauzeitung: SBZ
(1932/2), p. 57 f. SBZ (1932/2), p. 68 f.
Motor, Ger. (1933) No. 6, p. 25 ff.
The Railway Gazette: RG (27.1.1933),
p. 23 f. Die Reichsbahn (1933), p. 7 ff.
Zeitschrift des Vereins Deutscher
Ingenieure (1933) No. 3, p. 57 ff.
RG (13.7.1934), p. 78 ff.
RG (18.5.1934), p. 896 ff.
RG (5.10.1934), p. 575 ff.
RG (22.5.1935), p. 582 f. Glasers
Annalen (1.10.1937), p. 116 ff.

RAILPLANE

1933 Pullman Car & Mfg. Corp.

BURLINGTON ZEPHYR

1934 The Budd Company

1

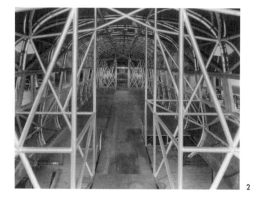

2

3

4

1933 Railplane The 'Railplane' was built by the amazing William B. Stout (cf. p. 18, 194, 212). He developed it for the Pullman Company (the consequence of a lecture delivered by Stout in Chicago in which he predicted a major upswing in civil aviation at the expense of the railway). "I would like – I said – to build the type of rail vehicle an airplane engineer would build, without having a railroad man around to tell how it should be done", this was the beginning of the project in Stout's autobiography (Stout: 1951, p. 270). Stout decided that he would first design a single railcar seating about 50 instead of a complete train. His maxim: consistent lightweight construction. The 'Railplane' frame was made of welded tubular steel, which was then covered with an aluminum skin. Even the bogies were made of tubular steel (photo-

graph p. 30). The engine, a 165 hp lorry engine, was mounted laterally on the front bogie and its power was passed to the driving axle by automatic power transmission (according to Stout this was probably the first time that automatic transmission had been used; it was built by a young Chicago engineer called Oskar Banker). The 'Railplane' had compressed air drum brakes. The 'Railplane' weighed an almost incredible 26 000 pounds unladen. Stout described its running qualities as quiet to a degree that had hitherto been unthinkable, with a high degree of comfort provided by the suspension. But those responsible at Pullman had some reservations about the low weight, partly because a non-motorized car built like this could not be placed between cars of the old, more solid type – another elegant example on the subject of

'tradition and breaking with tradition'. The 'Railplane' remained unique; Pullman built the M-10000 not long afterwards, and Stout was called in to advise in its design and construction.

1934 Burlington Zephyr On 26 May 1934 the 'Burlington Zephyr' travelled from Denver to Chicago, 1000 miles non-stop at an average speed of over 120 kph. This record-breaking journey marked the start of the second year of the World Fair 'A Century of Progress'. The three-part train was seen by over 2 million exhibition visitors. It was pointed out that by being so popular American trains like the 'Burlington Zephyr' also helped to promote the 'modern' furnishing style (cf. Reed, 1975).

The Burlington 'Zephyr' was built by Budd in Philadelphia, a firm that had acquired an inter-

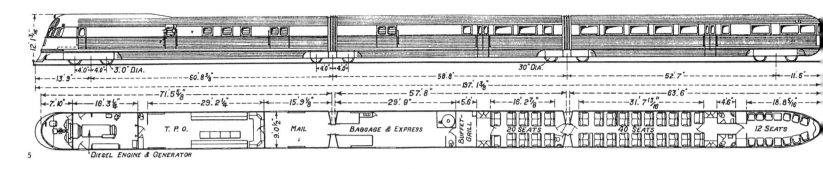

5

6

national reputation for lightweight construction. The frame was made of lightweight metal, and the skin was spot-welded horizontally corrugated stainless steel – an expensive, non-rusting structure. The train had a low centre of gravity (high speed on curves) and weighed only 100 tons (in other words little more than a one conventional Pullman car). The 'Zephyr''s appearance was new: brightly shimmering metal with almost no paint, covered undersides to the cars; the driver sat deep in the canted cab with the radiator for the engine above him, quite different from the steam locomotive driver, who was enthroned on high. The shape had been tested at the Massachusetts Institute of Technology in Chicago. Interior design was by Paul Cret, an important industrial designer who wrote about this job in the 'Magazine of Art' in 1937 (see

text on p. 268). The Burlington 'Zephyr' was an enormous success and turned out to be too small from the beginning (72 seats). At first a fourth car was added, and then more trains were built with 8 and 12 cars, until 1935. The 'Zephyrs' ran on the Denver–Chicago, Chicago–Minneapolis and Burlington–St. Louis routes. The original 'Zephyr' has survived and can be seen in the Museum of Science and Industry, Chicago.

Railplane: The Railway Gazette:
RG (8.12.1933), p. 864;
Stout, W.B. (1951), p. 269 ff.

Burlington Zephyr: RG (11.8.1933),
p. 228; RG (18.5.1934), p. 904 ff.
RG (22.3.1935), p. 584 ff.
RG (14.6.1935), p. 1184 f. Magazine
of Art (1939) No. 1, p. 17 ff.

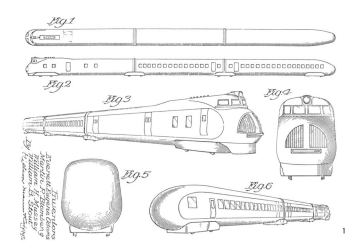

1933/34 City of Salina Between 1920 and 1934 the number of miles travelled by train sank to a third. Even large railway companies could no longer afford steam-driven locomotives. The answer lay in the development of rapid, light railcar trains.

In May 1933 Union Pacific commissioned Pullman and AC & F to design a three-part train. Both firms had only a few weeks time and worked with important engineers or designers: Pullman with W. B. Stout, AC & F with Otto Kuhler. Pullman won the contract with a project based on the 'Railplane' (cf. p. 136). As early as February 1934, after less than a year under construction, the train was delivered to Union Pacific.

The layout of the train corresponds with that of the 'Zephyr', which was built independently at the same time: power car with mail section, two passenger cars. This unit is also 'fully articulated', i.e. the cars are permanently coupled together and supported on common bogies. The shape of the train was developed in the wind tunnel at the University of Michigan. In the course of development work the driver's cabin was set higher, which made the basic shape of the front section look like an inverted airship. The two carp-like air inlets for cooling the engine made it look extremely monumental, indeed aggressive. Its appearance was misleading about the relatively modest engine performance of 600 hp, but conversely did correspond with the considerable top speed of 180 kph. Structure and covering were in the lightweight metal alloy Duralumin. Stainless steel was not available (the know-how and patents for high-precision spot-welding were held by Pullman's competitor Budd, cf. p. 137). The cars were constructed as self-supporting boxes. As in the 'Railplane' the cross-section of the cars tapered towards the top; the cars were 20 cm narrower and 90 cm lower than standard Pullman cars. A remarkable feature is the smooth outer skin – apart from the rivet heads with almost flush, permanently glazed windows (air conditioning) and a rubber skin at the points where the cars join. At first the bogies were covered, but this turned out to be impracticable (difficult to inspect, damage from flying stones).

In contrast with the shining 'Zephyr' this train had characteristically bright colours. Front, roof, undersides and rear were brown, the sides canary yellow with a bright red border. The interior, designed by Marie Harriman, was light and clean, with indirect ceiling lighting, ceiling

1   M-10 000 'City of Salina', drawing from specification for US Design
Pat. No. 100 000 (1936).

2   Union Pacific: subsequent
model M-10 005 'City of San
Francisco', 1936, carcass, aluminum.
Photograph: Pullman Corp.

3   Rear of the 'City of Salina'
train, riveted aluminum structure.
Photograph: Pullman Corp.

4   Union Pacific Railroad:
M-10 000 'City of Salina', general
view, 1934. Length of train 204 ft
(about 65 m), unladen weight 85 t,
121 seats. Photograph: Pullman
Corp.

5   Illinois Central: rendering of a
streamlined train, 1934.

6   Illinois Central: 'Green
Diamond', lounge in rear car. Photograph: Pullman Corp.

7   Union Pacific: M-10 005, 1936.

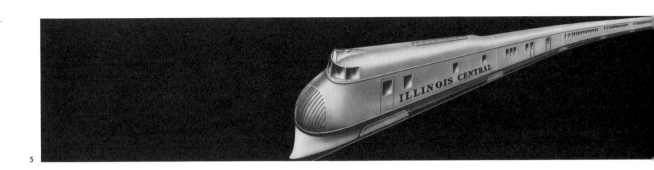

5

6

7

and side wall intensifying from white to dark
blue and golden-brown seats. A small kitchen
and tableware designed especially for the train
catered for passengers' physical welfare. Nevertheless, the 'City of Salina' was not a luxury
train.
Because of its instant success Union Pacific
built a few more trains with up to nine cars and
more powerful engines until 1935. Formally the
train turned out to be effectively the prototype
for American diesel trains. Its shape was protected (US Design Patent No. 100 000, issued to
design engineers Adams, Blomberg, Mussey
and Stout). The patent claim, based on the
drawing reproduced in ill. 1, simply said: "We
claim: – the ornamental design of an articulated
rail car or similar article as shown."
Union Pacific: The Railway Gazette:

RG (16. 7. 1933), p. 805;
RG (10. 7. 1936), p. 88 ff.

Illinois Central: RG (15. 5. 1936),
p. 978 ff.

AUTOMOTRICES

1933, 1935 Renault VH and ABJ
1937 De Dietrich

1933 Renault VH and ABJ In July 1933 'Chemins de Fer de l'Etat' opened the new Lisieux–Trouville route offering something completely new: an hourly service. You could take the railcar without constantly needing to consult the timetable "presque aussi facilement que l'on prenait le métro" (ed. Usines Renault: Les Automotrices. A la conquête d'un Nouveau Domaine, 1935, no page).
This new mode of transport was very successful and was adopted by other lines, and also by other railway companies (the French railways were nationalized, i.e. the SNCF was established, under Léon Blum in 1937).
After the first prototypes (1931) and a first series (1933) Renault handed over the streamlined railcars ABJ (one section) and ABV (two sections) driven by heavy oil (12 cylinder motor of

265 hp) to the railway companies in 1935. The frame was built of welded steel. The bodywork had a very smooth surface and a very small cross-section. In contrast with the VH types, which had the radiator under the roof, it was placed under the front windows in the ABJ and the ABV. The underside of the power unit was largely covered.
The ABJ type was 26 m long (without buffers), weighed 27 t unladen and reached a top speed of 120 kph.

Renault: The Railway Gazette: RG (23.3.1934), p. 514 ff. Renault (internal publication): Les Automotrices (Paris 1935); RG (24.1.1936), p. 183; La Traction Nouvelle (1936) No. 3, p. 74 ff.

De Dietrich: Le Génie Civile (14.10.1922), p. 380 ff. Omnia (1934) No. 173, p. 144 ff.

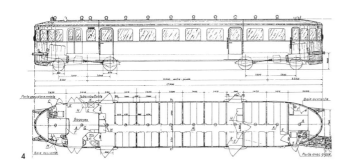

4

1   Renault VH railcar, first series, 1933. Radiator on the roof.

2   Renault railcar, frame (steel, welded).

3   Renault ABJ railcar, 1935. Usines Renault picture caption: 'Pénétration dans l'air'.

4   De Dietrich car factory, Niederbronn (Alsace): diesel railcar, 1934, plan and side view.

5   De Dietrich car factory, Niederbronn (Alsace): diesel railcar, 1937. Page from brochure. De Dietrich was another supplier in the railcar market, along with Renault, Bugatti, Décauville and other French manufacturers. Photograph: De Dietrich, Niederbronn (F).

5

1933 Autorail One of the most legendary models by Italian-Alsatian design engineer Ettore Bugatti (1881–1947) is the 'Royale': it had an 8-cylinder motor with a cubic capacity of almost 13 litres (1926). Six of these luxury cars, which still change hands today at very high prices, were built, but only three were sold at the time. To use the rest of the completed engines Bugatti – to a certain extent as a by-product of automobile manufacture – built an express railcar, the 'Autorail Bugatti'.

Bugatti made the vehicle in various versions. Common to all types was the arrangement of the engines (in the middle between two bogies) and the driver's cab ('kiosk') jutting up above the top of the car. This was also in the middle, meaning that it was possible to travel in both directions with just one cab. Bugatti had also

taken over a second feature of the popular (rubber-tyred) 'Michelines' as well as this extraordinary characteristic (whose rigorous and simplifying gesture is probably typically French): the four-axle bogies used throughout.

This disposition makes the 'Autorail Bugatti' the exact opposite of the 'Roter Pfeil' for example: the latter has the passenger area between the drive units, but the Bugatti railcar has the drive units between two passenger compartments (making an unrestricted view forwards and backwards a primary feature and giving a special feeling when travelling).

The 48-seater railcar (built in a single section) was extremely fast, with a top speed of 160 kph and in 1935 even broke the world record for diesel driven rail vehicles (196 kph). Between 1933 and 1946 – uninterruptedly throughout the

war – Bugatti built more than 80 Autorails in six versions: the single-section basic type 23 m long with two 200 hp motors, the 'Double' at twice the length (42.4 m, four motors), the 'Triple' (60 m long, four motors), the 'Présidentiel' (22.4 m, four motors) and finally a shortened and a lengthened variant each with two motors ('Léger', 19.3 m and 'Surallongé', 25.3 m).

The 'Autorail Bugatti' cannot have been developed in a wind tunnel; the sharp edge between the downward-running roof line and the side wall too obviously conflicted with eddy-free airflow for that. As always with Bugatti form seems to have developed from instinct to a large extent. But it symbolized the performance of these railcars in a powerful fashion. Remarkably, Sir Nigel Gresley, the British pioneer, drew directly on Bugatti's model (cf. p. 175).

2

3

1   'Autorail Bugatti' in the ETAT brochure, c. 1935. E. Strebel Collection.

2   'Autorail Bugatti', 'Présidentiel' version for ETAT arriving in Paris c. 1935. On the roof in the middle of the car is the hood on the driver's cab. E. Strebel Collection.

3   Photograph of a model of a steam locomotive by Bugatti (not built), second half of the thirties. E. Strebel Collection.

4   Page from a brochure issued when a Bugatti railcar broke the world speed record, 1935–1936. E. Strebel Collection.

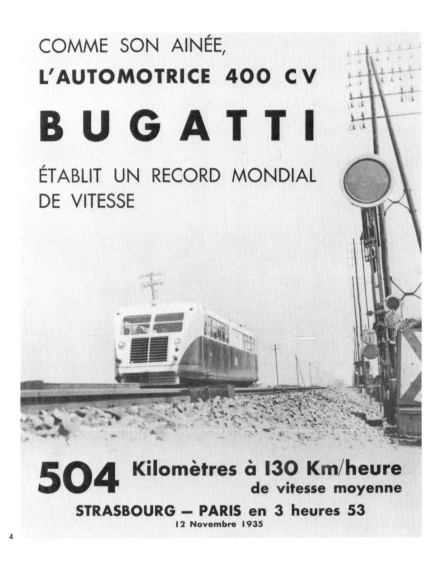

4

The Railway Gazette: RG (26.3.1933), p. 709f. RG (11.9.1936), p. 420ff. La Traction Nouvelle (1936) No. 5, p. 146ff.

AUTOMOTRICE FIAT

1933 Littorine
1936 Express Railcars

1933 Littorine The first Fiat automotrice ran from Rome to Littoria, hence the name 'Littorina' for the whole railcar category in Italy. They worked almost exclusively on branch lines ('secondarie', and were arranged to use the minimum of staff. The driver's cab was open to the passenger area. Theoretically the driver could also act as ticket collector. The Littorine had two driver's cabs and did not need to be turned round at termini. The first version, ALb 48 ('Automotrice Leggera Benzina', 48 seats), clearly shows its debt to the motor coach. It was driven by a petrol motor set on a bogie, and the radiator prominently displayed at the front seems to have been deliberately given the job of emphasizing the vehicle's relationship with cars. A striking feature of this type is the run of windows with slender intermediate supports. It is

reminiscent of a tram. Obviously the roof had no supporting function, but the weight simply rested on the substructure.

In a somewhat later version, the ALb 56 (56 seats) of 1934, the windows are separated from each other by sections of wall and its vertically opening windows show an increasing inclination to the formal language of the railways. A contemporary version used particularly in Sardinia is strongly reminiscent of American models, for instance the 'Burlington Zephyr', with which it was by no means comparable in terms of power, speed or purpose (short journeys). This FMS ('Ferrovie Meridionale Sarde') diesel-powered vehicle of the ALn type could not be coupled and thus could only work as a single unit. The necessity of joining individual railcars together to form large composites soon emerged.

These new units could be coupled and had connections for electricity and compressed air.
Each unit was driven by its own motor; the motors were controlled by the driver, who now drove by instruments, not by 'ear' (like a motorist).

1936 Express Railcars Fiat built the ATR 100 (ATR: 'Automotrice Rapido') express railcar for the Milan–Florence–Rome route, as well as the 'Littorine'. The train was painted dark blue at the top and red below, and had Jacobs bogies like other comparable units (cf. e.g. p. 134).
The most recent version documented here was the only one manufactured, used above all for members of the government. The unit's opulent furnishings included a sleeping compartment.

1 Fiat 'Automotrice' ALb 56. 56 seats, 1934.

2 Fiat lightweight diesel railcar ALn for FMS, 1935.

3 Fiat 'Automotrice' ALb 48. Lightweight railcar with 48 seats, 1932, 120 hp petrol motor, top speed 110 kph.

4 Fiat 'Autotreno Rapido', special train for members of the government, 1939.

5 Fiat 'Autotreno Rapido' ATR 100. Permanently coupled three-section train with Jacobs bogies, 1936.

6 Fiat 'Automotrice' ALn 556 (1937–1939).

4

5

6

L'Ingegnere (1933), p. 299f. Schweize-rische Bauzeitung (1934/1), p. 72.

SCHWEIZERISCHE BUNDESBAHNEN

1935 RCe 2/4 Roter Pfeil

1938 R 8/14 Schienenblitz, Tatzelwurm

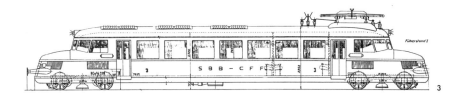

1935 Roter Pfeil 1929–1930 was the year of highest passenger-kilometres for the Schweizerische Bundesbahnen, then a decline started because of the economic situation. The railway board reacted in the same way as their counterparts in other countries and commissioned the development of lightweight railcars. Weight per seat was an important figure in terms of economy in service. For a locomotive-hauled train it was at least 1000 kilograms, and the 'Roter Pfeil' achieved half that, even though it was not consistently built using the lightweight construction method.

The RCe 2/4 railcar, which became a legend under the name 'Roter Pfeil' (Red Arrow), has perhaps remained the most popular Schweizerische Bundesbahnen vehicle. It was commissioned in 1933; the first two cars were delivered

as early as 1935 (of a total of seven, and two diesel versions). The vehicle could achieve 125 kph.

The architecture of the 'Roter Pfeil' is based on two main principles. First of all the two bogies are as far apart as possible at the ends of the car to achieve an even ride without lateral rocking movements. Secondly, and associated with that: as the drive units were mounted in the hoods above the bogies the interior floor of the vehicle could be lowered by half a metre; it was only 72 cm from the top of the rails, rather than the usual 125 cm.

The frame was like an offset girder-built underframe built of welded sheet steel. The skin was made up of welded steel sheets as well; the weight saved by using a light metal was considered insignificant. The well-known Swiss quality

of reserve is shown in the sober calculations and lack of interest in modernity at all costs. Only individual sections, for example the hoods over the motors, were made of light-weight metal. Railway experts acknowledged the "propaganda value of a free forward view for the passengers", which meant that points lost to the motor car could be won back (Schweizerische Bauzeitung vol. 105, 1935, p. 158). Although the 'Roter Pfeil's' driver's cab was not accessible to the public it was separated from the passenger area only by a glass window, and thus made it possible to look at 'the end of the tunnel', for example.

1938 Schienenblitz The 'Roter Pfeil' was more attractive than its capacity from the beginning: 70 seats were far too few, and it was

5

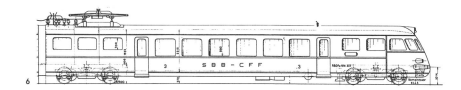

6

1   'Flêche du Jura', 'Jura Arrow',
Ce 2/4, 1939.

2   BBC study for a railcar with separate motor unit that could be coupled
and uncoupled, c. 1933. Photograph:
Verkehrshaus Luzern.

3   Side view of the 'Roter Pfeil'.

4   RCe 2/4 'Roter Pfeil' electric
railcar, 1935, 70 seats. Two versions
with diesel motors were built for
the non-electrified route through the
southern foothills of the Jura.

5   Diesel electric railcar by the
French Décauville company for the
Chemin de Fer du Nord, 1933, and
for Paris–Lyon–Méditerrannée (PLM),
1936 (picture). The motor unit came
from Switzerland: one Saurer BZD 300
hp V-12 diesel motor per bogie, electro-mechanical parts by the Oerlikon
machine factory. 62 seats, unladen
weight 40 t, 110 kph. Formal similarity
to the motor car.

6   RABFe 8/12 'Tatzelwurm',
'Schienenblitz', side view.

7   General view (c. 1938).

7

increasingly used for excursion traffic. For this
reason the Schweizerische Bundesbahnen commissioned the design of a three-section express
railcar unit. It was developed in 1936–1937,
three trains, known as 'Schienenblitz' (Rail Light-
ning) and 'Tatzelwurm' (Flying Dragon), were
built, and became almost as popular as the
'Roter Pfeil'. RABFe 8/12 means that the composite train had twelve axles, of which eight were
driven. The train was very powerful (4 motors,
2360 hp in total) and could accelerate rapidly
(to 120 kph in 60 seconds and 150 kph in
100 seconds). Here too the floor is low, which
made for short stopping times. The 'Roter Pfeil'
was felt to be only partly streamlined at the time
by those responsible, but the new express train
took over this attribute completely (and cor-
rectly).

SBB 'Roter Pfeil': The Railway Gazette:
RG (7. 9. 1934), p. 404; Schwiezerische
Bauzeitung: SBZ (1935/1), p. 157 f.
SBZ (1936/1), p. 33 ff. RG (24. 1. 1936).
p. 186 f. SBZ (1936/1), p. 264; SBZ
1936/2), p. 86 f.

Décauville: RG (23. 3. 1934), p. 528;
La Traction Nouvelle 'TN' (1936) No. 4,
p. 122 f.

SBB 'Schienenblitz': SBZ (1938/1),
p. 125 ff.

SBB 'Flêche du Jura': SBZ (1939/2),
p. 84 f.

TATRA
1936 Slovenská Strela

GREAT WESTERN
1933 AEC Diesel Railcar

1   'Slovenska Strela' – 'Slovakian Arrow', general view. The shape is spoiled by the shield.

2   The roof over one of the two driver's cabs.

3   Front section, metal sheets with joints filled before painting. Photograph Tatra.

4   Building the 'Slovakian Arrow', sheet iron frame with welded sheets. Manual assembly. the ovals mark the buffers, not the headlights. The 'Jaray' shape is easily recognizable. Photograph Tatra.

5   Great Western Railway (GB): 'Experimental Streamlined Heavy Oil Rail Car', 1934. Shape developed in the wind tunnel in 1933.

6   GWR diesel railcar no. 1 (1934): side view and elevation.

7   GWR diesel railcar no. 6 (1935): side view and elevation.

8   GWR diesel railcar no. 19 (1939): side view and elevation: contrary to the usual development (Fiat, Breda etc.) the GWR railcars became more angular with time.

9   A railcar from the first series next to a steam locomotive.

1936 Slovenská Strela The 'Slovakian Arrow' was developed for branch lines in 1936. It was a further development of the Czech railcar with central driver's cab permitting a view over the roof in both directions (cf. 'Bugatti' railcars, p.142), of which hundreds had been built: actual rail omnibuses for simple shunting using few staff. The 'Slovakian Arrow' was built for the Prague–Ostrava–Bratislava route. Like Tatra cars it was constructed by Hans Ledwinka (see p.206). At first suspension and guiding were separated in its bogies. It had a completely new kind of power unit: to avoid using a gear box it started using an electric driving motor (stator) whose energy was produced by a diesel motor. After reaching its operating speed (after about two to three minutes) the stator disengaged and the diesel motor took over

the drive directly. The vehicle travelled at up to 130 kph.

A drawing of the railcar from the 'AG für Verkehrspatente', i.e. Paul Jaray's office, in the possession of Freiherr von Koenig-Fachsenfeld raises the question of what contribution Jaray made to this design. Was he involved in the design as a whole or only the pressure fan on the roof of the car (patent Jaray)? Photographs of the 'Slovakian Arrow' under construction clearly show the two connected elements characteristic of Jaray's thinking.

Tatra 'Slovenska Strela': La Traction Nouvelle (1937), No. 7, p. 38 f.

5

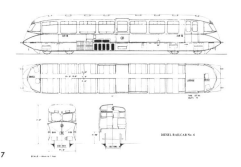

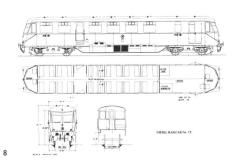

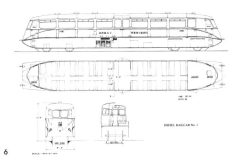

DIESEL RAILCAR No. 1

6

DIESEL RAILCAR No. 6

7

DIESEL RAILCAR No. 19

8

9

AUTOMOTRICE BREDA

from 1933 Littorine
1936 Elettrotreno Rapido

1 Breda ALn (Automotrice Leggera Nafta, i.e. diesel). Series 2000, 72 seats, one motor, unladen weight 19 t, 110 kph, 1933.

2 Breda ALb 56, two petrol motors, 56 seats, unladen weight 26 t, 140 kph, 1935.

3 Breda ALn 56 (heavy oil), unladen weight 28 t, 1935–1938.

4 Interior of the ALn 56. Italian railcars usually had only one class.

5 Breda ETR 200 (Elettrotreno Rapido) in the assembly shop (Breda, Sesto San Giovanni/Milan).

6 Breda ETR 201 (Elettrotreno Rapido 201) for the Bologna–Rome line, 94 seats, six electric motors, 160 kph, 1936 (record 1939: 203 kph). A train of this type was shown at the New York World Fair in 1939. The important architect Giuseppe Pagano was involved in the design.

1–6: Breda Spa, Milan

The Railway Gazette (22.9.1933), p. 418; Schweizerische Bauzeitung:SBZ (1937/2), p. 289; SBZ (1939/2), p. 25.

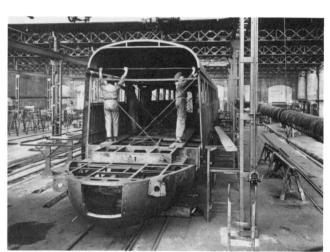

TGV, ICE, ETR, SBB

1980 TGV
1985 ICE

1988 ETR 450 Pendolino
1991 SBB Lok 2000

1 Trans-Europe-Express, German model, VT 11.5, 1957, inspired by Kruckenberg's express railcar (cf. p. 131). Photograph: SBB.

2 Elettrotreno Rapido ETR 450 'Pendolino', Italian high-speed train, in regular service since 1988. Photograph: SBB.

3 SBB 2000 locomotive, built by the Schweizerische Lokomotiv- und Maschinenfabrik SLM, Winterthur. Bodywork designed by Pininfarina Spa, Turin (c.1987), in use since 1991. Photograph: SLM.

4 Intercity-Experimental ICE, German high-speed train, 1985, in service since 1991. Photograph: Henschel Thyssen.

5 Train de Grande Vitesse TGV, French high-speed train, in service since 1980. Developed and manufactured by GEC Alsthom. Photograph: SNCF.

1980 TGV From the passenger's point of view European railways stagnated for decades (the Japanese 'Shinkansen' was in a class of its own for years). Progress like better safety systems was 'invisible' to the public. To avoid losing the competition with the car and short-haul flights completely, state railway systems started to commission a new generation of trains in the seventies. This had been preceded by the new process of laying rails without joints; 'diddleadut...diddleadut...diddleadut...', the rhythmical hammering that had been the acoustic symbol of rail travel for decades gradually decreased, and can be heard only on branch lines, if anywhere, today. Acoustic 'streamlining' was followed by visual streamlining and the streamlining of the timetable. The new trains are built with a driver's cab at each end, which renders

laborious locomotive changes at termini superfluous.

The French state railway SNCF was the first in Europe with the TVG 'Train de Grande Vitesse'. New track was laid for the trains, 'taking' rises and dips straight, rather then going round them. This was the really new feature of the TVG; beyond the ultra-modern electro-mechanical section it acquired one characteristic that had applied to the express railcar units described above for decades: lightweight construction, Jacobs bogies, reduced car cross-sections, a shape with reduced air resistance (but not rigorously optimized). The French designer (of English descent) Jacques Cooper (b.1931) was responsible for the design of the TVG. He looked for a shape intended to convey ideas derived from the motor car ("dessinez-moi un train qui ne

ressemble pas un train" said his commission in 1968). The TVG is designed to run at about 260 kph but holds the world record for a train with a measured top speed of 512 kph (!).

1985 ICE The German ICE ('Intercity Experimental') was developed completely with an eye to minimum air resistance (including minimum eddy effects when passing through stations). The five-section composite has two driving units, but these are cut off straight at the back to provide a smooth transition when units are assembled (in contrast with the TVG). Details like the bonded flush windscreen and the laterally curved windows in the driver's cab also show its difference from the TVG: everything in the ICE is inscribed within the formal skin: flaps, headlights, panes and ventilation grilles. Top

3

4

5

speed 350 kph. The driving units were developed by Thyssen Henschel among others, and thus by a firm (Henschel) that built an express locomotive as early as 1904 (cf. p. 156 f.). Some new track was also built for the ICE. It has been in regular service since 1991.

1988 ETR 450 Pendolino   The Italian ETR 450 ('Elettrotreno Rapido') 'Pendolino' by Fiat Ferrovia has a special mechanical device that causes the cars to lean inwards when negotiating curves, making higher speeds possible. This required two bogies on each car, and so the Jacobs method could not be used. The 'Pendolino' does not have actual drive units or locomotives; the drive motors are decentralized over the bogies. The trains consist of five or eleven permanently coupled units. Of the three

trains the 'Pendolino' has the most compact front, surprisingly close to the M-10 000 ('City of Salina') in its powerful expressiveness. But with a top speed of 250 kph it is a good half as fast again as American 'Streamliner' of the thirties.

LOCOMOTIVES

Streamlined locomotives were the answer
to the railcar train units that the public was so
enthusiastic about. Sometimes existing steam
locomotives were covered retrospectively,
sometimes they were new constructions in
streamlined form. Aerodynamically speaking
the German locomotives were the most
consistent and the American ones the most
eloquent. The British produced an elegant
synthesis of tried and tested technology and
modernized shape, while the French examples,
almost all individual specimens, are of differing quality.

EARLY STREAMLINED FORMS

1894 PLM   1904 Wittfeld/Henschel

1899 Heilmann   1907 Krauss-Maffei

1

2

1   Königliche Preussische Staatsbahnen: steam locomotive S 9
No. 562, Wittfeld-Henschel type,
1904. Driver's cab at the front, stoker's
cab separate in the usual place.
Photograph: Henschel.

2   Paris–Lyon–Méditerranée (PLM)
railway company: 4 cylinder com-
pound express steam locomotive with
slightly streamlined front and funnel,
1894. Part of the reason for the design
was the Mistral, which often blows
very violently in the Rhône valley.
Photograph: La Vie du Rail.

3   Jean Jacques Heilmann: steam-
electric locomotive, second version
1899, 100 kph. Photograph: La Vie du
Rail.

4   Königliche Bayerische Staatsbahnen: steam locomotive with
wedge-shaped smoke-box door and
streamlined funnel, built by Krauss-
Maffei, top speed 155 kph, 1907.
Photograph: Krauss-Maffei.

Henschel: The Railway Gazette
(25. 5. 1934), p. 93; RG (20. 1. 1935),
p. 1059; Henschel-Heft (1935)
No. 5, p. 26 ff.

3

4

NORMAN BEL GEDDES

1932 Locomotive Number 1

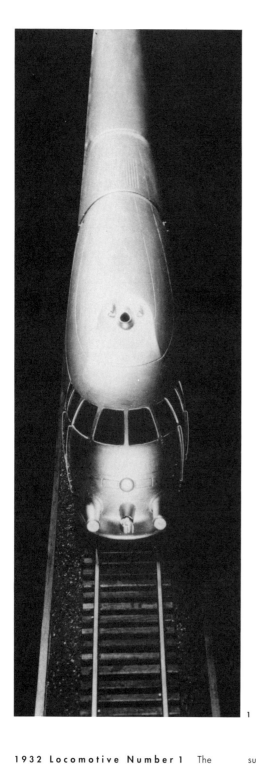

US Design Patent No. 92511, patented 19 June 1934.

1/3 Norman Bel Geddes: Locomotive Number 1, 1932. Photograph of model (from 'Horizons'). Photograph M. Goldberg.

2 Norman Bel Geddes: Locomotive Number 1, 1932. Longitudinal section and elevation, drawing for 'Horizons', pencil on transparent paper.

1–3: Bel Geddes Collection, H. Ransom Humanities Research Center, University of Austin/Texas, by permission of Elizabeth Lutyens Bel Geddes.

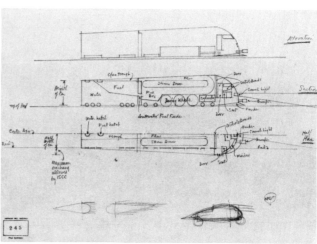

1932 Locomotive Number 1 The train introduced by Norman Bel Geddes in his trailblazing book 'Horizons' (1932) was probably his vision that has the most lasting effect. And he was dealing with a technology that was not for the future: the steam locomotive. Geddes' train anticipated the appearance of the express diesel rail unit with remarkable accuracy.

"Speed will increase as weight and wind resistance are reduced." (Horizons, p. 69). the design is based on this simple insight. The parts of the locomotive are covered with a 'streamshell': firebox, boiler, smoke-box, dome, funnel and of course details like the bell and headlights as well. Something that was practised on German locomotives in particular is anticipated here: covering up points that need frequent access for service with metal shutters. Another far-reaching

suggestion was placing the driver's cab at the front, thanks to an automatic stoking device; this greatly increased safety because of the incomparably better view. A striking feature is the spoiler on the front of the locomotive, which links the traditional cow-catcher with modern aerodynamics.

The cross-section of the locomotive tapers down over the tender to the cars, which are elliptical in cross-section; Geddes made them about 45 cm lower than usual. The lowest possible weight was to be the crucial construction feature. The outer skin was to be as smooth as possible: the windows flush, no protruding handles, connections between cars covered with an elastic skin. Sealed windows and air conditioning (tried out on American trains for the first time in summer 1931) were an essential consequence of all this

for Bel Geddes. Geddes generally thought that the greatest possible comfort was more use to a railway company than the largest possible number of seats. A day room with movable armchairs, an observation car with solarium and compartments to be used during the day or at night (one lavatory with WC for every three passengers) were to be available for journeys across the American continent lasting for days. The end car with observation lobby anticipated the one installed in the 'Zephyr' in 1934 (cf. p. 137).

Built-in light fittings, cheerful colours, telephone and telex were mentioned by Bel Geddes almost as though they were to be taken for granted, in the same breath as a device using illuminated letters to provide the most up-to-date business and political news.

3

Bel Geddes, N.: Horizons
(Boston 1932), p. 64 ff.

NORMAN ZAPF
1934 Commodore Vanderbilt

HENRY DREYFUSS
1936 Mercury

1934 Commodore Vanderbilt The locomotive 'Commodore Vanderbilt', which hauled the famous 'Twentieth Century Limited' train, was the first in which the new formal language of express railcar trains was transferred to the old technology of the steam locomotive. The task was to give the existing engine of the 'Hudson' type a similar new appearance. This ended up as a streamlined skin: the mechanical part of the locomotive was not to be changed. Designer Norman Zapf solved the problem with the aid of the wind tunnel at the Case Institute in Cleveland.

His design set a precedent in the United States. It was the first example of what later became known in colloquial language as 'bathtub shrouding'. Zapf successfully transferred the streamlining of the first diesel trains to a steam locomotive. Their size, associated with coarseness before the re-design, was monumentalized by calming the lines. This effect is by no means to be taken for granted and proves Zapf's skill in his choice of resources. It seems strange that the 'Commodore Vanderbilt' was re-covered for a second time in 1939, this time by Henry Dreyfuss (see p.162), despite the fact that it drew a very positive response from the public.

1936 Mercury The 'Mercury' train ran on the lucrative Cleveland–Toledo–Detroit route, under the auspices of 'New York Central'. It was built in 1935, and this was the first time a designer had the opportunity to design a whole train, inside and outside. The contract went to the young New York designer Henry Dreyfuss (1903–1971), one of the first American industrial designers, who were introduced in 'Fortune' magazine in 1934 as exponents of this new profession. The 'Mercury' train was created from a locomotive built in 1926 and seven existing cars. Dreyfuss's aim in designing the exterior was the greatest possible uniformity of locomotive and cars (for example, the tender is designed like a car; the whole train has the same cross-section). The compact exterior of the locomotive drew criticism as well as admiration. The 'Mercury' locomotive was the high point of the method of cladding an existing locomotive 'from the top' (second application of 'bathtub shrouding'). Sigfried Giedion used a photograph of the 'Mercury' as an example of the 'over-expansion of volume' when criticizing the American interpretation of industrial design in matters of 'streamlining' (Das Werk 1946, p.155 ff.).

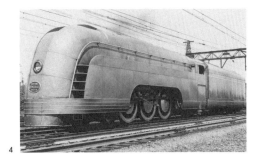

It is possible that even Dreyfuss shared the res-
ervation, because in his next commission for
New York Central he abandoned the 'bathtub'
shape in favour of the 'bullet' shape for the
'20th Century Limited' (cf. p. 162). An uncom-
monly striking feature of the 'Mercury' were the
wheels: they were silver-painted discs (not
spoked wheels), and they were illuminated by
spotlights at night. This is the most exciting
variation on the obviously typical American
approach of not covering the driving wheels of
steam locomotives, contrary to pure streamlined
form, but conversely to make them the locomotive's 'character mask'.

HENRY DREYFUSS

1938 20th Century Ltd., New York Central Railroad

Henry Dreyfuss: three type J-3a locomotives for the 'Twentieth Century Ltd.'
on the 'New York Central System'.
The locomotive 'Commodore Vanderbilt' was re-covered for a second time
in this form in 1938 (cf. p. 160).
A. B. Gottwaldt Collection.

1938 20th Century Ltd. The New
York–Chicago rail connection, conceivably the
most 'American', was fought over by two rail
companies because of its prestige, the 'New
York Central System' and the 'Pennsylvania
Railroad'. Both companies ran a luxury train
between the two metropolises on their own track,
with their own stations and different routes.
The two companies' trains competed in terms of
comfort and 'appeal'; in terms of time they each
took about the same time for the journey, which
was a good thousand miles. The 'Pennsylvania'
train was the 'Broadway Ltd.', fitted out by Raymond Loewy and hauled by the K4S locomotive
(see p. 166). The 'New York Central System'
turned a little later to Loewy's friendly rival Henry
Dreyfuss. The J-3a locomotives illustrated here
of the Hudson type shrouded by Dreyfuss and

the cars they drew replaced old rolling stock
and pulled the new '20th Century Ltd.' train in
Dreyfuss's luxurious design (a train of this name
had been running since 1902 and continued
until 1967). Dreyfuss departed from the shape
selected for the 'Mercury' and chose a bullet
shape here. This locomotive with a vertical crest
on the forward-bulging boiler looked quite
unmistakable. It is not difficult to imagine how
the railway companies wooed their passengers
when comparing it with the K4S.

The Railway Gazette: RG (24.7.1936),
p. 150; RG (27.5.1938), p. 1029;
RG (9.9.1938), p. 450 ff.
Dreyfuss, H.: 10 Years of Industrial
Design (New York 1939);
Dreyfuss, H.: Designing for People
(New York 1955).

OTTO KUHLER

1935 Hiawatha   1939 Black Diamond

1937 Royal Blue   1941 Tennessean

1

1935 Hiawatha Otto Kuhler immigrated from Germany in 1923. He was one of the busiest designers of cladding for steam locomotives and diesel railcars for various American railway companies in the thirties. He was not interested in 'streamlining' as an academic problem (he doubted whether it had a significant physical effect), but as a design problem. He wanted to give rail travel back the romanticism that it had lost, and in his eyes streamlining was a device that made this possible. He exploited it with all the self-confidence of a prestigious bespoke tailor. The 'Hiawatha' steam trains commissioned by the Milwaukee Road were enthusiastically received by the public in spring 1935, and brought an immediate improvement to the railway company's fortunes: it had been running at a heavy deficit. The cars were designed in the same way as the locomotives: their interior had a touch of glamour and 'high life' (the bar, for example) that was within everybody's reach. In this respect the 'Hiawatha' trains went consciously further than the 'Zephyr', for example, or the 'City of Salina'.

Kuhler selected an usual colour scheme for the trains that was generally accepted. The crest on the locomotives was black, the sides of the boiler light grey, bounded at the bottom by two brown strips, between which Milwaukee's traditional colour put in an appearance in the form of a luminous orange band. The locomotive's connecting rods and all the wheels of the train were painted dark brown. Compared with the cool, technical material style of the 'Zephyr', for example, the 'Hiawatha''s polychrome was a consciously populist choice.

1937 Royal Blue Kuhler created the first streamlined steam train for the east on similar principles, 'Royal Blue' for the Baltimore and Ohio (1937). Locomotive and cars were already in existence, and were modernized; the locomotive was covered, the interior of the cars rebuilt. Kuhler himself considered the 'John Wilkes' steam locomotive for the 'Lehigh Valley' company to be his most successful creation (1939). It too is a clear demonstration of his method, which was not primarily on a technical basis, but mainly 'impressionistic'.

2

3

4

1   Otto Kuhler: 'Hiawatha' steam locomotive with assorted cars, 1934–1935, formally modelled on the first diesel 'streamliners'.

2   Otto Kuhler: Baltimore & Ohio Railroad, locomotive, 1937.

3   Otto Kuhler: Baltimore & Ohio Railroad, 'Royal Blue' locomotive, 1937.

4   Otto Kuhler: 'Tennessean' locomotive, Southern Railroad, 1941.

5   Otto Kuhler: 'Black Diamond' locomotive, Lehigh Valley Railroad, after rebuilding, 1939.

5

Kuhler: The Railway Gazette (10.11.1939), p.612f. Kuhler, O.: My Iron Journey (Denver 1967).

Hiawatha: RG (24.5.1935), p.1037; RG (9.6.1939), p.937.

RAYMOND LOEWY

1936 Locomotive K4S
1939/41 S-1/T-1

1936 Locomotive K4S and S-1/T-1

Franco-American design pioneer Raymond Loewy (1893–1986) worked for the Pennsylvania Railroad from 1932 (his first commission for this company was a station wastepaper basket). He intended his K4S locomotive design to be an extremely safe machine. He considered the fact that the driver's cab constantly filled up with smoke as a result of uncontrolled air currents and turbulence was a danger factor. To gain an insight into the airflow conditions at the front of an existing steam locomotive Loewy travelled on a straight stretch of track between Chicago and Fort Wayne, hanging on to the front rail with one hand and holding a pole with a strip of material fastened on to it in the airstream in the other. He insisted that this empirical experiment provided him with fundamental insights.

This commission produced the K4S locomotive, which created a considerable stir – not just because of its shape, but because of one structural detail: the horizontal smoke deflector plate behind the funnel, which caused lift because of its shape and carried the smoke away above the driver's cab.

The S-1 was a further development of the K4S in formal terms. One locomotive only was built, and at the time it was the largest and one of the fastest locomotives in the world (length with tender 42 metres, output 6000 hp, top speed 190 kph, weight 500 tons). Loewy arrived at an optimum shape for the S-1 by means of wind tunnel experiments on the clay model (Guggenheim Aerodynamic Laboratory, University of New York). It is typical of Loewy that he did not touch the traditional disposition of the parts;

the driver's cab is behind the boiler and the furnace – cf. p. 158 in contrast with this. But a masterly feature of the S-1 is the way in which the linear decoration becomes an integral part of the form. The single headlight becomes a dynamic element, bound into the overall form by the use of striking profiles, and it almost seems to 'throw itself forward', or project itself, and the stay bar underneath it becomes a light stirrup piece curving around the shaded undersection of the steam boiler cladding. Loewy was a master of the distribution of light and shade.

Raymond Loewy, 1979: "I remember a day in Fort Wayne, Indiana, at the station: on a straight stretch of track without any curves for miles; I waited for the S-1 to pass through at full speed. I stood on the platform and saw it coming from the distance at 120 miles per hour. It flashed by

1   Pennsylvania Railroad: steam locomotive, predecessor of the K4S (1920s), photographed in Montauk.

2   Raymond Loewy: covering for the steam locomotive as in ill.1 (1936). The horizontal smoke deflector plate above the funnel takes the smoke up over the driver's cab.

3   Locomotive T-1, 1941, frame cast in one piece, length of section illustrated over 20 m.

4   Raymond Loewy Ass.: T-1 express locomotive (1941). Further development of the S-1, about a dozen completed. Wheel arrangement 2-2-2-2. Side covering was reduced in comparison with the S-1 to prevent the bearings from running hot and make servicing easier. The enormous locomotive's frame was cast in one piece. Extremely strong development of the front section ('Shark Nose').

5   Raymond Loewy: S-1 steam locomotive (1 only manufactured), further development of the K4S with strongly protruding steam boiler covering. Wheel arrangement 3-2-2-3. Overall length with tender 42 m. Because of its colossal size (curve radii) the locomotive was used above all on the straight Ohio–Chicago run. The 'American Railroads' slogan was used only for the New York World Fair of 1939, at which the locomotive featured. The Pennsylvania Railroad was in overall charge of developing the locomotive but other railway companies were involved financially.

4

5

like a steel thunderbolt, the ground shaking under me, in a blast of air that almost sucked me into its whirlwind. Approximately a million pounds of locomotive were crashing through near me. I felt shaken and overwhelmed by an unforgettable feeling of power, by a sense of pride at the sight of what I had helped to create in a quick sketch six inches wide on a scrap of paper. For the first time, perhaps, I realized that I had, after all, contributed something to a great nation that had taken me in and that I loved so deeply ... I had found my way of life and felt thankful to all those bright men who had transformed my sketches into reality. It is not maudlin to remember moments like this: they happen so infrequently."

Loewy, K-4S, S-1, T-1: The Railway Gazette: RG (1.5.1936), p.867f.
Loewy R.: The Locomotive, its Esthetic (New York 1937). RG (9.9.1938), p.450ff. RG (24.8.1939), p.698f.
Schweizerische Bauzeitung (1939/2), p.251f.

1934 Loewy: GG-1 The Pennsylvania Railroad railway company was one of the first in the United States to electrify its network. Loewy was commissioned to rework the existing electric locomotives. In his book 'Never leave well enough alone' (New York 1951) he wrote about the design with which he had been presented as follows: "Before: the air vents for ventilation are conspicuous. They interrupt the flow of the lines." And his own design, of which 57 were built: "After: air vents scarcely visible, they have been included in the horizontal line." (R. Loewy, Never leave well enough alone, plate 2).

The shrouding for this extraordinarily impressive locomotive (30m long) was constructed in a completely new way. Loewy proposed a welded shell structure for the body rather than riveted

plates. The whole 'body' of the locomotive could be lifted by crane as a one-piece shell and placed on the electro-mechanical section and the chassis.

Because the GG-1 was extraordinarily quiet, track inspectors kept being involved in accidents. Loewy's decoration, the so-called 'cat's whiskers', five gold stripes on a dark green ground, were intended as a visual warning signal. Similarly the headlight 'swept' to and fro over the tracks at night to alert grazing cattle.

Loewy GG-1: The Railway Gazette (18.9.1936), p.472ff.

SBB 'Landi-Lok': Schweizerische Bauzeitung: SBZ (1927/2), p.294; SBZ (1938/1), p.235.

5

1   Pennsylvania Railroad: electric locomotive, P-5a. Riveted steel plates, two driver's cabs.

2   Pennsylvania Railroad: same locomotive type with new shape, c. 1932 (designer unknown). The driver's cab is in the centre. Wheel arrangement 2-3-2.

3   Electric locomotive with even more uniform style, larger version (wheel arrangement 2-3+3-2), riveted structure.

4   Raymond Loewy: redesign of the locomotive shown in ill. 3, 1934. Welded structure. Stylistic retouching and more careful decoration give a more uniform general impression.

5   Ae 8/14 locomotive, 1931 version, twin-section articulated locomotive with 2×7 axles, of which 2×4 are driving axles. The most powerful electric locomotive in the world, built for the St. Gotthard run. Photograph: SLM Winterthur.

6   Ae 8/14 locomotive, externally modernized articulated locomotive with the same conception as the older model. View before covering is fitted, Maschinenfabrik Oerlikon manufacturing shop. Photograph: SLM Winterthur.

7   Ae 8/14 locomotive, a national achievement as a superlative in terms of power, built for the Schweizerische Landesausstellung in 1939; hence the name 'Landi-Lok'. Photograph: SLM Winterthur.

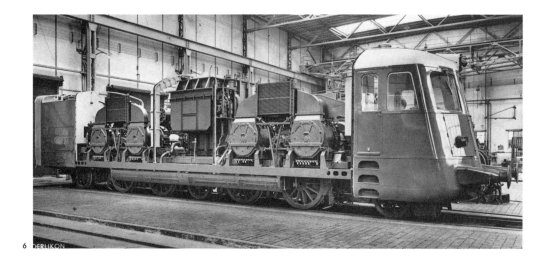

6 OERLIKON

7

1 Express steam locomotive 221.A.11, 'Atlantique' type (wheel arrangement 2-2-1) for the PLM (Paris–Lyon–Méditerranée) company, subsequently streamlined in 1935. Raymond Loewy had admired the PLM locomotives as a child (cf. p. 156), and praised this piece of work as follows in 1937: "Note perfect blend of engine and tender. Visibility from engineer's cab excellent. Streamlining good." (R. Loewy, 1937, ill. 34).

2 Subsequently streamlined express steam locomotive 231.725, 'Pacifique' type (wheel arrangement 2-3-1) for the P.O.-Midi railway company, 1936. Photograph: La Vie du Rail.

3 Subsequently streamlined express steam locomotive 231.761, 'Pacifique' type (wheel arrangement 2-3-1) for the French ETAT state railway, 1936. Photograph: La Vie du Rail.

4 Subsequently streamlined express steam locomotive 231.761, 'Super-Pacifique' type (wheel arrangement 2-3-1) for Chemins de fer du Nord, 1936. Photograph: La Vie du Rail.

5 ETAT steam locomotive, 'Huet' shrouding system, one only manufactured, 1936. Photograph: La Vie du Rail.

6 Express steam locomotive (wheel arrangement 2-3-0) for the French ETAT state railway, one only manufactured, 1937. Photograph: La Vie du Rail.

PLM 221.A.11: The Railway Gazette: RG (17.1.1936), p. 108 ff. Schweizerische Bauzeitung (1938/1), p. 83.

NORD 3.1251-3. 1290; RG (22.1.1937), p. 145 f.

ETAT A-1 231-761; RG (19.3.1937), p. 537 f.

P.O.-MIDI 231-726; RG (5.8.1937), p. 909.

ETAT 230; RG (5.8.1938), p. 250 f.

1

2

3

4

5

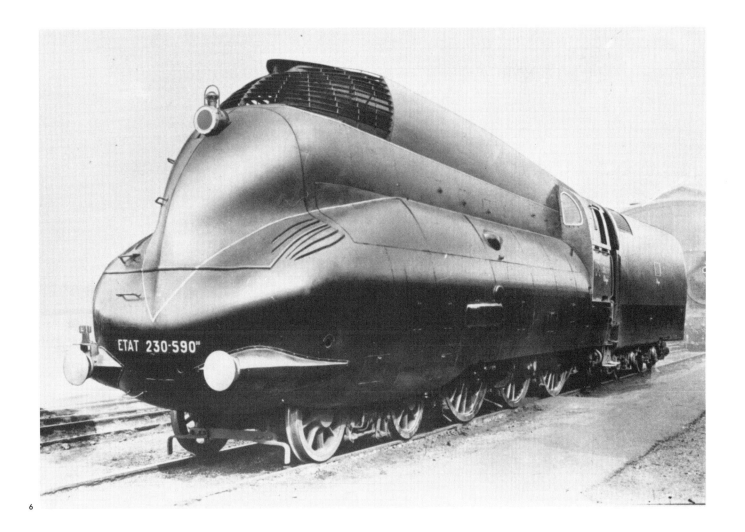

6

DEUTSCHE REICHSBAHN

1935 Henschel-Wegmann Steam Locomotive, 61001/002

1939 Krauss-Maffei Steam Locomotive

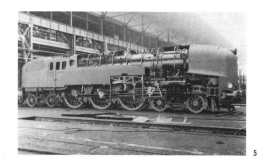

1   Krauss-Maffei locomotive 03 1083 before the 'Stream-Shell' was fitted. Photograph: Krauss-Maffei.

2/3   Krauss-Maffei locomotive 03 1083, 1939. Consistent covering, including driving wheels. Photographs: Krauss-Maffei.

4   The same locomotive with open smoke box doors. Photograph: Krauss-Maffei.

5   Locomotive 61001 for the Henschel-Wegmann train in the factory, Kassel 1935. Wheel arrangement 2-3-2. Streamlined covering only partially fitted. Photograph: Henschel.

6   Locomotive 61002, the second of the two Henschel locomotives, leaving the factory in Kassel, 1935. A. Gottwaldt Collection.

1935 Henschel-Wegmann The two Kassel engineering firms of Henschel and Wegmann wanted to use a joint construction to prove the effectiveness of a steam-driven train as opposed to express railcar trains like the 'Fliegender Hamburger'. They thought that this would give them an advantage with directors of the Deutsche Reichsbahn because of the use of indigenous coal as a fuel, rather than (imported) diesel oil. The Reichsbahn commissioned a short train (four cars) from them, intended to run between Dresden and Berlin. The 'Henschel' locomotive was 18.5 m long and had a working weight of 128 tons, thus smaller and lighter than Borsig and Krupp's large-scale, record-breaking locomotives, but – measured against a load hauled of only four cars – it was still considerable. It was a tender-locomotive (coal tender and

water tank as part of the locomotive) with similar back and front, each provided with a headlight. The locomotive was almost equally well suited to travelling forwards or backwards. The cars were built of light-weight steel and conventionally had only four axles, thus not twin articulated, but with flush joints between the locomotive and cars and between the individual cars. The Henschel-Wegmann train was all in all not as consistently designed as other composite trains, but the locomotive was very fast, with a measured top speed of 187 kph. Its performance lent appropriate expression to the expressive shape. Because of the high speed, the driving wheels were also extraordinarily large (diameter 2.3 m) but – in contrast with the American 'Mercury', for example, (cf. p. 163) they were largely covered.

The train was painted purple and cream below, and the roof was silver. It was delivered in May 1935 and went into service in 1936. It did not prove to be more economical in the long term.

6

Henschel-Wegmann train: Henschel-
Hefte (1933) No. 4, p. 41f. The Railway
Gazette (26.1.1934), p. 133f.
Henschel-Hefte (1935) No. 5, p. 7ff.
Henschel-Hefte (1936), No. 11, p. 61ff.

Deutsche Reichsbahn: RG (21.6.1935),
p. 1209ff.

LONDON-MIDLAND-SCOTLAND (LMS)

1937 Coronation Scot

LONDON NORTH-EASTERN (LNER)

1935 Silver Jubilee
1937 Coronation Express

1 London-Midland-Scotland 6220 'Coronation', Pacific type (wheel arrangement 2-3-1), design for the cladding, 1935.

2 London and North-Eastern (LNER) 10 000 Hudson type (wheel arrangement 2-3-2) 'Flying Scotsman', 1929 (rebuilt 1937). The picture shows its state in 1929.

3 LNER No. 2003 'Lord President', Mikado type (wheel arrangement 1-4-1), rebuilt 1941 with a different wheel arrangement.

4 LNER No. 4498 'Sir Nigel Gresley', A4 Pacific (wheel arrangement 2-3-1), 1937. One of 17 built in its class. The locomotive 'Sir Nigel Gresley' is still in existence today.

5 LNER No. 2512 'Silver Fox' A4 Pacific (wheel arrangement 2-3-1), one of four built, 1935.

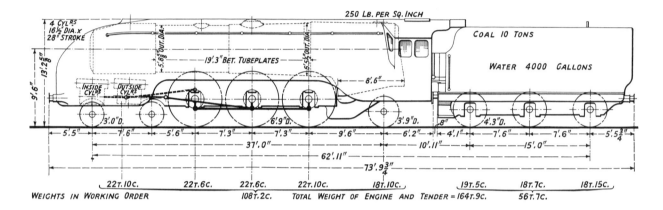

1937 Coronation Scot The British railway companies were significantly different from their French and German counterparts in that they introduced series steam locomotives with streamlined covering at a relatively early stage. Two companies competed with each other to produce the most beautiful and rapid trains: 'London-Midland-Scotland' on the London–Glasgow run (with the 'Coronation Scot', and 'London and North-Eastern' for London–Edinburgh (with their 'Coronation Express'). Both trains were very successful with the public.
The LMS 'Coronation' locomotive was designed by chief engineer Sir William Stanier. It was shipped to the United States for the New York World Fair in 1939 and toured the United States.

1937 Coronation Express The LNER locomotives were designed by design engineer Sir Nigel Gresley. A Gresley locomotive, the 'Mallard', broke the world speed record for steam locomotives in 1938 with a measured top speed of 126 mph (over 200 kph). Gresley was clearly influenced by the French 'Autorail Bugatti' in designing these locomotives.

LMS 'Coronation Scot': The Railway Gazette: RG (10.6.1938), p. 1118 f.
RG (5.8.1938), p. 288 f.
RG (13.1.1939), p. 51 ff.

LNER No. 10 000: RG (30.1.1931);
RG (26.11.1937), p. 926 f.

LNER A4: RG (20.9.1935), p. 450 ff.
'Coronation Express'; RG (2.7.1939), p. 31 ff.

2

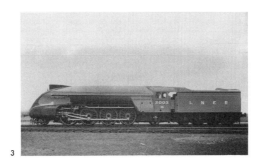

3

4

5

STANDARD ENGINE

1937 EMD 5

MIDDLE EAST, ASIA, AUSTRALIA

1934 Japan

1935 Manchuria

1938 Iraq

1939 Australia

1   EMD-5 standard diesel locomotive (Electro-Motive Division of General Motors), introduced 1937 on the 'Baltimore and Ohio Railroad'. Expensive to acquire but economical to maintain and run. Three 'Illinois Central Railroad' locomotives outside Chicago. D. Phillips collection.

2   Steam locomotive for Iraqui state railways, built by Stephenson c. 1938

3   'Asia Express' for the Dairen–Hsinking route, South Manchurian Railway Company, 1935.

4   Streamlined train for the Japanese State Railways with converted 2C1 locomotive, gauge 1067 mm (narrow gauge).

5   Express locomotive for the South Australian Railway Company, 1939.

2

3

4

5

Streamlining produced kaleidoscopic diversity
in motor car design. Much remained on paper,
a great deal was realized. The scale of suggestions run from the uncompromising manifesto
to mass-production cars (still the most-manu-
factured today). It is not necessary to be an
uncritical car lover to see a fascinating side of
design history in what is unfolded here. The
scale runs from eccentric bizarreness to sculptu-
rally pure works of art. Some radical pieces
were never built, but there is still plenty that is
exciting.

EARLY EXPERIMENTS

1895–1914 Motor Design Competitions

2

1

1895–1914 Motor Designs In 1895 the Magasins du Louvre announced a motor-car design competition. Contrary to original intentions the jury awarded only one prize, to Pierre Selmersheim. Only a photograph of the model has survived of his design; it was presumably made of wax, and the front had sunk a little at the time the photograph was taken. The most striking feature of the design is that it is on two levels. The driver is supposed to sit at the top at the back ('as if on the bridge of a ship') and the passengers would have been undisturbed at the front and down below (early manifestations of the observation lobby and the thrust-forward interior).

'Jamais-Contente' by racing driver Camille Jenatzy was the first motor car to travel at over 100 kph. It was built at the C.I.T.A. coachbuild-ing plant in Liège and its pointed torpedo shape embodies the turn of the century view of what a shape that is to achieve maximum speed should look like.

A few years later the insight was beginning to be generally accepted that the form offering the least possible wind resistance was squat at the front and tapered towards the back (Bergmann, Berlin 1911 and Conte Ricotti's Alfa Romeo, with bodywork by Castagna, Milan 1913). In the latter case it is obvious how difficult it was to fit what was then the ideal streamlined body on to a chassis without a kick-up frame. For years it was also not possible to bend a safety-glass windscreen.

Lüthi-Hubmann's Swiss patent (1914) made some impact on the international scene, and an attempt was made (although ultimately without success) to relativize Paul Jaray's contribution with reference to this patent.

3

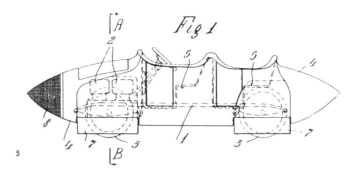

5

4

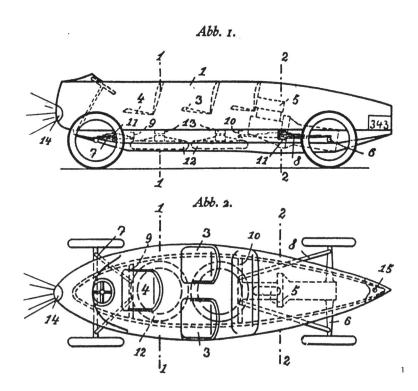

Abb. 1.

Abb. 2.

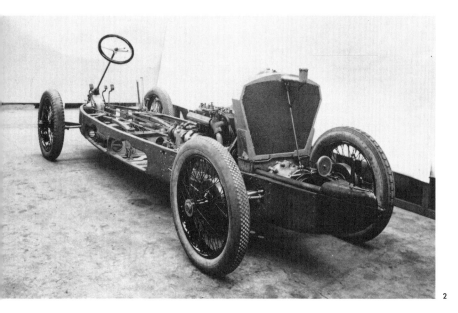

1921 Tropfenwagen Edmund Rumpler (1872–1940) was born in Vienna and as a young man (from 1897) worked as a design engineer for the 'Nesseldorfer Waggonfabrik' (later: Tatra-Werke) in Moravia and from 1902 at the Adler-Werke in Frankfurt am Main. He founded Germany's first aircraft factory in Berlin in 1908 ('Luftfahrzeug Bauanstalt').

The 'Rumpler-Taube' became famous as a first-generation fighter aircraft in the First World War (despite its name it was designed by Igo Etrich). Under the Treaty of Versailles Germany was not permitted to build aircraft. Rumpler transferred his activities to the motor car, and later to refrigeration technology.

Rumpler started work on what was to become the 'Tropfenwagen' ('teardrop car') during the war. The car made streamlining a subject for public discussion in Germany. But if one reads Rumpler's thoughts that led to the conception of the car it is clear that other criteria were more important for him than aerodynamic purity.

His arguments started with the chassis. He wanted to create a car in which the passengers sat in the best-sprung area between the axles; in conventional vehicles only the chauffeur sat there, and the passengers sat over the rear axle. In his desire for an even distribution of weight between front and tail he chose a rear unit with composite engine, transmission and drive (the chauffeur weighted the front axles). The single-wheel suspension using full floating axles (his invention!) was important to him because of the road surfaces in his day; his argument was that it would prevent the wheels from jumping so much when the ground was uneven, a frequent problem.

The lack of a propeller shaft improved the interior performance, and the 'teardrop form' improved the exterior. The car had a fraction of the wind resistance of normal bodywork. The wing-shape of the roof silhouette was said to produce lift (in fact: weight reduction), and the same was true of the mudguards, which were shaped like rudimentary wings.

Rumpler: "The rear-axles shafts, on whose ends the wheels of the car sit, swing around the centre of the rear axle like the wings of a bird, and the rear axle is set on the longitudinal and central axis of the car." And: "In fact the 'Tropfenform' automatically pointed us in the right direction. The fast car requires that the driver's seat is placed as far forward as possible, so that hazards confronting the car from side streets can be noticed as soon as possible."

1   E. Rumpler: drawing from
the patent specification, elevation and
plan. Central engine, boat-shaped
tail, unusual arrangement of seats,
free-standing wheels. According
to Rumpler the roof was not drawn
because of a mistake by the
draughtsman. German Imperial
Patent 346 341.

2   Rumpler-'Tropfenwagen', underbody from behind.

3/4   Rumpler-'Tropfenwagen', bodywork on chassis.

5   Rumpler-'Tropfenwagen', version with extended roof and spoked
wheels, photographed in England.

2–5: Museum für Verkehr und Technik,
Berlin.

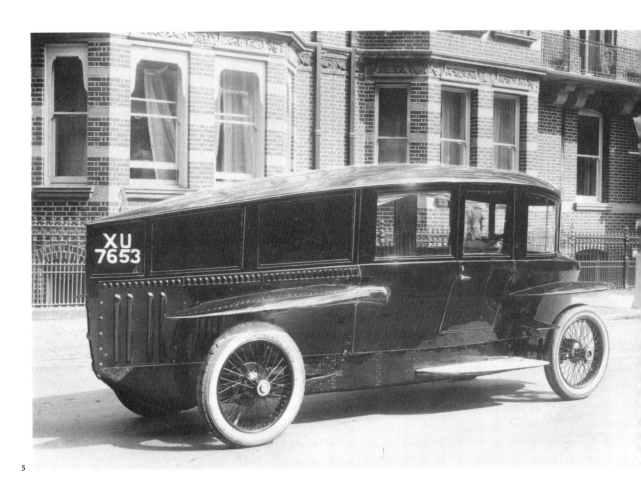

5

This car's technical profile was remarkable. But
in practice there were considerable disadvantages. The car weighed 1.7 t unladen, which
made it far too heavy for the engine output
(36 hp) and too large (height 1.92 m, wheel base
3.34 m), despite a top speed of 115 kph. And the
six-cylinder Siemens engine was not fully developed. Disputes about the patent-worthiness of
the shape, with Paul Jaray among others, were
settled against Rumpler. Only about 100 of the
cars were made between 1921 and 1925 – and
not all of them were sold; two of them are still
in existence (Museum für Verkehr und Technik,
Berlin; Deutsches Museum, Munich). Some specimens were burned for a short but apocalyptic
take in Fritz Lang's film 'Metropolis', and thus
survived on celluloid.

Schweizerische Bauzeitung (1923/1),
pp. 7–9.

1 Emile Claveau: 'Voiture de Caractère Aérodynamique', prototype, introduced at the Paris Salon de l'Automobile, 1928. Engine in front of the rear axle, low seat position, open wheels without mudguards, open headlights.

2/3 Claveau car, two sides of a brochure, 1928.

4 Sir Dennistoun Burney: streamlined car with 3 l engine at the rear, 1930, photographed in London. The car was in production until 1934, but produced only on a small scale.

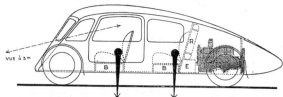

2

3

1927 Emile Claveau The rear-engined car illustrated was presented for the first time in October 1926 (Salon Paris). Its designer and builder, motor-car engineer Emile Claveau, had taken out a patent for aerodynamic bodywork as early as 1923 (French patent No. 226 566). Claveau felt that cars at that time were nothing more than a heterogeneous mixture of traditional elements. He made it his aim to fuse them into a whole. An up-to-date car should reach a high speed (on bad roads as well), carry the largest possible number of passengers in maximum comfort, offer maximum safety and all this for minimum purchase and maintenance costs. The means of achieving all these by no means nugatory aims changed for him after 1931: this was the date at which Claveau became an advocate of front-wheel drive and bodywork with

enclosed wheels. In 1927, the year he introduced the car illustrated here, Claveau's programme was as follows: aerodynamic shape, independent suspension on all wheels, easily accessible interior, all mechanical devices to be brought together, low centre of gravity, self-supporting bodywork construction, low weight, simple assembly, mass production, simple shape, possible to repair oneself.

In cross-section the body sits pronouncedly between the wheels, not over them. Thus the car had an unusually low centre of gravity and a small front area (which is very striking for example in comparison with the Rumpler car). On the other hand the open wheels and lamps were a distinct aerodynamic disadvantage. Claveau was less a strict proponent of aerodynamics than a design engineer.

After the war he designed a limousine with V-8 engine and lightweight metal bodywork, presumably financed by the Péchiney aluminum company (Claveau 'Descartes', 1946, one prototype built).

4

Claveau: Omnia (1926) No. 78,
p. 556f. Omnia (1932) No. 149, p. 149;
Motor Kritik (1932) No. 21, p. 490f.
Journal de la S.I.A. (1932), No. 12,
p. 1956 ff.

Burney: Omnia (1932) No. 149, p. 150.

PAUL JARAY

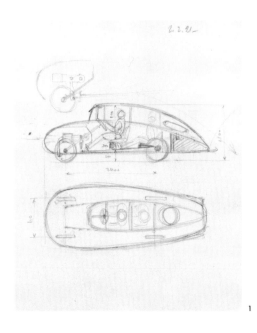

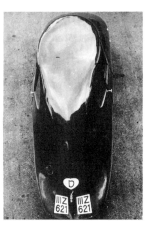

1 Paul Jaray: sketch for a streamlined motor car with two seats arranged one behind the other, pencil in an octavo notebook. Drawn during Jaray's exhibitions in the Luftschiffbau Zeppelin GmbH, February 1921. Basis for Jaray's 1921 master patent.

2 Paul Jaray: table summarizing motor car shapes patented by Jaray, c. 1935.

3 Stromlinien-Karosserie-Gesellschaft, Zurich (Paul Jaray and Paul Susmann): wooden frame for the Chrysler Type 72, photographed in the courtyard of the Haizer und Herrmann coachbuilding company in Zurich, 1927 or 1928.

4 Paul Jaray driving his car on a 'Ley' chassis, 1923.

5 Jaray's 'Ley' car, rear view, 1923.

6 The Jaray 'Ley' car (left) and the Jaray Chrysler car by Lake Lucerne, rear view, c. 1928.

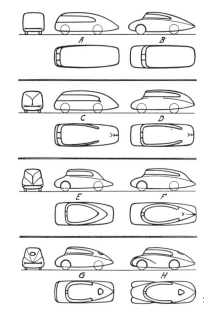

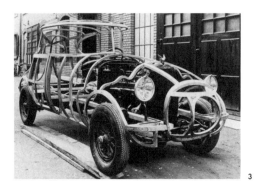

1921 Streamlining according to Jaray

The history of the car is rich in attempts – some of them radical – to get away from the traditional box shape; some of them are recorded in this publication. The Austrian engineer Paul Jaray (cf. p. 16) went further at an early stage than many engineers and designers have done since. Jaray's 'Ley' car of 1923 is – seen through today's eyes – a grotesquely high vehicle. But the shape of the front of the car, with the 'radiator jet', the headlights set flush in the sheet metal skin and the wheels fully enclosed by the body, which is rounded on all sides were decades ahead of general developments. (The motor car was slow to develop away from the motorized coach: passenger compartment plus engine plus mudguards and running boards to the present-day shape – and the problem is still

by no means solved, quite apart from justifiable doubts about the sense of the way in which the car is used today).

Jaray's invention of 'pontoon bodywork' – a name that he did not use himself – was a revolutionary deed if one realizes that the residual mudguards were still one of the most significant parts of car bodywork even in the fifties (cf. for example p. 228).

Jaray's first master patent on the subject of streamlining was headed 'motor vehicle for the conveyance of persons' (German Patent, application 8. 9. 1921, registered 31. 1. 1922). It dealt with two types of motor car: an 'ideal type' derived from the airship and a realistic type (suitable for road traffic).

The shape of the former was based on Jaray's perception of how an ideal streamlined body

should look when close to the ground: like the upper part of an airship, with a very slightly curved floor. This means a semi-circle in cross-section (of variable diameter), with the longitudinal section in the shape of a bisected spindle. For practical reasons (sightlines for the driver) Jaray excluded the possibility of making the whole of the vehicle a 'half streamlined body' – as he called it. Instead of this he based his whole concept on a shape put together from two bodies. The bodywork substructure of the motor car was a 'half streamlined body', with the 'wind protection hood' set on top of it as a second volume. The shape of the latter was derived from the airship gondola, except that in this case top and bottom are reversed. Jaray used this shape in order to avoid lateral air displacement, which he considered responsible for

6

the disturbance of dust on country roads (something for which he blamed the 'boat shape' of Rumpler's teardrop car).

In contrast with this Jaray's streamlined body had the advantage that it "drove the air it displaced essentially upwards and brought it back down to the ground at the tail with the minimum of disturbance" (from the patent specification). Jaray's argument was based not least on this reduced disturbance of dust, which was a difficult problem on the unmetalled roads of the period.

But the difficulty of the 'half streamlined body' resided in the great breadth of the semi-circular cross-section (and purely practically in the mechanical problems of how such a heavily curved door was to be constructed). For this reason Jaray described a variant in the patent

specification as well as this ideal form. For this he replaced the bisected streamlined form of the underbody with a 'streamlined brace', i.e. with a cut-out wing profile. Its smooth side walls curved into the wind protection hood that was placed on top. The cross-section of the hood was again in 'spindle shape' with an approximately parabolic and a rear end that ran to a point; this rear point met the horizontal rear edge of the lower 'streamlined brace' fairly precisely. The 'Ley' car was of this type, as were most motor cars made in the Jaray shape.

'Internal aerodynamics' are important for the understanding of the Jaray shape: these included air for cooling the engine as well as for ventilating or heating the interior. Engine cooling was achieved by means of a tunnel between the air inlet 'radiator jet' at the stagnation point of

the front of the car and the radiator set behind it; after the air had flowed through the radiator it was removed through openings in the floor of the engine compartment. Ventilation of the car interior was achieved by means of a ventilation flap at the second stagnation point on the car, in the centre of the (steeply inclined) windscreen; fresh air entered the passenger compartment at this point and created excess pressure that (theoretically at least) prevented penetration by exhaust gases.

Jaray approached the problems of the motor car above all at the formal level; he was an aviation engineer, not a builder of motor cars. For this reason he came across conditions affecting his cars that he would not have been able to alter fundamentally even if he had wanted to. His first streamlined cars were built on existing chassis

7

8

9

without kick-up frames that were thus much higher than chassis later in the twenties. Comparison of the 1923 Ley car with the 1928 Jaray Chrysler speaks for itself.

Jaray applied his concept to cars of all kinds of design: the conventional arrangement of engine at the front and drive to the back wheels, front-wheel drive cars (e.g. Audi) and rear-engined cars (designs for Tatra). In the course of the thirties Jaray became a supporter of a rear drive unit consisting of engine, gearbox and differential, but he still saw his shape as suitable for all styles.

As an aerodynamics expert for Zeppelin Jaray found himself confronted with the necessity of giving essential parts protruding from the overall shape of the airship the minimum wind resistance (struts, engine gondola suspension devic-

es, landing gear). With cars he worked on the principle that protruding parts were avoidable and that the optimum streamlined shape should cover the mechanical parts as a 'greater shape'. In practice this turned out to be difficult not least because of the car's sensitivity to side winds or because of lift at the front of the car. And so Jaray too felt obliged to take out supplementary patents protecting features like the headlamp arrangement on the Jaray Chrysler car: a streamlined internal form fitted between the reintroduced front mudguards and the bonnet. For Jaray the limousine was a closed car, a car that had been 'made closed'. The superstructure was a supplement governed by airflow to the normal car, which was still open around 1920; the hood protected the occupants from wind, weather and cold, and offered the luxury of a heater.

This premise changed rapidly in the twenties. Jaray's approach was soon superseded. The view of someone like William Stout was now much more valid: he saw a car as a 'living room'. The greatest defect of Jaray's concept is necessarily restricted space. For this reason it scarcely has a part to play in modern motor-car construction.

7 Paul Jaray's own car: specially produced on a Mercedes-Benz chassis, built 1933 by Huber and Brühwiler, Lucerne; exterior view.

8 Paul Jaray's own Mercedes-Benz, detail of windscreen with impact pressure flap, 1933.

9 Interior of Jaray's own car on a Mercedes-Benz chassis.

10 Paul Jaray: design for a Tatra limousine with rear-engine drive, 1934.

11 Karosserie Vetter (Stuttgart): Opel 21 with Jaray bodywork, one only manufactured, 1936.

12 Karosserie Spohn (Ravensburg): large Maybach coupé designed by Jaray, 1935. This fast car was originally intended as a police vehicle for the new autobahns, but only three were built. The boxer Max Schmeling bought one of them.

13 Maybach car by Jaray, rear view.

1–11: ETH-Bibliothek, Wissenschaftshistorische Sammlungen.

12/13: MTU Friedrichshafen.

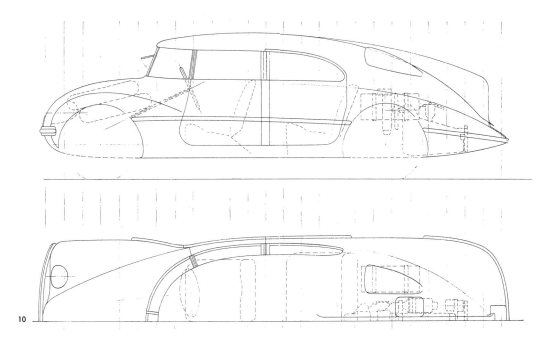

10

11

12

13

Der Motorwagen (1922) No. 25, p. 333 ff. Schweizerische Bauzeitung (1923/1), p. 7 ff. Deutsche Motor-Zeitschrift: DMZ (1924) issue 5/6, p. 41 f. Motor Kritik: MK (1933), p. 395 ff. MK (1934), p. 30 ff. DMZ (1934) issue 4, p. 66 ff. Automobil-technische Zeitschrift (4/1934), p. 105 f. Scientific American (4/1934), p. 221; Motor und Sport (1934) No. 34, p. 9 f. Jaray, P.: Zur Aerodynamik der Rennwagen (special ATZ edition 1935); Industriearchäologie (1984/4), p. 2 ff.

K-TAIL

1933/36 Wunibald Kamm
1936 R. Koenig-Fachsenfeld

AVA CAR

1938 Karl Schlör

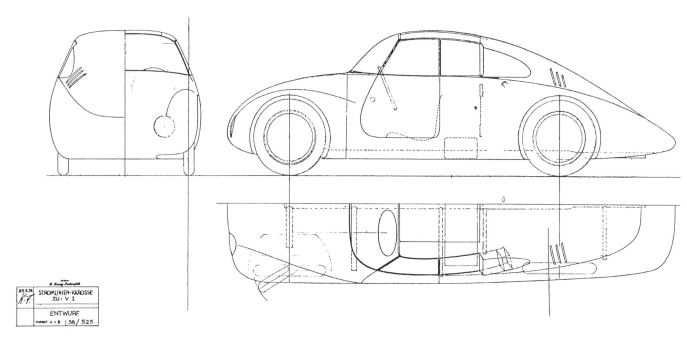

1/2 Karl Schlör: AVA experimental car on Mercedes-Benz 170 H chassis (rear engine), 1938, bodywork by Ludewig (Essen).

3 R. Koenig-Fachsenfeld: lateral section of the V-1 sports car, with spherically curved windscreen (cf. p. 28), 1938. Sammlung Freiherr R. Koenig-Fachsenfeld.

4 Wunibald Kamm/'Forschungs-institut für Kraftfahrwesen und Fahrzeugmotoren an der Technischen Hochschule Stuttgart' (FKFS): patent drawing for German Imperial Patent No. 743 115: motor-car body.

5 W. Kamm/FKFS: car on Mercedes-Benz 170 V chassis (front-engine). Two adjustable anti side-wind fins on the roof (FKFS, German Imperial Patent No. 730 027, 8.3.1939).

1933/36 Kamm and 1936 Koenig-Fachsenfeld There was a practical conflict inherent in transferring ideal streamlining from the airship to the motor car. The cross-section of the vehicle could taper only slightly from the main frame, so that the airflow did not break away at high speeds. If this rule were followed it would produce a car that was impractically long in normal traffic or undesirably reduced headroom for rear passengers. This was a problem presented by numerous Jaray bodies. Professor Wunibald Kamm (1893–1966), founder of the 'Forschunginstitut für Kraftfahrwesen und Fahrzeugmotoren an der Technischen Hochschule Stuttgart' (FKFS) and Freiherr Reinhard Koenig-Fachsenfeld (1899–1992) arrived at a different formula at about the same time as each other, but independently. Kamm is said to have

mentioned it in his lectures (according to Kieselbach) as early as 1933, but did not apply for a patent until later (Koenig: German Patent Specification submitted 17.2.1936, Kamm: German Imperial Pat.-No. 743 115, application 18.2.1936, published 28.10.1943). Working on the basis that the tapering ratio between the greatest height of the body and the length of the tapering section should be about 1:3 to retain a tight airflow (which would have meant a length for the tail of several metres under classical streamlined form), they found that the aerodynamic quality of the shape hardly suffers if it is cut off vertically at the tail. Thus the bodywork tapered from its largest cross-section as acutely as was necessary to keep a tight airflow (by 15 degrees), and was then cut off vertically. This shape has since been known as the 'K-shape', which refers

to the uncertain origin of the invention (Freiherr Koenig-Fachsenfeld or Kamm). It differed from the classic Jaray shape in that it offered more interior space, and looked more squat.

1938 Karl Schlör from Westhofen-Dirmstein (b. 1910) worked at the 'Aerodynamische Versuchsanstalt' Göttingen (AVA) as a young engineer under Ludwig Prandtl. During his time there he worked on an ideal (unitary) streamlined body, the AVA car, which was built as a single model on a Mercedes-Benz chassis. The car did not have a very powerful engine but achieved a top speed of 132 kph with an outstanding aerodynamic drag factor of 0.189. Its spherically curved windows were made of acrylic glass – appropriately to the contemporary state of technological development.

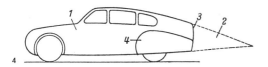

Kamm, W.: Das Kraftfahrzeug (Berlin 1936); Kamm, W. and Schmied, C.: Das Versuchs- und Messwesen auf dem Gebiet des Kraftfahrzeugs (Berlin 1938); Die Strasse (1939) issue 4, p 104 ff. Automobiltechnische Zeitschrift: ATZ (1939), p. 489; ATZ (1939), p. 493 ff.

Schlör: Reinicke, H.: Bestimmung des Luftwiderstands vom Schlörwagen 1939, ATZ (1/1948).

Koenig-Fachsenfeld, R.: Aerodynamik des Kraftfahrzeug, Band I und II (Frankfurt am Main 1951); Koenig-Fachsenfeld, R.: Aerodynamik des Kraftfahrzeug, Band III und IV (Heubach 1984).

1   Norman Bel Geddes: diagram of Curtiss's experiment with the reversed car body (from 'Horizons').

2   Norman Bel Geddes: Motor Car No. 8 (1931), rear view.

3   Norman Bel Geddes: Motor Car No. 9, pencil sketches, 1933.

4   Norman Bel Geddes: Motor Car No. 9, sheet with plan, longitudinal section, view and aspect and sequence of cross-sections, 1933.

5   Norman Bel Geddes: Motor Car No. 9, rear view.

6   Norman Bel Geddes: Motor Car No. 9, model (cast aluminum with plastic windows).

2–6: Bel Geddes Collection. H. Ransom Humanities Research Center, University of Austin/Texas, by permission of Edith Lutyens Bel Geddes.

1

2

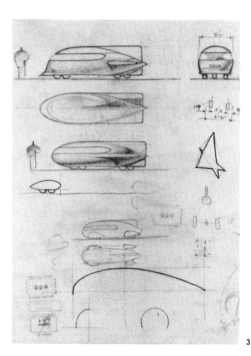

3

1931 Motor Car Nos. 8 & 9   The motor-car and bus designs that Bel Geddes introduced in 'Horizon' in 1932 were not based on research in a wind tunnel or other scientific facilities, but on the results of other people's research. He was convinced of the rightness of the 'teardrop' premise.

The crucial factor for Bel Geddes was an experiment by aircraft engineer Glenn Curtiss, who had turned a traditional car body round and mounted it on a chassis, then proved reduced wind resistance. From this Bel Geddes derived a new form of road vehicle with a squat front and tapering tail. A picture of an ice-floe in a river that adopted a 'teardrop' shape when melting seemed to be proof of the correctness of this shape (which is not true: ice melts in this shape only in certain cases). The choice of this basic

form did not relate to Jaray's patents in any way.

"At first sight, you may not think this design looks pleasing or much like a motor car. You may think it odd" (Horizons, p. 57). But for Bel Geddes Motor Car No. 8 was a consistent design, with eight seats within the same size as a normal vehicle, rear engine, wheels completely integrated into the body and sophisticated details like adjustable headlights. After publication in 'Horizons' his studio continued to work on the subject, looking for a more consistent and perhaps more pleasing formalization. 'Motor Car No. 9' (1933) was made up solely of 'teardrop' internal forms and based on circular cross-sections.

Bel Geddes, N.: Horizons (Boston, 1932), p. 44 ff. Bel Geddes, N.: Magic Motorways (New York 1940).

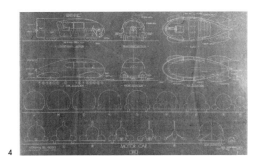

4

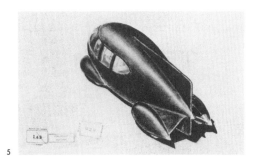

5

6

DYMAXION CAR
1933 R. Buckminster Fuller

SCARAB
1932 William B. Stout

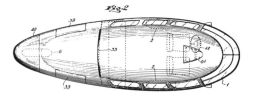

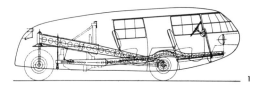

1 'Dymaxion Car', top view (from the patent specification (US Patent 2101057, application 18.10.1933). On the roof is a periscope (pos. 61) for rear-view purposes (no rear window). Longitudinal section. The car was about 6 m long. Rear wheels suspended on diagonally rising forked perforated bearer with the central engine between the forks.

2 'Dymaxion Car', one of three vehicles built, on the banks of Lake Michigan, 1933.

3 Schematic drawing: demonstration of the manoeuvrability of the rear-steered 'Dymaxion Car' compared with a traditional vehicle.

4 Stout 'Scarab', drawing from the patent specification; section through the tail, engine arrangement, wheel suspension, tubular steel body structure. Front view with demonstration of single-wheel suspension (US Patent 2047336, 1934).

5 Stout 'Scarab', Stout's own car (only vehicle built), rear view, 1932. Photograph: Detroit Historical Department.

6 Stout 'Scarab', interior: small folding table, movable seats, flat floor. Photograph: Detroit Historical Museum.

7 Stout 'Scarab' III (1944), prototype with integral fibre-glass structure (bodywork and underbody), anticipating the fifties in design terms. Photograph: Detroit Historical Museum.

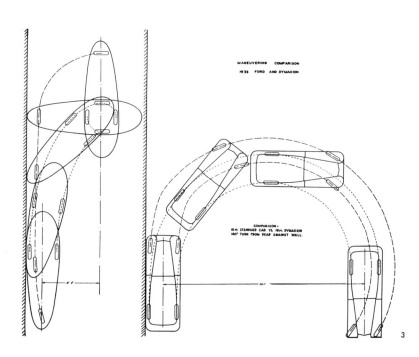

1933 Dyamaxion Car Engineer Buckminster Fuller (1895–1983) introduced the 'Dymaxion Car' to the public at the 'Century of Progress' exhibition in Chicago in July 1933, outside architects' George and Frederick Keck's 'Crystal House', which placed what were probably the exhibition's most radical innovations together. Marine engineer Starling Burgess was involved in the development of the car. It was a three-wheeler with a rear Ford V-8 engine. Transmission and steering were totally non-standard: the front wheels were driven, and the rear wheel was steered. The body was strongly reminiscent of a modern aircraft fuselage. The car was entered from the rear, and the driver's seat was in the sloping cab. The vehicle was built for optimum aerodynamics (although it must be assumed that this affected frontal air resistance above all,

and that the vehicle must have been extremely susceptible to side winds). Fuller worked on the ratio of wind and rolling resistance: in a conventional car it was 1:1 at 60 kph, and 4:1 at 100 kph. The 'Dymaxion' car was intended to produce only a quarter of this wind resistance and travel at 40 rather than 18 miles per gallon. The lightness of the vehicle (1700 pounds) was also a contributory factor. Fuller considered that front-wheel steering was an outdated survival of the horse-drawn carriage, and compared it with the rear steering of ships and aircraft (but the vehicle must have been extremely unstable when travelling at speed). The patent specification mentions " ... the body having the form of a unitary aeronautic streamline body with substantially unbroken curvature from end to end (...), and its maximum cross-section occur-

ring at about one-third of the distance from the bow end".

1932 Scarab The 'Scarab' brought together completely new insights about an efficient chassis and bodybuilding with a radical and unusual overall architecture for the car.
The car illustrated here was Stout's own vehicle, a prototype. It did not go into production in this form, but in an edition of 100 vehicles that was rather more adapted to the American taste – as a construction that seemed a little less coherent, but was still astonishing (cf. p. 19). The wheels of this unitary car were placed at the extreme corners of the body; they were low-pressure aircraft wheels (comfort). The car was the same length as customary American models, but so roomy inside that all the seats inside with the

6

7

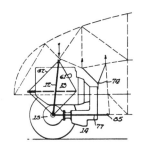

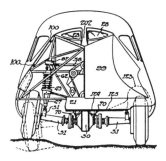

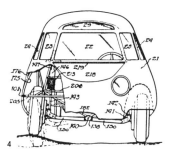

4

5

exception of the driving seat could be moved around the flat floor and grouped around a little folding table. The 'Scarab' is streamlined in shape within Stout's own view, but not on the basis of 'teardrop' form (cf. Stout text, p. 266). The shape of the 'Scarab' is remarkable because it is curved on all sides and because the sides are so strongly slanted inwards, a means of presenting less resistance to side winds.

The body was built on a tubular steel frame, a spatially effective structure rather like an insect's shell, hence the name 'Scarab'.

Like the 'Dymaxion' car it had a rear Ford V-8 engine. But here the common features end: the 'Scarab' chassis was infinitely more elaborate. The body frame was to a certain extent suspended on four columns, with four MacPherson strut units with conical springs extending to a

very high level. The body is supported by them, and as the suspension points were substantially higher than the centre of gravity of the car this could develop only minimum moments of tilt on bends. The use of conical springs, individual suspension of all four wheels and the nature of the tyres are adapted from aircraft construction.

Buckminster Fuller: Architectural Record (8/1933), p. 147; Buckminster Fuller, R.: (1973), p. 136 ff.

Stout: Stout, W. B. (1951), pp. 255–257; Scientific American 'SA' (3/1934), p. 126 f. SA (3/1935), p. 152.

ANDREAU

1 J.-E. Andreau: French Patent No. 790518: "Perfectionnements apportés aux véhicules automobiles carénés" (1935). Fig. 2: ideal streamlined shape with 'nil lift angle' rising to the rear. Fig. 3, 4: ideal vehicle with mathematically calculated rear fins and chassis cladding offering minimum wind resistance.

2/3 Design for Bugatti after Andreau, drawn at coachbuilders Chausson (Paris), 1935.

4 Prototype on Citroën chassis, plywood, 1944.

5/6 Mathis VL 333 (3 seats, 3 wheels, 3 litres/100 km), 1947. Aluminum body, not produced in series.

7 Peugeot 402-'Andreau', one of about six cars built, 1936. The design was originally developed for a car with an 8-cylinder engine, but the prototypes had a four-cylinder engine. Andreau's very academic approach is combined with a high level of artistic attraction – a typically French phenomenon in the field of engineering science. Photograph: Peugeot.

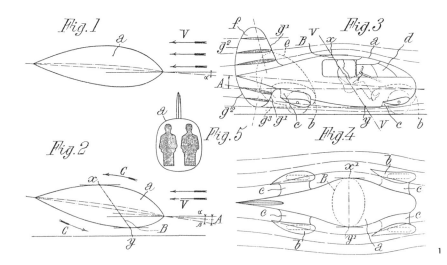

1

2

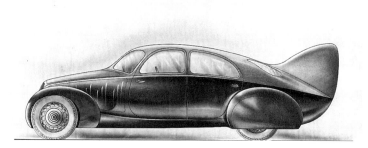

3

1935 Voitures Carénées French aviation engineer Jean Edouard Andreau submitted a patent application in 1935 that presented a remarkably independent reply to aerodynamic problems and differed in one fundamental point from the Jaray tendency, for example. Jaray was looking for an ideal form close to the ground on the basis of a bisected streamlined body, while Andreau's research moved in a quite different direction.

He applied the well-known fact that turbulence drag is at its lowest if an aircraft wing rises slightly to the rear to road vehicles. To keep the ground effect (excess pressure and additional lift) to a minimum he slightly increased the angle of inclination. Andreau also worked from the basic form of a spindle-shaped rotational solid. As this shape, which runs out to a point at the

back, was aerodynamically inappropriate for road vehicles (no lateral stability), a rear keel was needed on top of the vehicle for stabilization purposes. In contrast with Jaray's horizontal tail edge, in this solution the vehicle ended in a vertical knife-edge. But this shape did not include the rear wheels in particular, which called for wheel cladding. This was made convex or concave to correspond with the streamlines adopted (fig. 4 in the patent specification, pos. b). Horizontal wing stumps covering the suspension were appended to create negative lift (pos. c). It is clear that, unlike Jaray, Andreau was not working on a basis of simplification, but searching for a shape that was correct in an almost biological way, and logical in its own terms. Extremely sophisticated thought was given to the largest 'central cross-section' ('maître-

couple'), which was very important to the French approach (e.g. also for Claveau, cf. p. 184). By placing the 'carène' diagonally the connecting points of the horizontal tangents ('lines' of the relative wind) form a diagonal plane (fig. 2, pos. xy). This corresponds with the human sitting position; thus the largest cross-section of the vehicle ran diagonally from the shoulder area to the feet. It is remarkable that Andreau used very far-reaching technical thinking about airflow to produce complex forms of extraordinarily zoomorphic appearance.

4   5   6

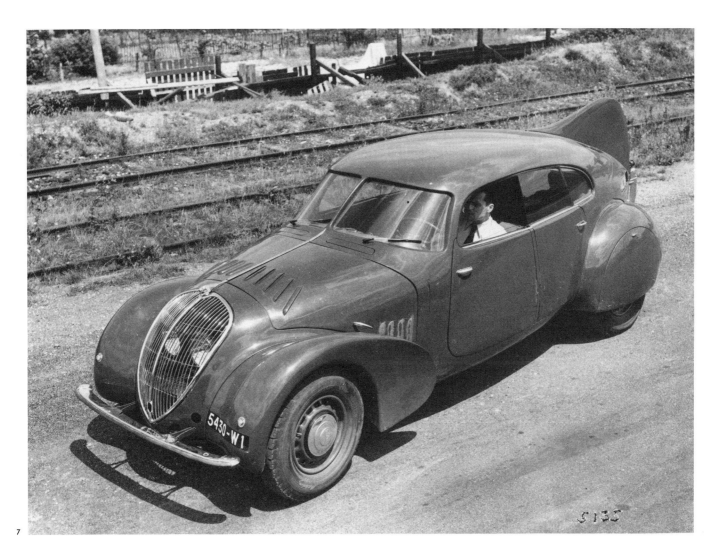

7

Motor und Sport (1934) issue 19,
p. 11 ff. La Vie Automobile
(10. 9. 1938), p. 329 ff. La Traction
Nouvelle (1–2/1939), p. 32 f.

SIA COMPETITION

1935 Société des Ingénieurs de l'Automobile

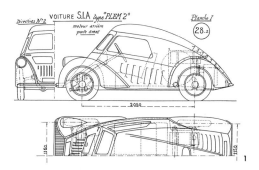

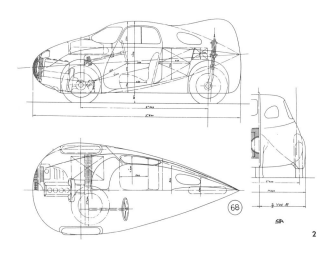

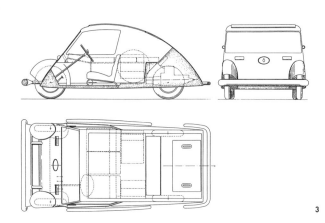

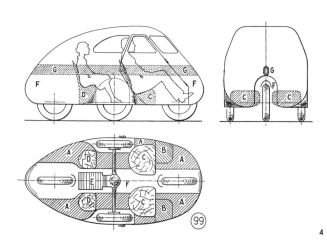

1935 Société des Ingénieurs de l'Automobile The French Société des Ingénieurs de l'Automobile (SIA) ran a unique competition for its members in 1935. They had to design a two-seater car that could reach an average speed of 75 kph, that could travel 100 km on no more than 5 litres of petrol and was to cost no more than 8000 francs (this was just under half the price of the new and exceptionally reasonable Citroën 7/11 Traction Avant). 102 designs were submitted – by prominent designers and complete unknowns – and published in a substantial volume. The list of competitors includes names like Andreau, Claveau, Grégoire and Le Corbusier/Jeanneret.

The competition was intended as a shot in the arm for the crisis-ridden motor-car industry; it was based on the insight that a real recovery would come only as a result of massive stimulation of demand, i.e. by mass production. This implied radical democratization of the motor car.

'Streamlining' was not a condition of the competition, but it is no co-incidence that it featured in a large number of the designs. It was a means by which a necessarily small and not very powerful engine could reach considerable speeds; additionally it provided a formal plane of reference for testing the 'modernity' and up-to-date quality of a design. "Une telle voiture est évidemment difficile à faire. Beaucoup de personnes y ont pensé, mais, jusqu'ici, aucune n'a poussé jusqu'à la réalisation commerciale" (from the competition publication). This latter statement needs amending: the Fiat 'Topolino' was developed at approximately the same time as the SIA

competition. It was a little two-seater with the same features as those required by the SIA, and it became the first popular Italian car in subsequent years (chief engineer: Dante Giacosa).

5

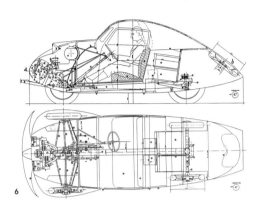

6

1   Plem: entry no. 28. Rear engine, access at the front.

2   Andreau: entry no. 68: three-wheeler car with front-wheel drive (cf. p. 197).

3   Le Corbusier/Pierre Jeanneret: entry no. 102. "Les auteurs indiquent que dès 1928 ils ont conçu un type de voiture qu'ils n'ont pas songé à présenter à cette époque, parce que trop différente des conceptions habituelles à ce moment: moteur à l'arrière, formes aérodynamiques, faible encombrement, quoique de très grand confort intérieur ..." (jury report). The design became known as the 'Voiture Maximum'.

4   Seyot: entry no. 99: 'Cycle Car', three-wheeler with unusual wheel arrangement.

5   Logo for the competition publication.

6   Gaultier & Angeli: entry no. 67: front engine and drive, wide track at the front, narrow behind.

7   Ryan: entry no. 84: 'Aérodynamisme 100%'. Direction of travel from left to right.

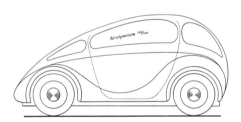

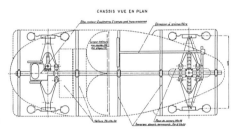

7

Société des Ingénieurs de l'Automobile: Album de la Voiture SIA 2 Places (Paris 1935); Omnia (1935) No. 182, p. 59 f. Omnia (1935) No. 184, p. 112 ff. La Vie automobile (25.12.1936), p. 342 f.

VOLKSWAGEN

1934 Ferdinand Porsche

AUTO-UNION

1938 Rekordwagen

1934 Volkswagen   In a report to the men in power in Berlin (early in 1934) Ferdinand Porsche (1875–1951), the independent design engineer, insisted that a 'People's Car' could not simply be a smaller version of a normal car. He suggested a car that would have normal dimensions but be light in weight, with a top speed of 100 kph, 4 seats and simple, robust and easy to service. Hitler took up the idea.

Porsche was commissioned to design the 'VW' in mid 1934. The original one-year development period turned out to be unrealistic. Even though this was not the original 'People's Car' ('Model T' Ford: 1908; Citroën 5 CV: 1921; Opel 'Laubfrosch': 1924; Austin 'Seven': 1922), the 'Volkswagen' project was unusual.

The German car industry still had no experience of fully industrialized mass production. Translating the performance specification into a design that was ripe for manufacture was carried out under a regime of highly restrictive costing and Porsche's resistance to the views of the relevant authorities in the motor industry.

Porsche visited the Ford factory in Detroit and other factories with assembly-line production in 1936 and 1937. The 'Volkswagen' was intended to be an exemplary demonstration of National Socialist material management: the car's components were to be made by various German manufacturers and assembled on a single site. This plan was abandoned for economic reasons; the VW town of Wolfsburg was founded in 1937 in an area that was scarcely industrialized on a site on the Mittelland-Kanal, and a complete manufacturing plant was set up within a year. Hitler originally intended to launch the car in 1938 as the 'Strength-through-Joy' car. This idea was abandoned, allegedly to Porsche's great relief (export!). But there was scarcely any significant production before the war (about 500 vehicles); the plant was badly damaged during the war. The 'Volkswagen's' actual success story began in 1948, when the idea was already 15 years old. By 1990 almost 20 million 'Beetles' had been completed, which meant not least unique popularity for a 'moderate' streamlined shape. Despite its historical and ideological connection with the Nazi dictatorship it has to be recognized that the 'Volkswagen' made an enormous contribution to the democratization of the motor car.

1 Volkswagen prototype, body-work carcass, c. 1937. No running boards; they were reintroduced only in the final phase of the project.

2 Volkswagen prototype in the wind tunnel, attempts to improve the aerodynamics, 1937.

3 The same prototype, rear view.

4 Volkswagen, production model 1939, did not go into series production until after the war.

5/6 Auto-Union-Rekordwagen, c. 1938. Centrally mounted engine, full aluminum shell. The bulging front created lift that was to be the undoing of racing driver Rosemeyer. Photograph: ETH-Bibliothek, wissenschaftliche Sammlungen.

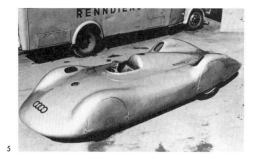

5

6

Schweizerische Bauzeitung (1939/1), p. 105 ff. The Automobile Engineer (2/1939), p. 47 ff.

MERCEDES-BENZ

1922 Teardrop Racing Car   1936/39 Supercharged Record-breaking Car
1935 Rear-engined limousine

1   Mercedes-Benz record-breaking car 1939; 3 l supercharged engine with special bodywork.

2   Mercedes-Benz record-breaking car 1936/37, 12 cylinder engine, top speed 372 kph (Rudolf Caracciola).

3   Mercedes-Benz Type 170 H, with rear engine, produced 1935–1939.

4   Benz teardrop racing car 1922–1925, 1924 version.

5   Rudolf Caracciola on the autobahn record run near Dessau, Mercedes-Benz record-breaking car, 1939 version.

All photographs: Mercedes-Benz-Archiv

5

CHRYSLER

1934 Airflow Model

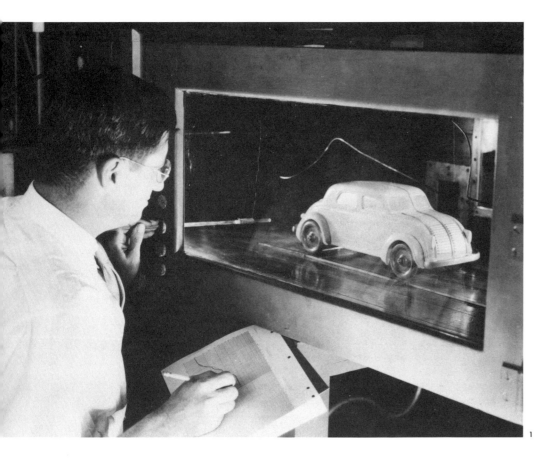

1   Engineer Oliver Clark wit the 'Trifon' model in the Chrysler Motors Corp. wind tunnel. Airflow measurement using a pitostatic tube, c. 1932.

2   Carl Breer, Chrysler's chief engineer, with the model of 'Trifon' or 'Airflow' and of an older Chrysler vintage, c. 1932.

3   Norman Bel Geddes: Chrysler 'Airflow', mock-up with modified front section, June 1934. Soon after the public's reservations about the innovative shape of the 'Airflow' made themselves felt Chrysler started studies aimed at changing it. However, they remained content with altering details, rather than adopting Bel Geddes' radical suggestions.

4   Photograph of an 'Airflow' with streamlined cladding (single study) with removable tail. It is possible to see the two-part 'Airflow' pane behind the bevelled windscreen. 1934.

5   Chrysler 'Airflow' in front of the high speed train 'City of Salina', 1934.

1–5: Chrysler Historical Foundation

1934 Airflow Model   The Chrysler 'Airflow' was considered a turning point in American design history. It established a new formal language for the American motor car: a move away from the 'boxy cars' of the twenties and early thirties and on to rounded sculptural forms that determined the image of the American car until the mid fifties.

As well as this the 'Airflow' represents the start of a new manufacturing process, particularly in terms of welding and modular construction. The name of the model set a programme for the car that was based on irreversible laws of physics and was thus intended to be an utterly convincing advertising line: 'Airflow'. Work on the project started after 1930, first for an important prototype, the 'Trifon'. Chrysler built their own wind tunnel, in consultation with pioneer aviator

Orville Wright. One of the main ideas behind the design was that the passengers should sit in the best-sprung area between the axles, and that the rear passengers should not be above the rear axle. Sprung comfort was one of the main concerns of Breer's team. Pushing engine and interior forwards was completely new for a car on this scale, and went against all the rules of aesthetics that the public had become familiar with. Streamlining was used both to perfect the new feature and to communicate it. There is no doubt that this was all too much for the public; the expensive new model became a financial fiasco for Chrysler. But the car started an extremely important movement. Chrysler's competitors launched models in 1936 that may have handled streamlining more gracefully (cf. p. 208), but 'Airflow' retains its historic significance.

Automotive Industries: AI (1934), p. 550 f. AI (1934), p. 766 ff. American Scientific (8/1977), p. 98 ff.

TATRA

1934 Type 77

1936 Type 87/Type 97

1947 Tatraplan

1934 Tatra Type 77 No other motor-car manufacturing firm introduced 'real' streamlining for series production cars as radically as the Czech Tatra company in Nesseldorf, under the direction of Austrian design engineer Hans Ledwinka (1878–1967). In contrast with other factories who tried to avoid Jaray patents, Tatra was a Jaray licensee. And indeed Paul Jaray himself was involved in the process and submitted a design from which elements were adopted for 'Type 77'.

'Type 77' (1934) was a large touring car (length 5.2 m, six seats, V-8 rear engine, air cooling, top speed 150 kph). It thus met the requirements for an 'autobahn car', a problem at the forefront of the technicians' minds at the time. The public found the shape exciting: its outstanding features were a short bonnet and side windows angled

inwards. Jaray's idea of a semicircular windscreen could not be realized with safety glass at the time, but even the windscreen that was used, strongly angled and in three sections, was unusual.

The tail with its fin (for particular lateral stability) and with no visible rear window (internal pane between passenger and engine compartments and view through ventilation slits in the rear hood) was absolutely sensational. Given this layout, placing the air-cooled engine behind the passenger cell was an ideal solution, in terms of noise suppression as well. Thus the 'Type 77' met the requirements of ideal streamlined form: compact front and extended tail; moving the interior forward into the best-sprung area between the axles established new standards of comfort. This was achieved at the

expense of consciously blocking traditional associations like: the longer the bonnet in front of the passengers the greater the prestige.

The photograph taken in the Tatra design office shows that this shape too was the result of a considerable amount of development. Even roadworthy prototypes did not look as convincing as the production model. Design decisions were concerned among other things with the rear wing (originally not fully integrated), the windscreen (originally slightly swept back in a V-shape), the air inlets in the roof (originally fitted inorganically). A point that was not even finally solved concerns the front mudguards, which could not be fully included in the linear flow because of the short bonnet. The fact that protruding mudguards were retained even by the Tatra development team shows how advanced and outside

3

4

5

1 Tatra 57 OV, prototype for a small car, 1933. Photograph: Tatra.

2 From the sales brochure: Tatra 'Type 77' on one of the first German autobahns (1934). 105 produced.

3 Tatra Type 97, with four-cylinder horizontally opposed engine, four doors. Production was stopped after about 500 cars at the instigation of the National Socialists because of excessive competition for the 'VW'. Photograph: Tatra.

4 Tatra Type 87, successor of Types 77 and 77a. All steel body, windscreen more steeply angled. Over 3000 produced.

5 Post-war 'Tatraplan', from 1947, full pontoon bodywork with 4-cylinder horizontally opposed engine. Photograph: Tatra.

6 Tatra development office c. 1933/4. Working model of type 77 in the foreground. Development work on wings/mudguards, side windows, windscreen, engine ventilation.

7 Tatra 77, tail area with air inlets for engine, slats for engine ventilation and rear view purposes; stabilization fins became a Tatra trade mark.

7

the current pattern of thinking Jaray's ideas of pontoon bodywork really were.

Tatra clung on to the idea of streamlining for decades, even after Czechoslovakia became a part of the Soviet power structure. The 77 model was soon replaced by the somewhat shorter model 87 (all-metal body). The 97 model (1936) went into production but was stopped after the 'Anschluss' of Czechoslavakia into the German Reich – it would have presented too much competition for the 'Volkswagen' project. The 4-cylinder 'Tatraplan' appeared in 1947: its name indicates association with aeroplanes. A new large V-8 limousine came on to the market in 1955 (Type 603), and became part of the regular image inventory of post-war Eastern European history as a prestige limousine for party functionaries and members of the government. Tatra

still exists today, and still makes a large rear-engined limousine (with an Italian Vignale body) as well as structurally remarkable commercial vehicles.

Automobiltechnische Zeitschrift (11/1941), p. 286f.

1 John Tjaarda: 'Briggs' stream-lined car with rear-mounted Ford engine, shown in 'A Century of Progress', Chicago, 1933.

2 Ford Lincoln 'Zephyr', front-mounted 12-cylinder engine, reverting to the 'Briggs' car in formal terms, 1936. Photograph: Ford Historical Foundation.

3 Ford Lincoln 'Zephyr' and the DC–3: in the glow of progress. Photograph: Ford Historical Foundation. (Lincoln Zephyr).

Motor (12/1933), p. 25.

1

2

3

WIKOV
1932 Streamlined Car

PEUGEOT
1936 - 02 Series

FIAT
1935 Fiat 500 Topolino
1937 Fiat 508 CS

1   Peugeot 402, 1936, from the
1938 catalogue.

2   Wikov streamlined car by
Wichterle and Kovarik (Wikov),
Prossnitz/Czech Republic, produced
in a small series, 1932.

3   Peugeot 402, 1936, detail with
headlights behind the radiator grille.
From the 1938 catalogue.

4   Fiat 500 'Topolino', two-part
plaster model, 1935. Photograph:
Centro Storico. Fiat.

5   Fiat 508 CS (Mille Miglia),
bodywork by Savio, first application
of the K-tail (cf. p. 190) in a somewhat
different form. 1.1 l engine, 42 hp,
140 kph. Photograph: Centro Storico.
Fiat.

6   Steyr 50, Austrian two-seater,
built by Karl Jenschke, 1936.

7   Adler Type 10, 'Autobahnadler',
1937. Built by Karl Jenschke. Platform
frame, body by Ambi-Budd, Berlin.
Touring convertible version.

Peugeot: La Vie Automobile
(10.2.1936), p.61ff.

Fiat: Motor Italia (1–2/1938),
p.24f. and 54.

STEYR

1936 Steyr 50

ADLER

1937 Adler Type 10

4

5

6

7

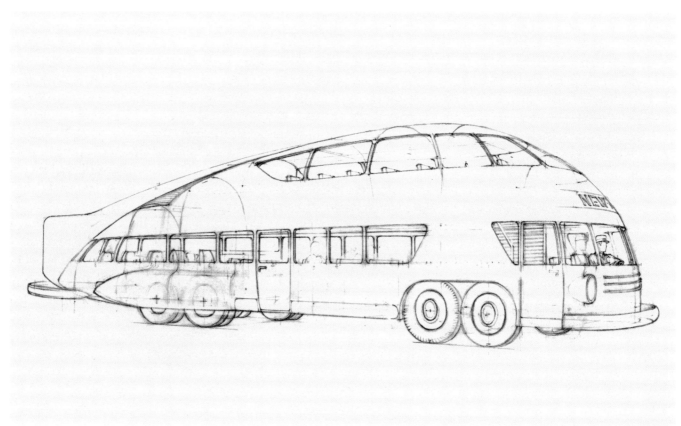

1   35-seater Mercedes-Benz express motor coach type LO 3100, 1935. Photograph: Mercedes-Benz-Archiv.

2   W. B. Stout: rear-engined 26-seater bus, 1934, unladen weight 7000 pounds, 110 kph. Photograph: Detroit Historical Department.

3   Karosseriebau Kässbohrer, Ulm: touring bus on a Mercedes-Benz chassis, 1936. Autobahn buses were run by the Deutsche Reichsbahn in the thirties. Photograph: Kässbohrer.

4   Norman Bel Geddes: 'Motor Coach No. 2', double-decker bus with rear engine on the right-hand side. Design drawing, pencil on paper, undated (1932). (Bel Geddes Collection, H. Ransom Humanities Research Center, University of Austin/Texas, by permission of Edith Lutyens Bel Geddes).

5   Isobloc bus with rear engine (Lyon), before 1950.

6   Karosseriebau Kässbohrer, Ulm: touring bus on MAN chassis, c. 1937. Photograph: Kässbohrer.

Deutsche Fahrzeugtechnik (9–10/1936), p. 94 ff.

5

6

CARROZZERIA TOURING

Superleggera

1   Carrozzeria Touring: Alfa Romeo 8 C 2900 B (1937). T. Anselmi Collection.

2   Carrozzeria Touring: Fiat 2800 (1939), aluminum body carcass. C. F. Bianchi Anderloni Collection.

3   Carrozzeria Touring: Lancia Aprilia Spider (1938) at the 'Targa Abruzzo' race (1939). C. F. Bianchi Anderloni Collection.

4   Carrozzeria Touring: Fiat 2800 (1939), the completed car. T. Anselmi Collection.

5/6   Carrozzeria Touring: BMW 328 sports car (1941). C. F. Bianchi Anderloni Collection.

1926 Superleggera In 1926 law graduates Felice Bianchi Anderloni and Gaetano Ponzoni acquired a Milan motor-car building company, which they re-organized and used to market the 'Weymann' patent in Lombardy. The 'Weymann' construction method, developed in England, was a light-weight construction method for touring cars using a wooden frame covered with artificial leather (thus no sheet-metal bodywork). This was the aim of the 'Touring' company, as it called itself: consistent light-weight construction. In 1932 an Alfa-Romeo built on this principle won the Mille Miglia (the first of a total of eleven Mille Miglia victories with 'Touring' bodywork).

In 1937 the company introduced the 'Touring Superleggera' method, a name which it adopted from that point: welded grid frames with alu-minum body work attached to them. It was an extremely lightweight construction method: the body of the BMW Spyder 328, illustrated on the adjoining page, weighed only 80 kilograms. Numerous 'Touring' designs were by Bianchi Anderloni's son, graduate engineer Carlo Felice Bianchi Anderloni (born 1916).

'Touring's' most important customers were Alfa Romeo, also based in Milan, and Fiat.

4

5

6

1 Pinin Farina: Alfa Romeo 6 C 2300 Pescara, 1935 (one vehicle only built).

2 Pinin Farina: Lancia Aprilia Berlinetta Aerodinamica, 1936 (possibly the first of three or four cars). Photograph: Pininfarina.

3 Pinin Farina: Lancia Aprilia, convertible with retractable headlights, 1939. Photograph: Pininfarina.

4 Pinin Farina: Lancia Aprilia convertible, 1938. Photograph: Pininfarina.

5 Pinin Farina: Lancia Aprilia Berlinetta Aerodinamica, 1937. Front view, taken at the 1937 Milan Motor show. T. Anselmi Collection.

6 Pinin Farina: Lancia Aprilia Berlinetta Aerodinamica, 1937. Rear view. T. Anselmi Collection.

Battista Farina (1893–1966) was the tenth of eleven sons (his nickname 'Pinin' means 'the little one'). He started to work in his brother Giovanni's Turin bodywork shop when he was just eleven. In 1920 he went to the United States to look at new production methods in the motorcar industry. In 1930 he became an independent coachbuilder. He was soon considered one of the best motor-car designers in Italy (and that means: in the world!). He worked for a number of firms in Italy and abroad, but it was his friendship with Vincenzo Lancia in particular that led to a long series of remarkable designs for the Turin firm. Pinin Farina was a large company even before the war, using industrial methods. The firm developed beyond the field of individual bodywork at an early stage: one important piece of expansion (and a major contri-

bution to the sheet-metal artist's reputation) was the development of designs commissioned by third parties (e.g. the SBB locomotive 2000, cf. p.153); they also set up their own production lines on which series vehicles (for example convertible models) could be produced for large manufacturers. Rather less well known is the fact that other bodywork designers worked for Pinin Farina at an early stage, e.g. Mario Revelli (cf. p.220), Mario Boano, Tom Tjaarda etc. In design terms Pinin Farina was a 'ricercatore' and an 'inventore', an inventor who was always trying out new things.

In about 1960 Pinin Farina handed over direction of the company to his son Sergio an his son-in-law Renzo Carli. The family name was changed to 'Pininfarina' by decree of Italian President Gronchi, which meant that the attrac-

tive name could still be used after the founder's retirement. In fairness it should be said that this is not just a myth; the firm still lives up to the reputation of its name by producing extraordinary designs.

6

CARROSERIE POURTOUT
Delahaye

FIGONI-FALASCHI
c.1938 Talbot Lago

1/2 Carrosserie Pourtout, Paris: Delahaye streamlined coupé, only one vehicle built, 1947. C. Pourtout Collection.

3 Carrosserie Pourtout: coupé with Peugeot 601 mechanical parts; this car belonged to film director Marcel Pagnol, and won the 'Prix d'Elegance' in about 1935.
The car also appeared in the film 'Le Schpountz', starring Fernandel. C. Pourtout Collection.

4 Carrosserie Figoni-Falaschi, Paris: special body on a Talbot-Lago chassis, c.1938. R. Tropeano Collection.

1

3

4

2

MARIO REVELLI DI BEAUMONT

I monòvolumi

1 Mario Revelli: Fiat Ardita 2500, design executed by Pininfarina, 1935.

2 Mario Revelli: Study for Fiat, dated 5.12.1933.

3 Mario Revelli: 'Creazione di Coupé Aerodinamico a Ruote Coperte su Alfa Romeo per Carrozzeria Viotti', gouache, 1935.

4 Mario Revelli: study for a unitary car, 1944.

5 Mario Revelli: study for a unitary vehicle (carrozzeria 'monocorpo'), c. 1933/34. Spare wheel as rear bumper.

2–5: B. A. Revelli Collection.

1

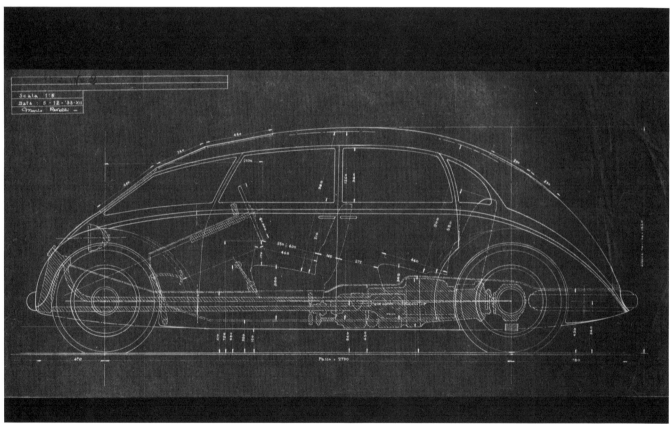

2

I monòvolumi Mario Revelli di Beaumont (1907–1985) built a racing motor bike with his brother when he was only seventeen, and he actually won a race with it in Monza in 1925. He was passionately fond of designing motor car bodies from a very early age, and always demonstrated far-reaching technical thinking. He designed elegant luxury cars and aggressive looking racing machines, but from a remarkably early stage (1933) he was interested in the idea of an externally compact, internally spacious unitary body, in some cases with the possibility of an underfloor engine. Revelli's patents include a rear-view mirror adjustable from inside the car (1927) and central locking for all doors (c. 1935). Revelli worked for Pininfarina, Fiat and General Motors among others (1952–1954) and Simca (1955–1963) as a free-lance designer. His signif-icance as a major Italian bodywork designer was recognized only a few years ago.

3

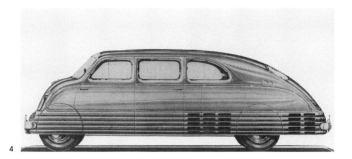

4

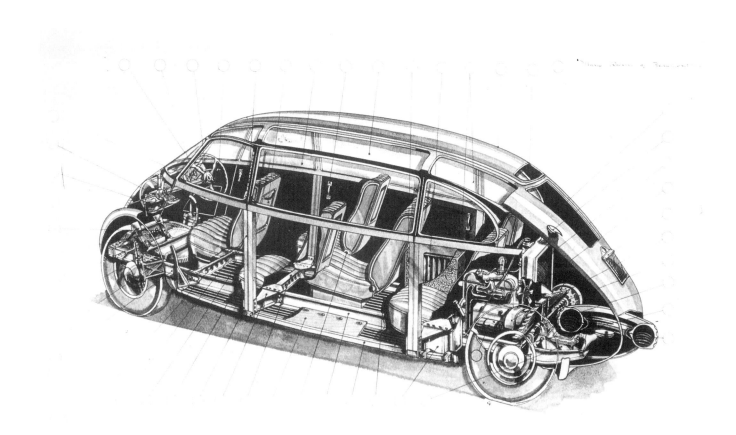

5

Until the integral body and frame was generally accepted (in the sixties), some notable coach-builders survived in Switzerland: Hermann Graber (Wichtrach) was the best known, but Worblaufen and Tüscher (Zurich) enjoyed good reputations. This trade was rooted in hereditary carriage-building; these were not industries, but craft workshops, at best small factories producing goods largely by hand.

In Switzerland motor-car bodybuilders had their heyday in the thirties. It was exceptional for cars to be designed with integral bodies and frames: they consisted of two main sections, the chassis and the body, which was fitted on top of it. The supporting frame for the body was generally made of ash, to which the laboriously beaten metal sheets were attached. Cars made by this method were not cheap; it took months

to complete a commission. But the economic crisis in the thirties favoured fitting bodywork on to chassis in the upper price range, as import duties for completed cars were deliberately set high to help the home industry to acquire more commissions.

The Zurich firm of Tüscher specialized in two- and four-door convertibles and made bodies for many American chassis (Cadillac, Buick, Chrysler), but also Jaguar, Alfa Romeo and other European makes. They also built commercial vehicles such as buses, a line that continued into the seventies. (The frame for these large vehicles was usually made of steel girders.) Most Tüscher designs were by Hans Dinkel and Paul Lötscher, and they include vehicles of outstanding elegance.

1/2   Chrysler Imperial 1938,
modified Chrysler front section, rear
designed and built by Tüscher.

3   Jaguar SS 3.5 l 1939, front and
rear designed and built by Tüscher.

4–6   Karosserie Tüscher: coaches for
various clients, 1940s.

1–6: H. P. Tüscher Collection

4

5

6

RAYMOND LOEWY

1933/1942 Evolution Charts
1936 Greyhound Bus

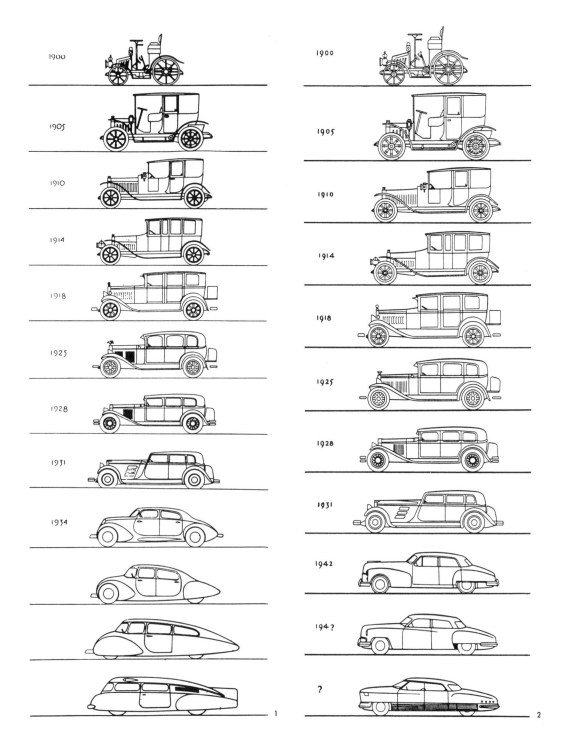

1933/1942 Evolution Charts
Raymond Loewy's 'Evolution Charts' have become famous as celebrations of progress. Loewy published one of these charts for the motor-car as part of his advertising work as early as 1933. This is also published in his illustrated autobiography 'Raymond Loewy: Industrial Design', though admittedly in a form that differs somewhat from the first version. If one compares the tow directly they show at the very least how difficult it is to extrapolate progress (or what is considered as such).
Loewy was not a visionary like Bel Geddes, but a pragmatist. In the course of his career he learned not to ask too much of the client, but to respect how much he could accept and under certain circumstances to approach a goal in several small steps. Loewy's formula 'MAYA'

(most advanced yet acceptable) expresses this attitude pithily.
The difference between the two charts as they diverged from 1933 is illuminating. The older chart culminated in futuristic cab-over-engine vehicles, rather like rear-engined motorway cruisers. The second chart, up-dated during the war, ended differently. The most up-to-date car at the time (1942) corresponds approximately to Loewy's own designs for the most recent Studebaker. The next car (194?) anticipated the 1947–1950 Studebaker models in a quite surprising fashion. These cars created a sensation shortly after the war (thanks to Loewy's design lead over the prevailing canon) Studebaker was the first firm to launch a new formal language after the war. But even this tempered progressive scale (front-mounted engine with bonnet)

was too racy for the American motor industry. Loewy was given the opportunity to design his masterpiece, the Studebaker Champion Commander (1951), but its passenger compartment had not moved as far forward as in the utopian final stage on the 1942 chart.
It is worth comparing this chart with Citroën designs (cf. p. 228). One difference in the approach is important here: Loewy saw streamlining as an aesthetic rather than a physical problem. He liked lines that tapered towards the rear because of their 'tumble-home', his American way of describing an accelerating perspective. But another remarkable feature of his oeuvre is the Studebaker 'Avanti' (1963), which can probably be considered the first expression of a wedge shape rising to the rear, in the first place symbolizing 'power', indeed an excess of power.

1   Raymond Loewy: 'Evolution Chart' for the Motor Car, first version (1933). (From Bush, 1975.)

2   Raymond Loewy: 'Evolution Chart' for the Motor Car, second version (1942). (From: R. Loewy: Industrial Design, Woodstock 1979).

3   Greyhound Lines: overland bus, works design, early thirties. D. Phillips Collection.

4   Raymond Loewy: Greyhound Bus, completely revised bodywork and mechanical parts (cab over engine), more slender logo, decoration emphasizing the lines, c. 1936. D. Phillips Collection.

3

4

NAMI 013 RESEARCH PROJECT

1947 Yurij Dolmatovskij

1

4

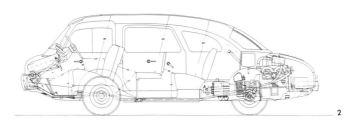

2

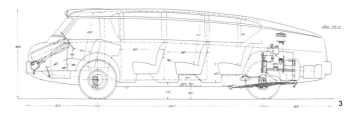

3

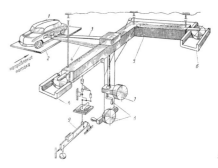

5

1947 Yurij Dolmatovskij The 'Nami' institute in Moscow undertook central research and development work for the various Soviet motor car factories from its foundation in November 1918 (and has continued to do this since the collapse of the Soviet Union). In 1947 it started on the Nami 013 project, which ran until 1952. The engineer in charge of the project was Yurij Aronovich Dolmatovskij (born 1913, author of numerous publications on motor-car construction, lives in Moscow). The Nami 013 project is an astonishingly radical example of streamlining used in a socialist country. Dolmatovskij said in a letter to the editors: "I was bowled over by streamlining from the earliest days of my work as a motor-car designer, and I still am." The Nami 013 project was based on elements (including the four-cylinder engine) from

the Volga Gaz M-20, which had been in production since 1944. But the Nami 013 was fundamentally different from all other Soviet products of its period because of its conception, which aimed for a balanced division of load over the axles. Striking features are the driver's compartment – placed over the front axle – and the passenger space, which is shifted well forward as a result, and placed between the axles; the motor is in the tail. This arrangement corresponds to a very large extent with the future shape for the motor car predicted by Raymond Loewy in about 1935 (see p. 224, ill. 1). But something that had to remain a merely a wish in the United States because it implied extensive interventions into conventional typology was to become reality because of the Nami institute's will. The vehicle did not go into series production

here either, but in contrast with Loewy's private vision, the state laboratory developed a prototype that could be driven, final structural drawings and a functionally sophisticated range of models: the Nami 013 was intended to be produced as a 7-seater, a 5-seater and in a taxi version. Numerous model tests in the wind tunnel were fundamental to the project. The prototype's petrol consumption (13 litres/100 km) was good result for the conditions of its day.

The 7-seater version would have been 4.9 m long and 1.66 m high – at the time the customary height for Soviet limousines – and was probably intended for VIPs. The built prototype for the 5-seater limousine had an overall length of 4.52 m, was 1.83 m wide, only 1.36 m high, and a wheelbase of 2.17 m. It weighed 1450 kg. The taxi would have been just as low, but still shorter

1   Nami 013, model photograph (state of development c. 1950.

2   Yurij Dolmatovskij: Nami 013, sectional drawing of the prototype, c. 1950.

3   Yurij Dolmatovskij: Nami study, sectional drawing of a 12-seater version, c. 1950.

4   Nami, model of the taxi version, c. 1950.

5   Nami Research Institute: scheme for the wind tunnel experiments, c. 1948.

6   Yurij Dolmatovskij: rendering for Nami 013, about 1950.

1–4, 6: Dolmatovskij/Engines Engineering

5: Publication Nami, Moscow 1950

6

and narrower (4.32 and 1.67 m respectively). The Nami institute still exists and collaborates now with Engines Engineering in Bologna (development of progressive car concepts for international markets, e.g. the concept for the 'Compy' small car with unitary bodywork, 1992–1993).

CITROEN DS 19

1945–1955 VGD Project – Voiture de Grande Diffusion

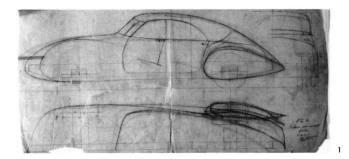

1

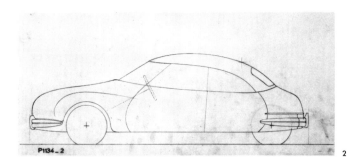

2

5

1 Flaminio Bertoni: design for a successor to the 'Traction Avant' (plan for model), 1945.

2 F. Bertoni: drawing of the planned Citroën with hydropneumatic suspension, 1947/8.

3/4 F. Bertoni: development of the Citroën DS 19, two stages or variants, 1947/8.

5 Serlf-portrait of Flamino Bertoni with two models for the Voiture de Grande Diffusion VGD project, 1948 (from Meyer-Spelbrink 'Das Citroën-DS-Buch'.

6 F. Bertoni/A. Lefèbvre: 'La goutte d'eau', 1:5 model of a middle-range Citroën car with centre of gravity set very far forward and narrow rear track, 1953.

7 F. Bertoni: ideal design for the large Citroën with unitary body, coloured pencil on paper, white high-lighted, 1950.

8 F. Bertoni: early ideal design for the later Citroën DS 19, hydropneu-matic suspension and unitary body, 1949.

1–8: Automobiles Citroën

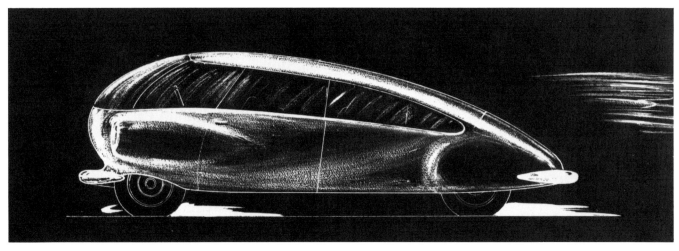

7

1945–1955 VGD Project It is well known that the name of Citroën stands for being extraordinary as a programme. For example, André Citroën (1878–1935), the founder of the firm, rented the Eiffel Tower for neon advertising, made pedal cars for children for propaganda purposes and was seen as a second Henry Ford (whom he knew personally) because he introduced assembly line production in Europe. He felt that everybody should be able to afford a car. He was looking for technical and formal innovation with reasonable prices in mind.

In 1933 he took on engineer André Lefèbvre (1894–1964), who came from Gabriel Voisin. Lefèbvre had an enormous success with the Type 7 and Type 11 front-wheel drive models ('Traction Avant'): rigid, integral all-steel body and frame, front-wheel drive, long wheelbase,

low centre of gravity and low look (no running boards), outstanding road holding and manoeuvrability. Lefèbvre obviously had the concept of the 'Traction' ready in his head: the development period was less than a year. The compression moulding dies for the car came from Budd/Philadelphia (cf. for example Burlington Zephyr etc.). The company was on the verge of ruin because of the enormous expense of converting the production lines for the all-steel integral body and frame. The various models in the 'Traction' series became a great success and were produced until 1957; it was one of the most popular cars in France. Planning for the successor model started as early as 1940: here more attention was to be paid to streamlining. The Italian sculptor Flaminio Bertoni, who designed the 'traction', was also responsible for the design

of the VGD project ('Voiture Grande Diffusion'). But Pierre Boulanger, Citroën's boss since André Citroën's death, gave priority to development of the TPV ('Toute Petite Voiture', later the 2 CV). After the war research on the VGD project intensified. Lefèbvre launched the top-secret hydropneumatic suspension project (project director Paul Magès). He and Bertoni worked on the basis of the 'Traction', but had something quite different in mind in terms of shape and construction: an up-to-date pontoon body (without added wings), curved windscreen, rounded front. Experiments were also conducted with flat-built, horizontally-opposed engines. It is fascinating to reconstruct the 'DS' design process; it was by no means steady. Bertoni and Lefèbvre had a 'teardrop shape' in mind, but then rejected it again. The public became impatient, and

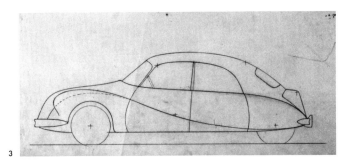

3

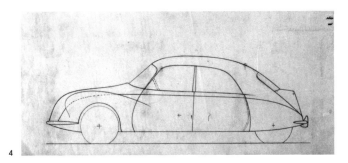

4

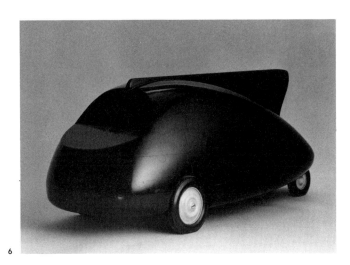

6

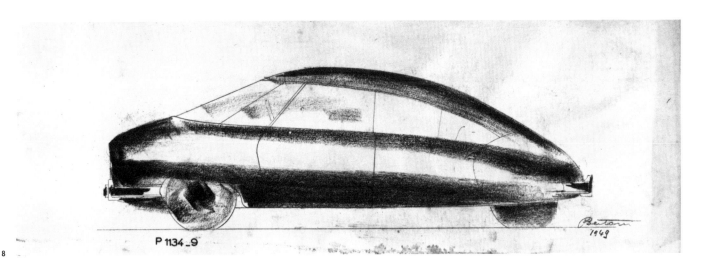

P 1134_9

8

so did the dealers, who only had the 'Traction' to offer, which was now looking somewhat elderly. The final shape of the car emerged relatively late, when developing a new engine had to be abandoned for reasons of time and a new body design had to be created because of the overall height of the old power unit. The car now gradually moved towards its unique architecture. Bertoni thought of a roof sloping sharply towards the back, in other words 'classical' streamlining according to Jaray. The unusual shape of the rear window had already been fixed. As there was too little headroom in the back the roof had to be raised by a hand's breadth and a hollow trim was placed over the window. Bertoni was not content with the car's appearance, the transition from the roof to the tail of the car was not organic. It was not until

shortly before the public launch of the car (Paris Motor Show, autumn 1955) that he found a solution to the problem, by placing conical flashing lights at the problematical point: this created a transition between rear window and plastic roof quite brilliantly, and also linked rear and side windows, roof and roof pillars, superstructure and substructure, detailed shape and overall shape.

It seems that the body was not developed in a wind tunnel. Despite this the car had uniquely low wind resistance; this was not least because of the almost completely covered underside of the car and the 'interior aerodynamics' (guided engine and brake cooling). The presentation of the car as 'Fusée' at the 1957 Milan Triennale: on a pedestal, 'flying away', with sealed wheel housings, was an interpretation that reinforced

the design idea. The DS ('Déesse', Goddess) is perhaps the only car that seems 'suspended' between its wheels, and makes floating part of its statement.

1   Citroën DS 19 in the light tunnel for a paint check, c. 1957.

2   'France d'aujourd'hui' exhibition in the Kunstgewerbemuseum, Zurich (1957).

3   Citroën DS 19, interior with original dashboard; single-spoke steering wheel, 1957.

4   Orson Welles and Liz Taylor in a DS 19, Paris 1960.

5   'Fusée'/'Rocket', DS 19 exhibition display with elevated body and sealed wheel housings, taken at the 1957 Milan Triennale.

6   Citroën DS 19s ready for delivery in the Quai Javel factory, Paris, (c. 1957).

1–6: Les Automobiles Citroën

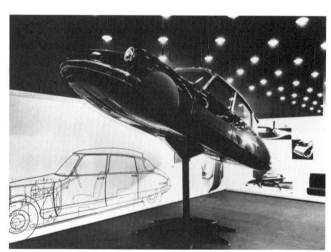

Lit. Serge Brioult, Pierre Dumont, Hans Otto Meyer-Spelbrink.

Omnia (1934) No. 168, pp. 593–595 ff.

6

Streamlining for motor cycles was much influenced by sport. It establishes unity of man and machine. Because of the inevitable vulnerability to side winds of the full streamlined shell there was a move towards the semi-streamlined shell after the war. This reduces wind resistance almost as well, but is less sensitive to side winds. In everyday use development of a sidecar was an obvious point of contact with aerodynamics.

MOTOR CYCLES
Full and half shells

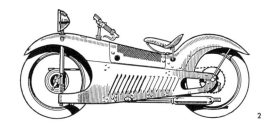

1   Motosacoche (Geneva): motor cycle with sidecar, series-produced vehicle, 1929.

2   'Majestic' motor cycle with shrouding, 1929.

3   Gilera 'Rondine', Italian world-record-breaking machine, 1937.

4   Paul Jaray: design for a motor cycle fully enclosed, c. 1937. (ETH-Bibliothek, wissenschafts-historische Sammlungen).

5   R. Koenig-Fachsenfeld: design for a fully enclosed motor cycle with streamlined helmet, 1939. (R. Koenig-Fachsenfeld Collection).

6   'Moto Guzzi' racing machine with half shell, 1955–1957. The partial fairing is effective as far as relative wind from the front is concerned, but does not have the problematical vulnerability to side winds shown when fully enclosed. This has remained the approach that has found lasting acceptance for racing machines.

Motor Kritik: MK (1937) No. 15, p. 531 ff. Motociclismo (8. 9. 1938), p. 12 f. Moto Revue (14. 7. 1939), p. 432; MK (1942) issue 13, p. 470 f.

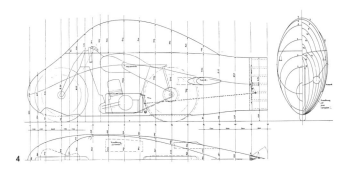

4

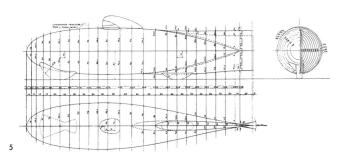

5

6

PIAGGIO

1946 Vespa

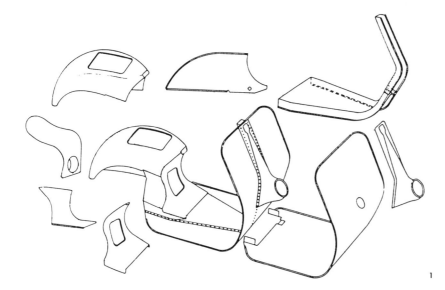

1

2

3

1   The structural parts of the 'Vespa' (from Rassegna 18).

2   Corradino d'Ascanio, first 'Vespa' prototype, 1946 (from Rassegna 18).

3   Corradino d'Ascanio: 'Vespa-Paperino', second prototype, 1946.

4   The 'Vespa' as part of the street scene, here in front of the Olivetti factory by architects Figini and Pollini in Ivrea (from KGMZ-Wegleitung 239, 1960).

1946 Vespa Corradino D'Ascanio (1891–1981) was a respected aviation engineer in Italy who made his mark above all with inventions in the field of helicopter building. After the war in 1945 he was commissioned by industrialist Enrico Piaggio (manufacturer of helicopters and aeroplanes) to develop a new kind of 'Scooter'. This was to accommodate the change from armaments to the production of civilian goods. The two-wheeled vehicle was to be simply built and economical in manufacture and use. D'Ascanio was thinking more of a car than a motor cycle when he started work. Motor cycles were largely a male preserve; they were heavy, not easy to drive and required appropriate protective clothing against dirt and weather. The new scooter was to be easy to use – which meant light in weight – it was to be equally suitable for men

and women and should be possible to ride without special protective clothing. The 'Vespa', which emerged from these requirements, is a brilliant combination of structural refinement, efficiency and economy.

Some sources suggest that the 'Vespa' engine was developed previously as starter for aircraft engines and taken over by D'Ascanio. This is not definitely established. But the engine was epoch-making because of its position: it was fitted right of the rear wheel, which means that it drives directly, without a chain, and is fixed to the wheel, i.e. suspended with it. The arrangement eliminated the spreading of dirt to clothes. It also permitted a sitting position that was quite different from that of the motor cycle. The owner sits on a 'Vespa' in the same way as a chair, and does not 'ride' it; this permits greater lateral

movement. This called for a new kind of structure: the motor cycle had a closed frame like a lattice, but the 'Vespa' had to be a shell that was open at the sides and with an integral body and frame, a 'scocca'. 'Monocoque' construction required a small number of pressed sheet parts that were welded into a three-dimensional structure. A small number of parts, light in weight, spot welding: a stable structure, ideally suited to large-scale serial production (like the 'VW', cf. p. 200). The small wheels, which were not set in forks, but mounted laterally on the hub, as in a motor car (wheels changed more easily) became the hallmark of the modern scooter. The name 'Vespa', wasp, derives from the broad rear section, which resulted from the technology used. The 'Vespa' is still in production, and aboutt 9 million have been built. It was much modified

4

in the course of these forty years, but retained
its basic features. The successor model is called
'Cosa' and is still related to the 'Vespa', which
became a symbol of Italy modernizing itself
after Fascism and war, and a transitional point
on the road to the affluent society.

Rassegna 18 (1984), p. 22 ff.

Streamlining developed slowly as far as aircraft were concerned. A great step was the transition from box to circular cross-section for the fuselage and the introduction of the cantilever wing. However, a fuselage that tapered continuously towards the rear was expensive to manufacture. As aircraft grew bigger a tube with the most constant cross-section possible became standard. Striking streamlining became less important; lift, the view from the cockpit etc. were and are other parameters that have increased in significance. Finally: military aircraft, even those flying at subsonic speeds, follow principles that are different from civil aircraft. It is nevertheless true that flying has made an inestimable contribution to stimulating the imagination to consider 'streamlining' in everyday life.

JUNKERS

1926 Junkers Flying Wing

DORNIER

1928 DO-X Flying Boat

NORMAN BEL GEDDES

1929 Air Liner No. 4

1   Hugo Junkers: design for an all-wing all-metal flying boat, 1926 (not built).

2   DO-X fuselage under construction (Altenrhein factory, Switzerland), unmistakable similarity to a ship.

3   Claudius Dornier: DO-X flying boat, 1928. Three levels, wing span 51 m, 10 engines, flying weight 48 t, capacity 170 passengers. Three aircraft built.

4   DO-X: engines on the wing, test run.

5   The DO-X on Lake Constance.

6   Norman Bel Geddes (with Otto Koller): Air Liner No. 4. Design for a tailless 'V'-winged flying boat with a wing span of 528 ft and capacity for 606 people (451 passengers, 155 crew), 1929. Graphic representation from below (not built). Photograph: Bel Geddes Collection, H. Ransom Humanities Research Center, University of Austin/Texas, by permission of Edith Lutyens Bel Geddes).

2–5: Flug- und Fahrzeugwerke Altenrhein

6

4

5

DOUGLAS COMMERCIAL

1934 DC-2, 1935 DC-3

BOEING

1933 Boeing 247

1939 Stratoliner

LOCKHEED

1934 Electra

1   Lockheed Super Electra, 1934, in competition with the DC-2. U. Haller Collection.

2   Boeing 247, 1933. All-metal low-wing aircraft with integral wings, the direct predecessor of the DC-1/DC-2. U. Haller Collection.

3   Boeing 'Stratoliner', introduced 1939, in competition with the DC-2/DC-3, but larger (33 seats) and with 4 engines. Clearly recognizable features are that cockpit has been shifted well forwards, the fuselage is streamlined, the engines are integrated with the wings and the undercarriage is retractable. D. Phillips Collection.

4   Douglas Sleeper Transport DST, 1935, sectional drawing of the fuselage with fitted bunks. The DC-3 was the day version of this type.

5   A Swissair DC-2 over the Alps, photographed c. 1947. Photograph Swissair.

6   An 'Eastern Airlines' DC-3 over New York. Polished light-weight metal shaped the collective idea of aircraft into the fifties, and was then gradually replaced by painted surfaces that were more easily maintained. D. Phillips Collection.

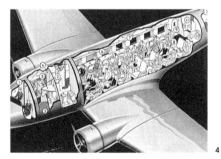

1934 DC-2, 1935 DC-3 The first commercial air route in the United States was between San Francisco and San Diego ('Ryan airlines', from 1925). In contrast with Europe, civil aviation became an economically relevant factor in the United States at a surprising late stage; even in the twenties aircraft were used almost exclusively for carrying mail. This did not change fundamentally until the arrival of the DC-3. The DC-3 ('Douglas Commercial' 3) became one of the most important aircraft in civil aviation because it was also distributed in Europe and the rest of the world.

The Douglas factory built a prototype for TWA in 1933, the DC-1, from which the series-produced DC-2 was developed in 1934 (14 seats, one seat on each side of the central aisle). A total of 220 DC-2s were built. The aircraft had

an all-metal fuselage and was conceived – a fundamental innovation – as a monoplane with low-set wings; the fuselage sits on the wings which are connected underneath the passenger compartment. In contrast with earlier aircraft, for example the Ford 'Tri-Motor', (cf. p. 19) the fuselage of the new generation of aircraft that emerged around the mid thirties was almost circular in cross-section. This was not yet quite the case for the DC-2, but it was for the DC-3, arising from the airlines' need to offer beds for passengers. The DC-3 was a version of the DC-2 that was 76 cm longer and 66 cm wider in the interior than the DC-2. The 21-seater DC-3 for its part was the 'dayplane version', fitted only with seats, of the enlarged DC-2 version 'Douglas Sleeper Transport'. It had three seats per row. The first DC-3 went into service in June 1936.

More than a thousand of this version of the aircraft were produced, a large number of them in military versions during the Second World War.

LOCKHEED

1

1   Lockheed C-69, prototype of the subsequent L-049 'Constellation', c. 1944. The aircraft was used as a troop transporter during the war. U. Haller Collection.

2   A KLM Lockheed Super-Constellation at Amsterdam-Schipol airport. In the foreground is a DC-7. Photograph: Royal Dutch Airlines KLM.

3   A TWA Lockheed 'Constellation' photographed in 1953 at Zurich-Kloten airport. Photograph: Swissair.

4   An 'Eastern Airlines' 'Lockheed Constellation'. Under the fuselage is a supplementary container for freight. U. Haller Collection.

2

1947 Lockheed Constellation Lockheed brought classical streamlining for aircraft to its zenith with the four-engined 'Constellation'. Development started in 1940, as a competitor to the Boeing Stratoliner and the DC-4. Its adoption as a civil aircraft was delayed by the USA's entry in to the war after Pearl Harbor; the aircraft was used by the US Air Force towards the end of the war and not handed over for civil use until 1947.

At a time when increasingly large aircraft were abandoning a spindle shape for the fuselage and developing into cylindrical tubes (e.g. the DC-6), the Constellation had an organic-looking shape with a gently curving back that was slightly reminiscent of a dolphin. This shape brought laminar flow, at the time considered to be an ideal worth striving for, almost within the designers'

grasp. It is to be assumed that this form was also chosen because of lower fuel consumption – important for intercontinental flights, but it is just as likely that style was an significant factor as well. Lockheed had already introduced double tail planes for other aircraft, and made them into a trade mark. The 'Constellation' now acquired a triple tail plane; symbolism and a certain appeal that radiated from an aircraft designed in this way was used to woo the public and carried more weight than aerodynamic function.

1954 Super Constellation As passenger numbers increased the 'Constellation' soon became too small. But several extensions of the fuselage, culminating in the largest version, the 'Super Constellation', soon demon-

strated the problems associated with a zoomorphic shape of this kind quite incontrovertibly. The constantly changing cross-section made economical flexibility for the shape quite impossible, and also made manufacturing each single aircraft an extremely expensive business. Manufacturers and airlines alike now increasingly sought their salvation in aircraft with a constant cross-section, which lent themselves easily to 'extended versions'.

3

4

MILITARY JET AIRCRAFT

1947 Bell X-1A   1954 De Havilland Venom
1949 Vickers Valiant   1958 Prototype N-20

1 'Bell X-1A' rocket aircraft, 1947. This US aircraft was the first to break the sound barrier. The pointed nose is appropriate to supersonic requirements (air displacement cone). U. Haller Collection.

2 De Havilland 'Venom', Swiss Army fighter, introduced 1954. Rudder unit attached to double fuselage; auxiliary tanks on the wing tips. Pilot sits right at the front; air intakes at wing attachment point, engine in the aircraft's longitudinal axis behind the pilot. U. Haller Collection.

3 Vickers Valiant Bomber. Max Bill made the following comment on this picture in 1952: "This aircraft with four jet engines shows a clear change since the rise of reaction technology. The four engines are built into the wings close to the fuselage. This bomber is built without any aesthetic intentions; it is not shown as an example here for that reason, but because its shape is beautiful nevertheless, in the hope that aircraft intended for use in peaceful traffic will become even more beautiful." (M. Bill, Form, Basle 1952).

4 Prototype N-20, 4-engined jet fighter developed in Switzerland. Engine arrangement comparable with the De Havilland 'Comet'. The aircraft did not go into production. Photograph: Eidg. Flugzeugwerk Emmen.

3

4

CIVIL JET AIRCRAFT

1949 De Havilland Comet 1960 Sud Aviation Caravelle

BOEING 747

1970 Jumbo Jet

AIRBUS A 320

1988 Supercritical Wings

1 De Havilland 'Comet' (extended version). First passenger jet in aviation history, 1949. Four jet engines in the wings replace the earlier piston engines, but are placed more closely together. Wing construction is made more difficult by this engine arrangement, and it was therefore abandoned for later jets. U. Haller Collection.

2 Airbus Industrie: Airbus A 320. The new generation of passenger aircraft has 'supercritical' wings enabling considerable fuel savings. The wings are swept back at an angle of 25 degrees and have a high aspect ratio (ratio of span to surface), i.e. a small wing surface and thus minimal surface friction drag. 'Winglets' on the wing tips prevent boundary vortices. They were not part of the original A 320 concept. The bulge in the fuselage in the wing area contains fuel among other things. U. Haller Collection.

3 Boeing 747 on the ground, Zurich Kloten airport before the tubular docks were introduced. Twenty times the seating capacity of the DC-3, and three and a half times as long. Photograph: Swissair.

4 Sud-Aviation 'Caravelle', 1960, 'Caravelle 12' version illustrated, 1970. Engines at the tail (low noise level in the passenger compartment). Nose identical with the British 'Comet' types. Wings set well back because the centre of gravity is well towards the tail; longitudinal ribs regulate airflow round the wings. One of the most beautiful aircraft in civil aviation. U. Haller Collection.

4

CONCORDE
1969/76 Supersonic Passenger Aircraft

NORTHROP B-2
1989 Stealth Camouflage Bomber

2

1   'Concorde' on take-off; mirage as a result of hot exhaust gases. Photograph: Air France.

2   'Concorde' in the air. Cruising altitude for transatlantic flights 18000 m. Photograph: Air France.

3   'Concorde', supersonic passenger aircraft, maiden flight 1969, went into service 1976. Joint Franco-British development to fly at twice the speed of sound. Flying time Paris-New York three and a half hours. 100 seats in very slender fuselage with long, pointed nose (necessary at supersonic speeds). 'Gothic delta' wing shape requires a steep angle of attack on landing, hence the nose folds down to guarantee the necessary downward view. Photograph: Air France.

4   Northrop B-2 'Stealth' ('camouflage bomber'), 1989. Wing span 52 m, length 21 m, unladen weight 48 t, maximum speed 1010 kph. This flying wing would be unstable and uncontrollable because of its shape if it were not continuously stabilized artificially by computer. The irregular shape was developed to avoid reflecting surfaces detectable by radar. The first radical negation of 'streamlining'. Photograph: 'Cockpit'.

3

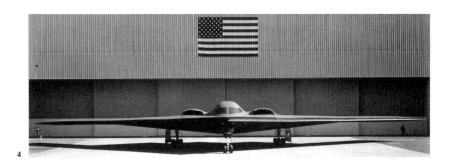

4

Sailing ships show two sides of flow mechanics at the same time: maximization of wind power in the sails, minimization of resistance in the water; here cutting through the medium with low resistance, there capturing energy. In the case of motor-driven ships the wind always came 'from the fore' as far as design engineers were concerned. They tried to minimize the air resistance caused by the relative wind. These efforts could be seen above all in the development of the funnels. In the early 20th century they were tall and had a circular or oval cross-section, but between the wars they became lower and more squat, approaching the ideal streamlined shape.

NAUTICAL EVOLUTION

1907 Lusitania
1935 Normandie

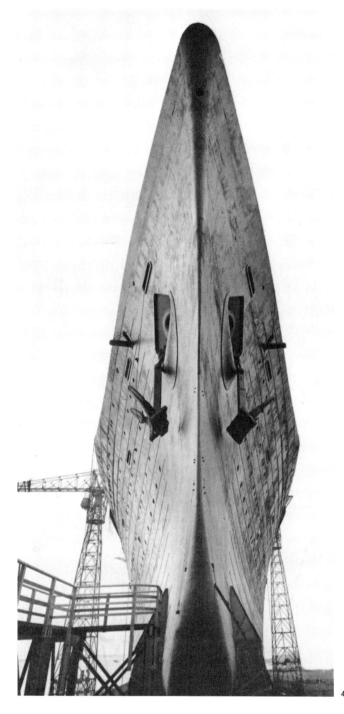

3

2

1

4

1   Lusitania, English luxury liner,
1907.

2   'Normandie', French luxury
liner, c. 1935, night photograph in
Le Havre.

3   'Normandie', aerodynamically
developed funnel.

4   Bow of the 'Normandie'.

5   Andreas Feininger: Staten
Island Ferryboat (from A. Feininger:
'New York', Ziff-Davis Publishing Co.,
N.Y. 1945).

5

NORMAN BEL GEDDES

1932 Ocean Liner

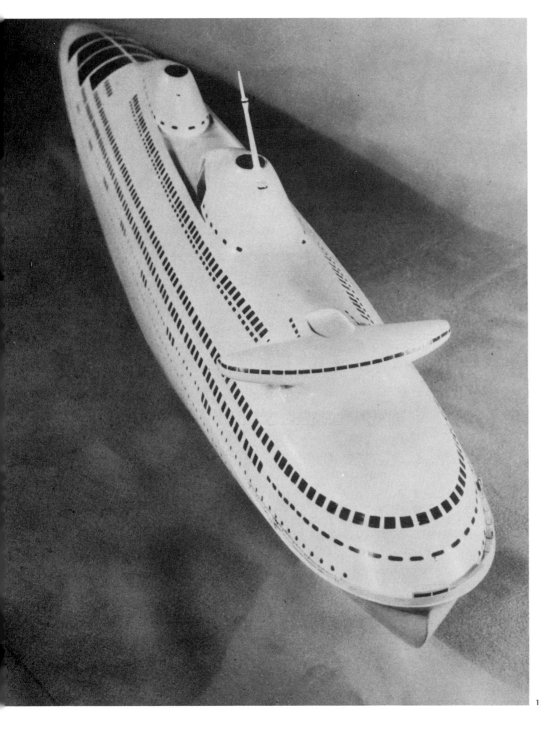

1   Norman Bel Geddes: Ocean Liner, model photograph, c. 1932. Photograph: M. Goldberg.

2/3   Norman Bel Geddes: Wenner-Gren yacht, model photographs, 1934. Photographs: R. Garrison. The design was commissioned by Swedish-American industrialist Wenner-Gren and was based on the idea of the Ocean Liner.

4   Norman Bel Geddes: Ocean Liner, longitudinal section (from 'Horizons').

5   Norman Bel Geddes: Ocean Liner, drawing for a rendering (?), pencil on transparent paper. Corrections to the bow, sketches of seaplanes on the lower edge, c. 1932.

1–5: Bel Geddes Collection, H. Ransom Humanities Research Center, University of Austin/Texas, by permission of Edith Lutyens Bel Geddes.

1932 Ocean Liner   By designing his 'Ocean Liner' Norman Bel Geddes touched upon one of the icons of the Modern movement: the airy ocean steamer taken by Le Corbusier and others as a model for New Building. Bel Geddes pushed the idea of what was really up to date even further and for technical reasons involving flow demanded that all parts that had hitherto been open to the relative wind should be encapsulated. Any protruding shape was to be avoided, everything should be inside the streamlined envelope, including the lifeboats. Only the bridge was to form an exception; it was shaped like a wing profile. In reality the ship would have been 350 metres long and about 50 metres high from keel to the top of the funnel (corresponds to 13 storeys). Each of the funnels was enclosed in a streamlined casing whose sweeping curve could accommodate a bar or an aircraft hangar. The sun decks were to be aft, with tennis court, swimming pool and even a 'sand beach'. In fine weather they were open under the surface lines of the streamlined envelope. In case of wind or heavy seas the open decks would be covered by a glazed curtain.

Bel Geddes estimated that his ship would save a day on the New York-Plymouth run. He was not fantasizing about an express ship, but about a journey that would be more comfortable, more attractive and 20 per cent faster. In his eyes this was enough to convince a shipyard of the economic advantages of this design.

Norman Bel Geddes: Horizons (Boston 1932), pp. 36–43.

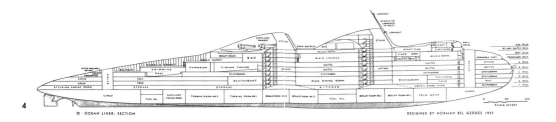

4

32 · OCEAN LINER: SECTION

DESIGNED BY NORMAN BEL GEDDES 1932

FILE 248
SK 011

5

HOUSEHOLD

Streamlining, which was physically restricted
in the wide variety of means of transport
that used it, continued as a 'style' in private
households and individual workplaces. The
spectrum of quality extended from the most
talentless kitsch to structures that were highly
sophisticated in their three-dimensional,
inwardly tense quality, from frivolous excesses to sublime, highly functional and aesthetic
modelling of a piece of apparatus, superbly
expressing the idea of synthesis.

1

2

3

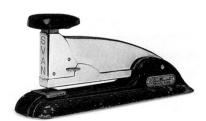

4

5

There is scarcely a single piece of household, kitchen, office or workshop equipment in which 'streamlining' actually had anything to do with flow mechanics – in other words the situation is quite different from that of the world of transport. Nevertheless streamlining was the formal language that countless products were now trying to imitate. There are several reasons for this, for instance: rounded forms reduce the danger of injury, are more pleasant to hold and easier to clean. Also individual function areas were arranged in the best possible way to make work easier – in fitted kitchens, for example.

In this context the spectrum of formal relationship influenced by streamlining extends from direct and imitative adoption of the 'teardrop shape' to more indirectly perceptible inner correspondence in the use of parts with smooth surfaces; great attention was also paid to the way in which they were joined. Previously objects had very often been assembled from greater number of smaller elements, which usually meant a considerable amount of manual fitting. Homogeneous covering – which came in around 1930 – reduced the number of parts, and these tended to develop into larger units. For example: sheet metal, which had previously been bevelled and soldered at the edges, now acquired shell form as a result of simultaneous shaping in several directions. New metallurgical compounds were essential for the preparation of sheet metal suitable for this 'deep-drawing' process. The pressed shell was also the shape for plastics of all kinds that was almost ideally suited to the manufacturing conditions imposed by pressing tools. This process went hand in hand with higher investment in tools and machines, and thus large-scale series production was again the economically imposed prerequisite. Price comparisons between products of the same kind from various periods prove clearly that under these conditions products cost increasingly less in real terms. Larger unit numbers – lower production costs – formal 'appeal' intended to encourage the customer to buy: these were the essential requirements for the 'consumer society' that was now coming into being, in the United States from the thirties onwards, and in Europe largely after the Second World War.

Whether streamlining was more a cause or a consequence of this process is probably a pointless question. The only plausible conclusion is that the process worked dialectically in both directions at the same time.

6

7

8

1   Electrotechnical regulator, cast
casing with ripple finish, Italy c. 1940.

2   Slide projector for cinema
advertising, grey cast iron casing with
ripple finish, Switzerland c. 1940
(manufacturer: G. Andreoli, Lucerne).

3   Zeppelin-shaped pencil-
sharpener, tin sprayed with silver,
Germany 1930s.

4   'Electrolux' cylinder vacuum
cleaner, diecast aluminum casing with
artificial leather covering, bakelite
cap, Sweden c. 1945.

5   'Svan' stapler, provenance
unknown, c. 1940.

6   Marcello Nizzoli, Olivetti
Studio 44 typewriter, Italy 1950.
From W. Braun-Feldweg: Normen und
Formen industrieller Produktion,
Munich 1954.

7/8   Walter Dorwin Teague: Kodak
'Bantam' camera 1936.

9   'Bewi' exposure meter,
Germany c. 1953.

1–5, 7/8: F.-X. Jaggi, MfGZ

6/9: Braun-Feldweg, 1956

9

2

3

1

1   Upright vacuum cleaner, model
375, motoer casing in cast aluminum,
Hoover Ltd., Great Britain 1948–1949.

2   'Sunbeam Mixmaster', Sunbeam
Co., USA c. 1950.

3   'Inca Super' kitchen scales,
diecast aluminum casing, Injecta AG,
Teufenthal, Switzerland 1953.

4   Alfred Edward Burrage,
'Picquot ware' kettle model K3,
Burrage and Boyd, Great Britain 1939.

5   'Rowenta' iron, Germany
c. 1960.

6   'Rotorix' mixer, sheet aluminum
casing, Interelectro AG, Switzerland
c. 1953.

7   Onion knife, polystyrene/
Swedish steel, Germany 1957 (manufacturer: F. Ritter, Munich).

1–7: F.-X.Jaggi, MfGZ

4

5

6

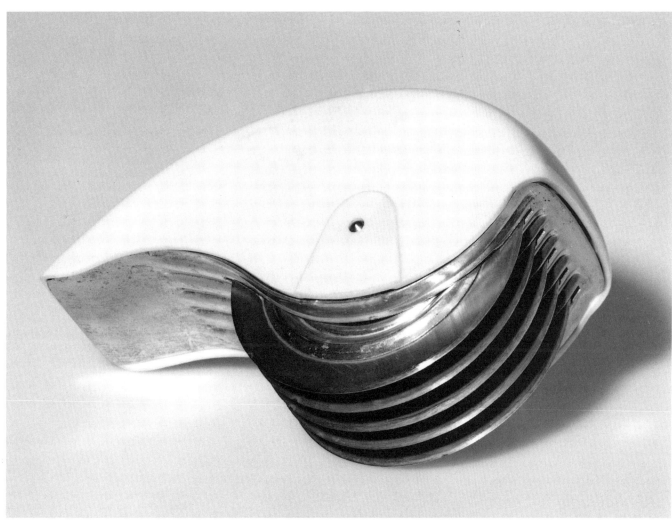

7

TEARDROPS, AERODYNAMICS AND MOTOR CARS

The falling drop – not a 'teardrop'!

Paul Jaray

In newspapers, and often even in the specialist press, in the context of efforts being made to use the concept of aerodynamics in motor car building as well, one often finds comparisons of aerodynamically efficient bodies with a falling drop of water.

And the name 'Tropfenwagen' – teardrop car – has even been coined for a boat-shaped car said to have been modelled on a falling drop of water. Over and over again when this type of car in particular is mentioned one reads that this is "a secret learned by listening to nature", because the falling drop is said to take on the most efficient form, that of a fish-like structure.

For example, one finds in the 'Deutsche Allgemeine Zeitung' of 7.10.1923:

"…The drop is streamlined by nature, i.e. it takes on a shape that produces the least resistance when falling, and its lines allow the air to flow past with the minimum of friction and formation of turbulence …" In the 'Technischer Umschau' of the 'Dresdner Neueste Nachrichten' of 19.10.1923 the following remark can be found in the essay 'Tropfen und Stromlinie': "… The drop is in fact nothing more than a natural streamlined shape, automatically produced by falling particles of liquid. We normal mortals are amazed because it is thick at the front and slender behind. But this proves only that our human instincts about resistance to movement by the air are incorrect …" The 'Technisches Blatt' of the 'Frankfurter Zeitung' wrote on 24.12.1921: " … the shape of a falling drop, derived from the laws of air resistance …" Even the engineering pocketbook 'Hütte', 24th edition (1923) says in a note on p. 428: "In bodies with the least possible form drag separation is completely or almost completely prevented by very slender and smooth tapering to a sharp rear knife edge or point. (Fish shape, shape of a falling drop.)" And in its 1921 September/October issue even 'Motor' magazine came up with this sentence in an essay by government architect Dierfeld: "By far the best results are gained from the so-called drop-shape, i.e. the shape automatically adopted by a raindrop falling to the ground. Essentially this form consists of a broad, almost hemispherical head followed by a long bulbously conical tip …" But the most detailed description of this – to mention it straight away – major error about the streamlined shape of the falling drop is given by Arthur Fürst in an

essay called "Die Wunder des Wassertropfens" in the 'Neue Badische Zeitung' of 23.10.1921: "… When a drop of water falls freely then its smallest particles shift under the opposite pressure of the air in such a way that they acquire minimum resistance when penetrating it. This produces the figure that is to be addressed as the actual drop shape. A freely falling drop does not have a point at the front, it is gently rounded and runs to a point at the back … It is clear … that this running to a point at the rear is outstandingly suited to dissipate air particles disturbed by the rapid passage and to avoid the formation of eddies, which are a very disturbing and restraining force. The curve at the front is much easier to construct …" (for a car) "than a point, and anyway a point would serve no purpose because the leading air wave adapts itself to the best form without this. We have reached all these insights by observing the shape of a falling drop of water, which must therefore be addressed as an excellent master …" At the end of the essay we even find the bold sentence: "This most modern of vehicles is for the time being the last result of the study of the water drop. Everyone must feel uplifted on becoming clear what an abundance of miracles is to be found in this highly unassuming formation: 'A profound glimpse into nature! Here is a miracle, only believe! …'"

Even the 'Hamburger Technische Rundschau' of the 'Hamburger Fremdenblatt', generally acknowledged to be well run and otherwise very accurately informed, has been misled in the same way. Here we read the following in no. 9 of 28.2.1924, p. 2 in a note on 'Tropfen und Stromlinie':

"The drop is in fact nothing more than a natural streamlined shape, automatically produced by falling particles of liquid. We normal mortals are amazed because it is thick at the front and slender behind. But this proves only that our human instincts about resistance to movement by the air are incorrect. Most cars are pointed at the front and blunt at the rear. This produces greater resistance when in motion, but above all very heavy formation of eddies, which can be seen by the extent to which dust is raised. A good streamlined or teardrop shape means that these eddies disappear almost entirely, so that very little dust is produced, even when driving very rapidly."

But this glimpse into nature was unfortunately not profound enough. And it is a miracle that this description that assumes the falling drop to be round at the front and pointed at the back managed to find its way into literature without any criticism. Nature itself has so far made no contribution to this apparent insight: in fact a falling drop is essentially spherical!

It therefore seems urgently necessary to cast closer light on the lack of connection between aerodynamic phenomena and the shape of the drop. The shape that offers least resistance to air or liquid, as seen in fish, for example, so-called 'streamlining', is impossible for a falling drop not least because it is entirely unstable, i.e. a body shaped like this and in free fall would turn over after the first few metres and then fly through the air with a rocking or swirling motion, mainly with its longitudinal axis lying at an angle to the direction of fall. So-called keels or fins are needed to stabilize such streamlined bodies. Like a fish's or a bird's tail they sit at the rear end of the body and prevent it from starting to move at an angle. Our modern airships have keels and fins like this as well. It would be inconceivable for an airship to travel in a straight line without this equipment. But this is already an indirect proof that a falling drop cannot be streamlined.

This will appear strange to many people who perhaps believe that they have even seen this alleged drop shape that is broad at the front and pointed at the back. This is quite explicable, because as long as the drop is hanging on an object and about to leave it because it is heavy enough, it is shaped like a pear or a bag. This is brought about by the joint effect of gravity and surface tension. But at the moment of release the drop is immediately transformed into a ball, and it then retains this shape, or an approximately spherical shape.

It is easy to observe this phenomenon using a stroboscopic disc – a spinning circular disc with an opening for observation – or intermittent light. It will be clear that the drop's deviation from the spherical is limited to very minor, rapid oscillations that make only insignificant changes to the spherical shape of the drop when in equilibrium. These oscillations are caused by external influences, e.g. the moment when the drop detaches itself, and are expressed in a kind of pulsation during which the sphere is distorted ellipsoidally by fractions of its diameter, diagonally and longitudinally to the direction of the disturbance.

But the falling drop's air resistance never produces a shape with reduced air resistance, or even the slightest pointed effect for the rear part.

According to Lord Rayleigh (Proc. Roy. Soc. 29.377.1879) a drop 5 mm in diameter is subject to an oscillation duration for the revolution-ellipsoid shape of the drop swinging around the spherical form calculated in the same way. Prof. Boys work should also be mentioned here, whose investigations – of the same kind – have been translated by Prof. Dr. Meyer in Freiburg im Breisgau. As well as these there are at least thirty publications dating from 1907 to 1915 also dealing with the subject of the spherical form of the drop. These experiments and publications, which have been kindly supplied to me by technical colleges in Stuttgart and Prague, Göttingen University and the Esslingen school (Baurat Buschmann), have only been confirmed by more recent investigations on my part. Finally it is also quite easy to understand that the state of equilibrium of the drop-body held together by surface tension must have the characteristics of the greatest volume with the smallest surface, i.e. spherical form. Thus it is easily clear that between the almost spherical form of the falling (or also the pearlike form of the hanging) drop and the streamlined shape of the body of a fish, for instance their is absolutely no relationship or link. It is wrong to present the drop shape as a model for good aerodynamic bodies.

It is clear that sooner or later there must be a change in the shape of the motor car to concur with the law recognizable throughout nature of the least possible expenditure of energy. The current external shape of the motor car no longer corresponds at all with the current position of science. But if one uses modern aerodynamic knowledge to reduce the actually very considerable air resistance of today's cars, then this can happen only according to the principle of streamlining (that is the lines of the individual fluid particles that everywhere retain the continuous course of the direction of flow), but not on the model of the drop in its true or supposed shape.

From: Deutsche-Motor-Zeitschrift, no. 5/6 1924.

THE NEW 'TERRANAUTICS'

The Findings of the Wind Tunnel Are Not Always Applicable to the Design of Motor Cars

William B. Stout

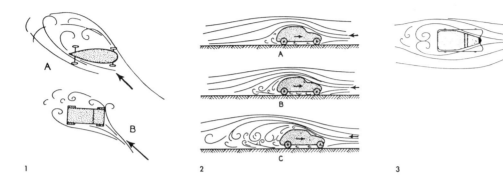

1   2   3

The matter of streamlining of motor cars has received so much erroneous attention, both from the automobile man who suddenly 'goes aerodynamic' and the aeronautic engineer whose emoluments from aviation have suddenly diminished, who go 'terranautic', that some points need very definite clearing up.

There are certain fundamentals that make the streamlining of a motor car an entirely different problem from that of an airplane, or any other vehicle. The first difference is that while the air always comes from the front in an airplane, it may come from any direction in a motor car or land vehicle.

An airplane floats free in the fluid in which it flies, and no matter what the direction of the wind as related to the ground, the wind as related to the airplane always comes straight on from the nose. You can visualize this by thinking of a motor boat on a river; when this boat is cleaving forward through the water it cuts the water directly on the bow equally on both sides no matter whether it is headed up-stream or downstream or cross-current.

Streamlined shapes as related to airplanes and boats therefore have no place on a motor car or railplane, where the vehicle is fastened solidly to the ground and the wind blows over it from any direction. In this case, streamlining must simulate more the turtle or the crab than the airplane or the bird, and certainly has nothing in common with the teardrop, except sorrow.

Figure1 shows the teardrop section A, and a square section, B, similar to the old type motor car with square corners. The shape A is that of a lifting wing and has three times the lift sideways that a square section, B would have. That means that if you make a motor car the shape of A in horizontal cross-section – similar to some English designs which have been promoted – the car will be three times as hard to hold on the road as the car B, and we already know that car B is fairly hard to steer in a side-wind as it is.

When in the streamlining of a car you also combine light weight and strength of airplane structure, then you most certainly must steer clear of high lift in the body section if you wish controlability; and not all cars of this type will be built with a weight of 7600 pounds as was an early model in this country to enable it to hold the road in side-winds. The plan view of the car must be so designed to give a minimum of side thrust in cross-winds; in other words, the shape must approximate streamlining by being completely curved in all directions with no sharp corners. Properly engineered, a great advantage may be had by streamlining.

In Figure2 is shown the effect of a flat curved back to a car. The shape of the front end is not important, as the air will bank itself up in front of an obstruction and more or less streamline itself; but in back is the important part. This must be so shaped that it will form no low-pressure eddies behind the car. However, this condition varies with speed.

In Figure 2 the curved flat top comes down to the rear of the car as shown. At low speed, as at A, the air follows down the back of the car very cleanly and with but a very small vacuum, except at the point of drag caused by resistance underneath the car between the road, standing still, and the rough bottom of the car moving. This, at slow speed, however, does not amount to much.

As speed is increased, however, as in B, this airflow changes. The air does not have time to follow down the steep flat stern of the car, and having no air coming in from the sides in an equal smooth curve, a vacuum area is formed with burbles and turbulence, shown by the picking up of leaves, snow or dust in this area.

Later on at a certain higher speed, the air will break completely away from the car in all directions, as in C, leaving a long continuous turbulence behind the car, all of this suction requiring additional horsepower. The streamlining of any car, therefore, must be judged by the 'cruising speed of economy' at which the manufacturer is aiming.

Figure 3 shows an automobile engineer's idea of streamlining; a very sharp pointed nose tapers away back to the stern. This is wonderful streamlining for a boat, where turbulence in the rear is not as important as is the cutting of the water at the front; but for air, the lines show a great vacuum area at the rear. If any manufacturer making this type of car ran his car backwards, at 60 miles per hour, the horsepower consumption would be not over half and his fuel economy equivalent.

In Figure 4 is an explanation of designing for certain economical speeds. A was our old type automobiles – square corners, with visor on top of the windshield (which, by the way, would consume about six horsepower), exposed lamps, bad air conditions between fenders and hood, and so on. On these old cars the best fuel economy was obtained at between 35 and 40 miles per hour.

Next, we came to the slanting windshield type with rounded corners and fenders straight into the hood. This next change in air resistance stepped the most economical speed up to approximately 48 miles per hour; the slanting back, or smoothed-in trunk, or even double spare tires on the rear adding to the economy. By a greater extreme of streamlining, as shown in C, it is very easy to increase the most economical cruising speed of a car to 60 miles per hour, or better. This will be the next step in motor car streamlining development.

The aerodynamic man will come along, however, and tell you a lot of things he has learned in the windtunnel and quote them for real motor cars. The wind-tunnel is a very great publicity center for motor-car development, and the motor car certainly offers a great field of research for the aerodynamic engineer; nevertheless, windtunnel figures on automobiles today are of absolutely no value from a quantitative point of view, on account of one single fact. So far no one has been able in the wind tunnel to simulate, or even approximate, the effect of the moving ground under the vehicle.

Tunnel figures are often given with two models—one upside-down – placed wheel to wheel, but this is not a simulation of the actualities because there is no ground effect when a model is tested in this way. If the model is tested on a floor, then the drag is not the same as it is in a motor car where the rough ground is continuously moving at high speed under the wheels. Even a method of doing it with a traveling belt has not been developed to a point where it means anything in accuracy.

However, great progress is being made if only in acquainting the public with the absolute necessity of cleaner lines for automobiles, of the possibilities of greater roominess inside, greater head room, greater luggage space, more luxury; and more than that, much easier riding through the adoption not only of streamlining but of the other principles which the automobile has already adopted from the airplane: Light structure, balloontires, pyroxylin finishes, and 'knees'

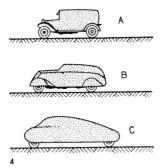

4

which are really airplane landing gears with
independent wheels attached to automobiles.
With all that aviation has to offer to the motor
car, we may look for tremendous changes in
this field during the next few years.
All eyes today are focused on airplane engineering as a way to lead all vehicles of travel
out of old conventions into a new possibility
of faster, better service at lower costs, and
decreased risks.

'Scientific American', March 1934, p. 126 f.

STREAMLINED TRAINS

Paul P. Cret

To appeal to a large public, facts must go through a process of preparation to make them more easily assimilable. The statement becomes a slogan, the theory a mere diagram. In the process, truths become advertising half-truths, something quite different from the original. One of the pet beliefs of the young student or of the amateur dabbling in art theory is that mere compliance with constructional requirements or necessities of use, at once invests an object or a building with aesthetic merit. We have all seen lengthy papers to this effect from the fertile pen of men who never created anything, and are woefully ignorant of the conditions of production of artifacts. Thus superficial perusal of the writing of Le Corbusier has promoted to the rank of accepted truths – among the laymen, of course – the proposition that a blind obedience to the laws of mechanical engineering endows the automobile of today with forms which put to shame the feeble efforts of the craftsmen and the architects of our time. In reality Le Corbusier states exactly the contrary, and has proclaimed many times that "Art begins where calculation ends". This does not embarrass the tyros in the least. They simply ignore the passages where their authority – an architect who knows that assembling materials for a book is not writing a book, and supplying certain comforts to automobile users, is totally different from designing a good-looking car – clearly shows that aesthetic qualities are of another order and have to be pursued by other methods.

A comparison of yearly models of automobiles for the last twenty yearwould show that mechanical progress does not advance evenly with aesthetic progress; it may lag behind for many years, until perfecting the forms of motor cars is pursued as an end in itself, by designers, modellers, sculptors, collaborating with the manufacturers. After devoting all his efforts to achieving a reliable motor, the manufacturer discovers the appeal of form to attract purchasers.

In the same way, railroads were for many years satisfied with very minor improvements in the design of their trains, inside and outside. The day coach received its present appearance a good many years ago. It is the competition of the motor bus, of the automobile, of the airplane which has recently suggested to some executives that the best defense against these inroads was an aggressive policy of improvement instead of complaints against unfair competition. Hence an effort to improve the speed, the safety, the comfort of some crack trains, and to place the traveling public in more cheerful surroundings.

The education of this public away from the Pullman style of 1880 had been started elsewhere. Hotels, residences, theatres, had shown that the day of green velvet as the acme of good taste has passed. Modern use of shining metals and bright colors had been carried to the motor car. The way was thus open to experimentation and to more individuality of treatment for the trains. One of the pioneers in this work was a Philadelphia manufacturer, the Edward G. Budd Manufacturing Company. Colonel Ragsdale of this firm had perfected processes for working and welding stainless steel, a material of greater strength than steel, so that standard structural shapes might be replaced by lighter sections of equal resultant strength, a saving in weight of equipment that, when multiplied throughout a train, resulted in great savings in operation costs. This gave to the architect, when called upon to intepret this very modern material, the opportunity to conceive an ensemble where modern fabrics, synthetic materials, would enhance the stainless steel of the framework.

It has been our fortune to design several of these stainless steel trains, the original Zephyr and later the Denver Zephyr and Twin-Cities Zephyr for the Burlington Railroad, and more recently, trains for the Santa Fe System.

For the Zephyr trains, our intent was to use the engineering design of the cars as a basis: the thin metal forms, the streamlined outer envelope, the inner surfaces of thin material frankly a veneer over the structural shapes, the intervening voids being filled with insulating material. The thinness of these veneer materials necessitated the use of countless screws whose heads must be part of the resultant impression, or of cover moulds of the same stainless steel, or of aluminum. In some of the cars, this veneer material – Masonite or Homasote, or where slightly larger dimensions were required (for ceiling surfaces), aluminum sheets – were finished with a dull surface enamel paint, sprayed on. In other cases these surfaces were in part covered with Flexwood. As the latter could be had in many veneers, in a wide variety of color and marking, it was possible to have the small rooms in a compartment sleeper, for instance, each in a different color scheme, thus doing away in large measure with the monotony of the earlier sleping cars.

Pile fabrics can be had in many colors, and in modern design, and since the Burlington officers preferred to sacrifice something of long-wearing dustconcealing qualities to cheerfulness and interesting color, and as the tones of the painted surfaces were also made colorful instead of drab, with sharp contrasting notes, the general impression of the interiors was one of bright color accented with lines of chromium or stainless steel mouldings.

Outside, the Zephyr trains are all stainless steel, with the lettering, of modern forms, in black enamel – a striking effect which has given to the Denver cars their names in a 'Silver' series – Silver King, Silver Queen, Silver Bar, Silver State, etc.

For the Santa Fe train, the problem was made interesting from the fact that the route of the cars lay through the old Pueblo Indian territory. For this reason, Indian motives were used in various places – in the carpet for the dining room, the inlaid wood map and bar decoration in the bar car, and in the observation car as originally planned.

Here the colors were those of the Pueblo – the brownish red tones taken from the old pottery, with notes of the bright blues, the blacks and the 'bayetta' red found in the old weavings. The ceiling lighting was a 'plumed serpent' from the Hopi tribal snake festival, to be lighted by blue lamps of low voltage. On the wall were painted representations of the ceremonial dolls of the Pueblo tribes. For the upholstery, two pile fabrics were designed, of mohair material to withstand railroad usage, but of color and design inspired by Indian weavings. One is an all-over design of walls of Troy, the other has bands with spots between, but each has a gray background and motives in bayetta red, indigo blue, and small notes of white.

Though the finished effect is one of colorfulness and gayety, with a sense of luxury and comfort, the approach of the designer is from the standpoint of what Stuart Chase calls the 'economy of scarcity', and all materials and the general design must be economical in the true meaning of that term – good value for the money expended.

Half a dozen of these trains are now in service. That they have been favorably received by the public is proved by increased passenger traffic and profits in spite of lower fares. It is not the place to discuss here the economic advantages of the Budd trains, mostly gained through a considerable reduction of the dead load in relation to the number of passengers transported. This aspect of the problem has been ably set in technical journals. Our object was merely to show that a new field is open to architects and decorators, and that aesthetic considerations have come into their own in a field where too conservative officials had thought for many years that they had little or no place.

'Magazine of Art', Washington, 1937, p. 17 ff.

SELECTED BIBLIOGRAPHY

The following list complements the literary references in individual essays (pp. 50–77) or in the relevant Kaleidoscope section (catalogue, pp. 113–263).

1. Periodicals (arranged chronologically)

Railways

Germany:
The Railway Gazette: RG (1.5.1935), p. 387 ff.
Zeitschrift des Vereins Deutscher Ingenieure (1938) no. 18, p. 515 ff.
Glasers Annalen (1.7.1939), p. 179 ff.
Motortechnische Zeitschrift, special edition (1941) issue 5

France:
Revue Générale des Chemins de Fer (July 1932), p. 3 ff.
Revue Générale des Chemins de Fer (January 1933), p. 3 ff.
Le Génie civile (7.10.1933), p. 341 ff.
RG (29.12.1933), p. 984 ff.
RG (5.10.1934), p. 564 ff.
RG (28.12.1934), p. 1092 ff.
La Revue de l'Aluminium (1934) no. 64, p. 2637 ff.
RG (27.12.1935), p. 1132 ff.
La Traction Nouvelle: TN (1936) no. 1, p. 2 ff.
TN (1936) no. 2, p. 38 ff.
TN (1937) no. 9, p. 78 ff.
Schweizerische Bauzeitung SBZ (1938/1), p. 26 f.
SBZ (1938/2), p. 165
TN (1938) no. 38, p. 38 ff.
Chemins de Fer (1952) no. 176, p. 117 ff.

Italy:
TN (1937) no. 7, p. 20 ff.
RG (10.5.1940), p. 56 ff.

USA:
Fortune (1934) no. 2, p. 40 ff.
TN (1937) no. 10, pp. 134–141
TN (1937) no. 21, pp. 96–107.

Motor Cars

Automobil Revue (4.6.1929), p. 8
Motor Kritik (1934) no. 2, p. 30 ff.
Die Autobahn (1/1934), p. 11 ff.
Illustrierte Automobil Revue (1/1935), p. 28 ff.

2. Specialist literature (by author)

- Anselmi, A. T.: Carrozzeria Italiana, Cultura e Progetto (Milan 1978)
- Bayley, S.: In good Shape (London 1979)
- Bianchi Anderloni, C. F. und Anselmi, A. T.: Carrozzeria Touring (Milan 1982)
- Brioult, R.: Citroën, l'Histoire et les Secrets de son Bureau d'Etudes, vols. I und II (Paris 1987)
- Bröhl, H. P.: Paul Jaray, Stromlinienpionier (Bern Eigenverlag 1978)
- Buckminster Fuller, R.: Raumschiff Erde (Hamburg 1973)
- Bush, D. J.: The Streamlined Decade (New York 1975)
- Clausberg, K.: Zeppelin. Die Geschichte eines unwahrscheinlichen Erfolges (München 1979)
- Cornolo, G.: Una Legenda che corre (Salò 1983)
- Dumont, P.: Quai de Javel Quai André Citroën (Paris 1973)
- Erdmann, K. D.: Der Erste Weltkrieg (= Gebhardt Hb der deutschen Geschichte 18) (Munich 1980)
- Essery, B. und Jenkinson, D.: LMS Locomotives, vol. 5 (St. Michael's, Lancashire 1989)
- Geisenheyner, S.: Militärische Luftfahrzeuge, die leichter als Luft sind, in: Armada International 9/91, pp. 26–30;
- Gottwald, A. B.: Schienenzeppelin – Franz Kruckenberg und die Reichsbahn-Schnelltriebwagen der Vorkriegszeit (Augsburg 1972)
- Gottwald, A. B.: Die Stromliniendampfloks der Reichsbahn (Stuttgart 1978)
- Güth, R.: Die Organisation der deutschen Marine in Krieg und Frieden 1913–1933, in: Militärgeschichtliches Forschungsamt (pub.), Deutsche Militärgeschichte 1648–1939, 6 vols. (Munich 1983)
- Haaland, D.: Der Luftschiffbau Schütte-Lanz Mannheim-Rheinau (1909–1925) (Mannheim 1987)
- Haresnap, B.: Stanier Locomotives (London 1970)
- Haresnap, B.: Gresley Locomotives (London 1987)
- Heydecker, J.: Der Grosse Krieg 1914/18. Von Sarajewo nach Versailles (Frankfurt 1988)
- Industriearchäologie (1984/4)
- Jeanmaire, C.: Die Elektrischen- und Dieseltriebfahrzeuge schweizerischer Eisenbahnen (Basel 1970)
- Kieselbach, R. F. J.: Stromlinienautos in Europa und USA (Stuttgart 1982)
- Kieselbach, R. F. J.: Stromlinienautos in Deutschland (Stuttgart 1982)
- Kieselbach, R. F. J.: Stromlinienbusse in Deutschland (Stuttgart 1983)
- Kleinheins, P., (ed.): Die grossen Zeppeline. Die Geschichte des Luftschiffbaus (Düsseldorf 1985)
- Knäusel, H. G.: LZ-1. Der erste Zeppelin. Die Geschichte einer Idee (Bonn 1985)
- Knäusel, H. G.: Zeppelin und Zeppelinismus, in: Trans: Magazin für Luft- und Raumfahrt (Berlin 1989)
- Koenig-Fachsenfeld, R.: Aerodynamik des Kraftfahrzeug, vols. I und II (Frankfurt a. M. 1951)
- Koenig-Fachsenfeld, R.: Aerodynamik des Kraftfahrzeug, vols. III und IV (Heubach 1984)
- Kurz, H. R.: Fliegende Züge (Freiburg 1986)
- Loewy, R.: Never leave well enough alone (New York 1951)
- Loewy, R.: Industrial Design (New York 1979)
- Luraschi, A. G.: Storia della Motocicletta vols. I–V (Milan, no year)
- Maillet, M.: L'œuvre d'André Chapelon à la SNCF et son Influence mondiale (Menton 1983)
- Margolius, I. and Henry, J. G.: Tatra, the Legacy of Hans Ledwinka (Harrow 1990)
- Meighörner-Schardt, W.: "...der Welt die Wundergabe der Beherrschung des Luftmeeres schenken." Die Geschichte des Luftschiffs LZ-2 (= Schriften zur Geschichte der Zeppelin-Luftschiffahrt 7) (Friedrichshafen 1991)
- Meighörner-Schardt, W.: Wegbereiter des Weltluftverkehrs wider Willen. Die Geschichte des Zeppelin-Luftschifftyps 'w' (= Schriften zur Geschichte der Zeppelin-Luftschiffahrt 8) (Friedrichshafen 1992)
- Metternich Graf Wolff, M.: Rumpler (Munich 1986)
- Meyer-Spelbrink, H. O.: Das Citroën Buch (Brilon 1989)
- Molino, N. und Pautasso, p.: Le Automotrici della prima Generazione (Turin 1983)
- Pedrazzini, C.: ATR 100 (Parma 1976)
- Pierluigi, A. und Guarneri, T.: Le Automotrici Breda delle FS Aln 56 e 556; (Rome 1981)
- Pininfarina: Pininfarina Sessantanni (Turin 1990)
- Ranks, H. E. and Kratville W. W.: Union Pacific Streamliners (Omaha 1974)
- Rassegna (1980) no. 2, Ferrovie Statali
- Rassegna (1984) no. 18, Veicoli
- Reed, R. C.: The Streamline Era (San Marino Cal. 1975)
- Robinson, D.: The Zeppelin in Combat. A History of the German Naval Airship Division 1912–1918 (Seattle/London 1980)
- Russel, J. H.: Great Western Diesel Railcars (Didcot 1985)
- Stout, W. B.: So away I went! (Indianapolis/New York 1951)
- Vilain, L. M.: Les Locomotives à grande Vitesses (Paris 1972)
- Wilson, R. G. and Pilgrim, D. H. und Tashjian, D.: The Machine Age in America 1918–1941 (New York 1986)
- Rowledge, J. W. R.: The LMS Pacifics (Newton-Abbot 1987)
- Schmalenbach, P.: Die deutschen Marineluftschiffe, (Herford 1977)
- Schmarbeck, W.: Tatra, die Geschichte der Tatra Automobile (Bad Oeynhausen 1977)
- Schmarbeck, W.: Hans Ledwinka, seine Autos – sein Leben (Graz 1990)
- Schönberger, A., (cd.): Raymond Loewy (Munich 1990)
- Schütte, J., (cd.): Der Luftschiffbau Schütte-Lanz 1909–1925 (Munich/Berlin 1926)
- Walle, H.: Das Zeppelinsche Luftschiff als Schrittmacher technologischer Entwicklungen in Krieg und Frieden, unpublished typescript (Freiburg 1992)

Note: Names of authors mentioned only in notes on essays have not been included in the index for reasons of space.

Angelo Tito Anselmi, 1931 After studying architecture in Milan worked as a technical and historical journalist, specializing in Italian motor-car history. Various publications and exhibitions on the subject. Also worked in Visual Communication. Lives and works in Milan.

Sabine Bohle-Heinzenberg, 1942 Studied art history and archaeology, doctoral thesis on 'Architektur der Berliner Hoch- und Untergrundbahn' (Berlin 1980). Assisted with exhibitions, including: 'Berlin 1900–1933, Architektur und Design' (1987) and 'Raymond Loewy. Pionier des Amerikanischen Industrie-Designs' (1990). Free-lance work for the Internationales Design Zentrum Berlin IDZ.

Franz Engler, 1949 Qualified architect (ETH) with his own office in Zurich (with F. Renaud). Many years of theoretical and practical work on technology and the history of technolgy.

Barbara Hauss-Fitton, 1959 Born and grew up in Michigan/USA. Studied art history in Amherst/Massachusettes and Freiburg im Breisgau, gained M.A. Assisted on the publication 'Ferdinand Kramer. Der Charme des Systematischen' (Giessen 1991). Lives and works in Lörrach.

Claude Lichtenstein, 1949 Architectural Diploma ETH. Curator at Museum für Gestaltung, Zurich since 1985. Various publications on art and design, including co-writing 'O. R. Salvisberg – die andere Moderne' (1985) and editing 'Ferdinand Kramer. Der Charme des Systematischen' (Giessen 1991). Lives in Zurich.

Devised by Claude Lichtenstein and
Franz Engler

Edited by Claude Lichtenstein

Design and typography: Atelier Lars Müller,
Baden, Switzerland
Cover design: Mihaly Varga, Zurich
Repro: Repro Art AG, Dielsdorf
Printing: Waserdruck AG, Buchs, Zurich
Binding: Buchbinderei Burckhardt, Mönchaltorf

ISBN 3-906700-71-2
Printed in Switzerland

Lars Müller Publishers
PO Box 912
5401 Baden, Switzerland

Phone 41 56 82 27 00
Fax   41 56 82 27 01

This publication is based on the catalogue
(ISBN 3-906700-47-X) for the 'Stromlinienform'
exhibition in the Museum für Gestaltung
(Design Museum) Zurich, Switzerland.
The exhibition was also shown in the Bauhaus
Dessau and the Karl Ernst Osthaus Museum
Hagen, both in Germany.

Translation: Michael Robinson
Barbara Hauss-Fitton (Streamlining
at the World's Fair: Chicago 1933/34 –
New York 1939/40)
Luca Turin/Barbara Hauss-Fitton
(Aerodynamics the Italian Way)

Credits
ABB Henschel, Kassel
ABB Verkehrssysteme AG, Zurich
Jean Andreau, Paris
Angelo Tito Anselmi, Milan
Hubert Auran, Noves, France
Automobiles Citroën, Paris
René Berger, Fällanden
Carlo Felice Bianchi Anderloni, Eupilio, Italy
Dr. Alois Bommer, Affoltern, Zurich
Robert Braunschweig, Bern
Archivio Storico Ernesto Breda, Milano
Hans Peter Bröhl, Aarwangen, Switzerland
Chicago Architectural Photographing
Company (David R. Phillips), Chicago
Chrysler Historical Foundation, Highland
Park/Michigan
Detroit Historical Museum
Deutsches Automuseum Schloss Langenburg
De Dietrich & Cie, Ferroviaire et Méchanique,
Reichshoffen, France
Yurij Dolmatovskij
Eidgenössisches Flugzeugwerk Emmen
Engines Engineering, Bologna
ETH Zurich, Bibliothek, Wissenschaftshisto-
rische Sammlungen (Dr. Beat Glaus)
ETH Zurich, Institut für Energietechnik
Colette Fawer, Geneva
FFA Fahr- und Flugzeugwerke Altenrhein AG,
Altenrhein
Centro Storico Fiat, Torino
FKFS Forschungsinstitut für Kraftfahrwesen und
Fahrzeugmotoren, Stuttgart
Henry Ford Museum, Dearborn/Michigan
Alfred B. Gottwaldt, Berlin
Dr. Ulrich Haller, Sempach, Switzerland
Harry Ransom Humanities Research Center,
Universität Austin/Texas
Historische Fahrzeugsammlung Simmelsdorf,
Germany
Industrie Pininfarina SpA, Torino
Infothek Carosserie Worblaufen, Effretikon,
Switzerland
Marguerite Jaray, St. Gallen
Peter Jaray, Baden, Switzerland
Andreas Jucker, Basel
K. Kässbohrer Fahrzeugwerke GmbH, Ulm
KLM Royal Dutch Airlines, Amsterdam
Krauss Maffei Verkehrstechnik GmbH, München
Krupp-MAK Maschinenbau Kiel AG, Kiel
Centro Storico Lancia, Torino
Dr. Erich Ledwinka, Graz

Franco Lombardi, Genova
Luftschiffbau Zeppelin GmbH, Friedrichshafen
Aldo Macchi, Birchwil, Switzerland
Dr. Wolfgang Meighörner-Schardt,
Friedrichshafen
Mercedes-Benz AG, Werkmuseum, Stuttgart
Teresa Millanta, Milano
Sepp Moser, Eglisau
MTU Motoren und Turbinen-Union,
Friedrichshafen
Musée de l'Automobile Française, Reims
(Philippe Charbonneaux)
Museo Nazionale della Scienza della Tecnica
'Leonardo da Vinci', Milano
Museum für Verkehr und Technik, Berlin
National Museum of American History,
Smithsonian Institution, Washington, D.C.
Piaggio V.E., Pontedera, Italy
Claude Pourtout, Paris
Renault, Histoire et Patrimoine,
Boulogne Billancourt
Bethel-Abiel Revelli di Beaumont, Torino
Marcel Ruff, Meersburg
Willy E. Salzmann, Zug, Switzerland
Ferdinand Schenk, Satigny, Switzerland
Schweizerische Bundesbahnen, Bern
Schweizerische Lokomotiv- und
Maschinenfabrik SLM, Winterthur
Schweizerisches Verkehrshaus, Luzern
SIA Société des Ingénieurs de l'Automobile,
Paris (C. Gueldry)
SMF Sondermodellefabrik AG, Giubiasco,
Switzerland
Stiftung Schloss Fachsenfeld, Aalen (Freiherr
R. Koenig-Fachsenfeld) Germany
Dr. Herbert Sprenger, Zurich
Dr. Thomas Staubli, ETH Zurich
Hans Strassl, München
Eduard Strebel, Schönbühl, Switzerland
Sulzer Escher-Wyss AG, Zurich
Technické Muzeum Tatra, Kopřivnice
(Karel Rosenkranz)
Touring Superleggera, Caronno Pertusella, Italy
Dr. Hans Peter Tüscher, Küsnacht, Zurich
Union Pacific Historical Museum,
Omaha/Nebraska
Volkswagen Automuseum, Wolfsburg